# BORN WITH POTENTIAL & PURPOSE

Steps To Discovering God's Amazing Plan
For Your Life

J. Arthur Gipson

Writer's Note: Scripture references are found in the back of the book, before the endnotes. Unless otherwise indicated, all Scripture quotations are from the Holy Bible, New Living Translation, NLT © 1996, 2004, 2015. All rights reserved. Scripture quotations marked (KJV) are taken from the King James Version of the Holy Bible. Scripture quotations marked (NKJV) are taken from the Holy Bible, New King James Version 1979, 1980, 1982. All rights reserved. Scripture quotations marked (NIV) © are taken from the Holy Bible, New International Version © 1973, 1978, 1984 by the International Bible Society. All rights reserved. Scripture quotations marked (ESV) are taken from the English Standard Version of the Holy Bible. All rights reserved. Scripture quotations marked (NASB) are taken from the New American Standard Bible © 1971. All rights reserved. Scripture quotations marked (GNT) are taken from the Good News Bible (GNB) © 1976 by the American Bible Society. All rights reserved.

## BORN WITH POTENTIAL & PURPOSE

Steps To Discovering God's Amazing Plan For Your Life

Book cover & logo: Berton C. Armstrong: bertoncarmstrong@gmail.com

All Rights Reserved © **2021 by J. Arthur Gipson**

**No part of this book may be reproduced or transmitted in any form or by any means, graphic, electronic, or mechanical, including photocopying, recording, taping, or by any information storage retrieval system, without the written permission of the author.**

**For information contact:**

Bpp4me@gmail.com

ISBN: 979-8-9850385-0-7

Printed in the United States of America

# TABLE OF CONTENTS

Preface .................................................................................................. 7

Introduction ...................................................................................... 11

Chapter One - Understanding Your Potential ............................... 17

Chapter Two - The Purpose of Potential ....................................... 41

Chapter Three - The Responsibility of Potential .......................... 74

Chapter Four - Releasing Your Potential .................................... 100

Chapter Five - Understanding Purpose - Part I ......................... 127

Chapter Six - Understanding Purpose - Part II .......................... 149

Chapter Seven - Purpose Lives On the Inside of You ................ 162

Chapter Eight - Comfort Zones Impact Your Potential & Purpose ........... 177

Chapter Nine - Wisdom and the Mind ........................................ 203

Chapter Ten - What's Blocking You From Maximizing Your Potential .... 232

Chapter Eleven - Born to Lead and Succeed ............................... 252

Chapter Twelve - God's Purpose is in the Name ........................ 271

Final Chapter - God's Plan for Your Life ................................... 285

Scripture References ..................................................................... 312

Endnotes ......................................................................................... 319

# Dedication

*Handwritten note:*

*John,*
*My Beloved Son, and assistant —*
*May you fulfill God's will in your season*

*— Myles Munroe*

**Dr. Myles Munroe: April 20$^{th}$, 1954 – Nov. 9$^{th}$, 2014**

Philippians 1:6:

*"I am certain that God, who began the good work within you will continue His work until it is finally finished on the day of when Christ Jesus returns (NLT)."*

# DEDICATION

*To: My Beloved Son*

*John,*

*The years of your service, support, prayers & love for Ruth & Me will continue to Bring a Harvest of Kingdom Favor to you and your Children. Thanks for everything.*

*Love you*

*Pastor Myles*

**Dr. Myles Munroe: April 20th, 1954 – Nov. 9th, 2014**

Philippians 1:6:

"I am certain that God, who began the good work within you will continue His work until it is finally finished on the day of when Christ Jesus returns (NLT)."

# Acknowledgements

I have the wonderful privilege of recognizing the love of my life, my wife Juliet. You are absolutely amazing as a friend, wife and mother. Your prayers, love, compassion, patience and understanding motivates me every day to release my potential. Thank you for your significant and devoted contribution to this book. I could not have done it without you.

I also wish to recognize my son and daughter, Jeaterai and Nicole. I am thankful for the privilege to be your parent. Over the years, we have spent a lot of time discussing the principles in this book. You were my first students. I am proud of your commitment to maximizing your potential along the path of purpose. Continue to do well.

I also recognize the tremendous gifts and contributions of the late Dr. Myles Munroe, who poured every ounce of his life into training me and thousands of others around the world. I am still amazed at the wisdom, knowledge and understanding that you possessed, as well as your unwavering dedication to representing the Kingdom of God. It is my sincere hope that a portion of your legacy will continue to live on in the content of this book, as my foundational concepts and understanding related to potential and purpose came from you.

To you my valued readers, may each one of you experience the joy of maximizing your potential and fulfilling your purpose for living during your lifetime.

Lastly and most important, I wish to acknowledge the contribution, wisdom, understanding and knowledge of the Holy Spirit. Thank you for sharing with me the wisdom of God, my Source and Creator. It is my hope that this book proves my dedication to serving the Lord Jesus Christ as an ambassador of the Kingdom of God.

# PREFACE

One of the greatest social tragedies of the 21st century is the reality that countless individuals worldwide have no desire to maximize their full potential because of a fear of disrupting their comfortable but unfulfilling environment. Whether self-imposed or forced because of undeniable external circumstances, the internal limits result in a life of average accomplishments, mediocrity, and complacency. Individuals of all ages, and in every socio-economic class find themselves trapped at a certain level in life without hope of finding true peace of mind and fulfillment of needs.

In my first book titled, 12 Steps to a Highly Rewarding Career – *Discovering the Secrets to Defeating Comfort Zones,* Dr. Myles Munroe wrote the following words in the Foreword:

> For over thirty years now, I have traveled to over fifty nations meeting, teaching, and training thousands of individuals to rediscover their purpose in life, understand their awesome potential and maximize their true ability. I have witnessed many who have discovered the secrets of success and rise above the surface of the average. However, I have also been saddened by the thousands who listen to the principles of truth that could set them free but refuse to take the step of faith and venture out beyond their self-imposed limits. I believe most of this fear to explore possibilities is generated by a very subtle culprit called the 'comfort zone.'[1]

Based on personal research, I believe that those profound words of Dr. Munroe remain true today. Many individuals in countries around the world are still victims of self-imposed limits that result in an average life and average accomplishments. Sometimes, challenging societal and economic conditions are reasons why these individuals seek the fulfillment of basic survival needs over the excitement of exploring their life's purpose. In other instances, individuals impose personal limits on their potential because of a strong desire to remain at the most comfortable position in life. The perceived level of comfort experienced in both cases creates mental safe havens. As a result, people gravitate to the mental safe havens because of a fear of stepping out beyond the unknown.

Unfortunately, the temporary mental comfort experienced when individuals create limits and linger in safe havens adds to the belief that the pursuit of purpose and released potential should not be high on the priority list. This mindset is one of the reasons why many people give less than their very best effort in life. Are you one of those individuals? Dr. Munroe encountered thousands of individuals worldwide, and he concluded that the acceptance of personal limits is a global human problem not entirely based on either the social or the economic conditions.

Perhaps, the economically challenged are most concerned with satisfying their basic needs for survival such as food, shelter, and clothing. Their definition of comfortable living is having enough food to eat, clothes on their backs, and a roof over their heads. Surviving extremely difficult economic conditions speaks to the resilience of the human spirit's will to survive. *"It's not where you start or even what happens to you along the way that's important. What is important is that you persevere and never give up on yourself,"* according to Zig Ziglar. In other words, one's economic position in life is not an indictment on their innate potential or purpose. <u>Can the economically challenged achieve a better quality of life by understanding their purpose and maximizing their potential</u>? As you continue to read, you will discover the answer to this question.

The economic middle class is another large group of individuals worldwide that are impacted by self-imposed limits on releasing their full potential. The middle class is separated from the lower class based on their income, ability to accumulate material possessions, and meet their basic needs for survival. The accumulation of material items and ability to meet living expenses tend to give a false sense of contentment in life. Many middle class individuals unknowingly sink into perceived safe zones when the preoccupation with enjoying material comforts take priority over the continual pursuit of purpose and the maximization of potential. <u>Can the middle class enjoy the benefits of material comforts, and find contentment pursuing purpose and maximizing their potential in life</u>? As you continue to read, you will discover the answer to this question.

The last grouping of individuals impacted by self-imposed limits is the wealthy and the societal elite. There are countless true stories about wealthy individuals that are unhappy because their lives are void of true contentment. While it is true that this class of individuals typically enjoys the best that money can buy, it is also true that money cannot buy true contentment in life. The problems occur when the wealthy believe that safe havens can mask the internal emptiness not satisfied by their social privileges, financial independence, economic power, and authority. Benjamin Franklin once said, *"He that is of the opinion money will do everything may well be suspected of doing everything for money."*

In other words, the pursuit and attainment of wealth is not an indication that a person is living a self-actualized life. This is true because a requirement of self-actualization is that you maximize your potential in the form of talents, abilities, or gifts. Having a specific amount of money on hand is not a prerequisite to reach this pinnacle in life. <u>Can the wealthy find contentment, and enjoy the benefits associated with their exclusive social class</u>?

The answer to each of the three questions underlined above is "YES." However, it is very important to understand the nature of your existence. Since each human possesses a body, soul, and spirit, please be aware that it is possible to satisfy the needs of the body and soul but fail to address the needs of the spirit. In other words, I believe that you must also satisfy your spiritual nature to be completely content with life. This requires that you have a healthy relationship with your Creator. Hopefully, you will begin to hear His voice calling, as you read through this book.

Potential and purpose are innate and associated with every talent, ability, and gift (TAG). Your potential is your natural gift from God for the benefit of yourself, family, community, country, and humanity. The world is waiting for individuals that are prepared, equipped and capable of contributing their unique value to further humanity. God is also waiting for you to accept the position that He reserved for you before you were born. The last question is, **are you ready to join the ranks of those that live an intentional life that leads to successful living?**

# Introduction

*"True wisdom comes to each of us when we realize how little we understand about life, ourselves, and the world around us."*
**Socrates**

There are many valuable contributions to humanity that are traced back to ancient civilizations. For instance, Ancient Egyptians were known for their advancements in sciences, architectural and building designs, as well as mathematics to name a few key areas. Equally as interesting is the fact that they had an acute awareness of the importance that self-knowledge plays in living an effective and productive life. Think about this point, the first pyramid existed in the mind of an individual before its manifestation. What caused that person to believe in the unseen thought before it materialized in the seen realm?

Is it possible that the Egyptians knew a valuable secret about the power of individual potential and purpose? Although the answer to that question is unknown, there are clear signs that they possessed advanced knowledge in the area of self-actualization. In fact, their actions, released potential, beliefs, advancements, and achievements, influenced the world during their era and beyond.

One of their most popular proverbs was, *"Know the world in yourself. Never look for yourself in the world, for this would be to project your illusion."* What is your interpretation of that proverb? Are you looking to find yourself by associating with others or do you believe that you can discover your purpose by aligning your decisions to coincide with the expectations of friends and family? The wise Ancient Egyptians believed that self-knowledge is found from within. Do you agree that the secret to your life is found behind the door of your heart? Please be aware that the Ancient Egyptians were not alone in their conclusions about self-discovery.

Following on the heels of Ancient Egypt, another great civilization rose in the West. Ancient Greece produced some of the greatest thinkers known to Western Civilization. Arguably, their most impactful contribution came in the form of a governmental system where citizens were empowered with the freedom to participate in their social and economic development. This system was given the name "Democracy," which means rule by the people. *"Democracy arises out of the notion that those who are equal in any respect are equal in all respects; because men are equally free, they claim to be absolutely free,"* according to Aristotle.

A main premise of democracy is the belief that all men are created equal and ought to have inalienable freedoms and rights to express themselves in a free society. When the phrase *"all men are created equal"* is interpreted in the context of geo-political governing systems, the full weight of the statement and its corresponding truth seems to only apply to those living in democratic societies. What about the millions of people living in countries around the world that embrace other forms of governing systems? Are these people created equal even though the ruling party or governing system rejects this truth?

Aristotle was careful to say, *"Democracy arises out of the notion..."* Therefore, the foundational pillar which solidifies democracy as a governing system for all people is the notion that all are created equal. Bear in mind that this wise philosopher did not say that democracy is the reason that all men are equal. What is the importance of this point? The answer is democracy stands firm on the foundation that every human being is made of the same natural material and require the same opportunities to succeed. Based on this foundation, the belief arises that all men deserve to have an equal chance to experience fulfillment in life through the expression of self under the protection of freedom, liberty, and justice.

For those individuals living under an oppressive governmental system without the freedoms and privileges of democracy, note that you have, at least, one thing in common with those in democratic societies. Before discussing the one thing, bear in mind that Ancient Greeks also developed a comprehensive value system of wise sayings that enlightened and challenged citizens to take responsibility for their self-awareness. The value system consisted of wise statements and principles espoused by recognized leaders in Ancient Greek society. Citizens from every social and economic class accepted and incorporated these values into their daily lives. Taking the same position as Ancient Egyptians, they concluded that the most profound principle of all was the admonition, "know thyself."

This thought-provoking statement drove Ancient Greeks to achieve significant advancements in the fields of governmental affairs, science, art, philosophy, and architecture. Implementing a democratic governing system and the adaptation of basic principles for successful living proved to be extremely effective for Greek citizens. However, many centuries later, numerous individuals in democratic countries have adopted lifestyles that are inconsistent, and counterproductive to releasing their full potential and discovering purpose.

Democratic societies create opportunities for individuals to reach the pinnacle of self-actualization and satisfaction with life. Nevertheless, these societies have also become breeding grounds for an entitlement mentality, complacency, and dependency. In addition, countless people seem to associate material things, social status, financial wealth, and relationships with "successful" people as the only factors that reveals one's value and potential. Sadly, many people also believe that pursuing a career path that will guarantee a comfortable living is better than pursuing a path that will lead to peace of mind. If you fall into this category, be aware that there is truth in this Ancient Egyptian proverb which says, *"Man must learn to increase his sense of responsibility and of the fact that everything he does will have its consequences."*

The bottom line is that every human is tasked with discovering self. This book is dedicated to helping you define your self-existence through the exploration of your talents, abilities, and gifts (TAGs). I will plant a seed in your mind that releasing your full potential and living a purpose-filled life is not only possible but necessary as well. Releasing your potential along the path of purpose leads to self-fulfillment, self-actualization, and peace of mind. It took me many years to understand life from this perspective and to accept the true meaning of self-actualization. I am amazed and disappointed that it took so long to make the connection that I have sought after since I can remember. Yet, on the other hand, I am thankful that the answers to many important life questions now resonates from the depths of my soul.

This book contains valuable information that will free your potential and make your purpose a reality. It is imperative to understand that the journey begins with the most important question related to "knowing thyself." What is the question? The question that has proven to be a mental stumbling block for centuries is "Who Am I."

This is a question that every human ought to have an answer to, but very few do. This epic question has survived the test of time because it relates to a fundamental and foundational issue that exemplifies the complexity of life. I have now come to understand, accept, and agree that mental struggles are shared by all people. It is ironic that in a diverse world approaching 200 countries with over 7.7 billion people, that an incalculable number of cultures and races share a mutual theme.

All people face the same issue regarding this problem whether rich or poor, young, or old, black, or white, male, or female. <u>Now, going back to the comment that there is, at least, one thing that those individuals living under a governing system other than democracy have in common</u>. It is essential for every human being to understand that answering the question "Who Am I" is a responsibility associated with having potential. Interestingly, this responsibility of potential is the one issue that binds all of us together and creates an equal platform for everyone.

There is good news for you. You will discover how to become the exception to the dilemma of discovering self. Reading this book will establish the proper foundation to help you discover and fulfill your destiny. You will begin to have a new appreciation for your personal value and importance. You will also gain tremendous insight concerning potential and your purpose for living. It is my hope that you are ready for the journey, because the "true greatness of your potential has yet to be revealed."

Additionally, you will discover that you are uniquely qualified to lead and succeed in your area of talent, ability, and gift (TAG). In fact, it is your birth right to be a leader in your area of gifting. From start to finish, you will begin to recognize that your life is not an experiment, but a purposeful existence full of opportunities to display your inherent potential. Additionally, you will learn how to turn those situations that block your path of purpose into positive learning experiences. The wisdom that you will acquire from the many quotes and life principles will increase your confidence and accomplishments. This wisdom will also give you the tools to become a possibility creator and an impossibility destroyer, as it relates to situations blocking your path of purpose. At the end of the journey, you will recognize the truth about your personal dominion and leadership role in society.

Are you a precocious young person looking to develop a plan for your life? Perhaps, are you a high school senior about to graduate and unsure about your future path? Do you fall into the category of being a dissatisfied employee working a dead-end job? Between jobs? Rich and famous but lack peace of mind. Powerful and important but secretly perplexed about your career path? Or, are you a retiree who still has more to contribute to society? Wherever you are on the path of life, think about these points:

Potential isn't measured by what you have done, where you are from or who you associate with. It is measured by the seeds of natural abilities buried in your recurring dreams and desires of the heart related to a predetermined area of specialization. This appointment with destiny exposes your true value and ensures your success in life. You were born for greatness and to have a fruitful life.

This book is dedicated to helping you discover your true value, God's plan for your life and the path that will ensure your success. It's not too late to plant your valuable seeds and receive the fruit of your potential. Remember the acronym TAGs (talents, abilities, gifts), as it will be used very frequently throughout this book. Let the process begin in you today. **Are you ready for an amazing journey and learning experience?**

# Chapter One

## Understanding Your Potential

*"Without continual growth and progress, such words as improvement, achievement, and success have no meaning."*
**Benjamin Franklin**

Smothered under the unrelenting oppression of apartheid, a powerful seed took root and grew into a pillar of strength that changed the course of life for millions of people. At the age of 45, he stood in the dock prepared to deliver his personal defense before the Pretoria Supreme Court. With the fate of his suffering people at stake, his bold leadership and commitment to paying the ultimate price for freedom was unwavering.

For over four hours, he delivered a passionate message outlining the grievances and unjust treatment of a voiceless people routinely terrorized by a repressive government. During his speech, he thoroughly articulated his evolving political response to the continuous tide of extreme social and racial injustices. Arguably, the most memorable words came at the end of his voluntary defense. His final statement in that emotionally charged courtroom was as follows:

> During my lifetime I have dedicated myself to this struggle of the African people. I have fought against white domination, and I have fought against black suppression. I have cherished the ideal of a democratic and free society in which all persons live together in harmony and with equal opportunities. It is an ideal which I hope to live for

and to achieve. But if needs be, it is an ideal for which I am prepared to die. ²

At the conclusion of the trial, the court found Nelson Mandela and other key members of the African National Congress guilty of crimes against the state. A life sentence was Mandela's punishment for being a founding leader of the military wing of the African National Congress. However, his fight for freedom and justice continued while incarcerated under inhumane conditions. His courageous stance against the extreme odds caused seeds of possibility to sprout in the hearts of the people he fought to free from tyranny. From a small prison cell, Mandela served as the inspiration behind a growing cry for justice and civil liberties. In his heart, he believed that his beloved South Africa had the potential to be a country for all people and races.

After years of oppression and segregation in South Africa, the international community eventually rallied behind the masses and their unrelenting cries for freedom. Together, they forced the South African political regime to enact unprecedented social, economic, and civic changes for millions. On February 11th, 1990, Mandela won his freedom from prison after 27 years of enduring harsh and unimaginable conditions. At the age of 76, he made history as the first black elected president of South Africa thereby signifying a radical end to apartheid. Armed with a mature understanding concerning the power of potential to overcome what appears impossible through natural eyes, *"It always seems impossible until it's done,"* according to Mandela.

## What is Potential

The bible records an encounter that Jesus had with a father whose son was controlled by an evil spirit. The concerned parent pleaded with Jesus, *"Have mercy on us and help us, **if you can**."* Jesus' response to this desperate plea offers considerable insight into the concept of potential. In fact, Jesus' reply appears as though he was surprised that the man said, *"if you can,"* because he understood the power of transformation that is associated with potential.

Listen to his response. *"What do you mean if I can?"* Jesus asked. He continued to say, *"Anything is possible if a person believes."*

Let's look at a very familiar phenomenon to explore the concept of possibilities. I am always amazed when I consider that we can communicate with someone that is thousands of miles away without the need for wires connecting the two phones. This is possible because the earth is naturally equipped with electromagnetic waves. Radio waves are an example of these invisible but powerful electromagnetic waves. Radio waves allow data or energy to be transmitted through the air waves using a transmitter and receiver. When the transmitter connects to the receiver, then communication is possible.

Now, this is a very important concept for you to understand. Did electromagnetic waves exist during the time that Jesus walked the earth? The answer is "YES." If so, then what prevented ancient civilizations from using it to communicate? Well, the technology that enables the utilization of radio waves was developed after German physicist, Henrick Hertz, discovered electromagnetic waves around 1864. Therefore, the conclusion is that when inherent potential is discovered, accepted, believed, and developed, then it enables you to connect to existing possibilities that are unseen but real.

Now, moving back to Jesus' comment, *"Anything is possible if a person believes"* is mind blowing. His comment suggests that if you can visualize it in your mind, accept it as a possibility, develop that thought and believe, then you are equipped to unleash the power in the form of potential to make it happen. Let me rephrase this concept for clarification. Jesus was saying that God has enabled you to manifest things that seem impossible to achieve. The question is whether you believe that you can achieve what you desire utilizing the power of your potential.

Merriam-Webster's online dictionary defines potential as *"existing in possibility."*[3] However, there are several other interesting ways to define this word. Potential is also defined as *"dormant ability."* This means that certain abilities exist in the unseen realm before manifesting into the seen realm. In other words, potential is present before the materialization or manifestation of your talents, abilities, and gifts (TAGs). Therefore, potential is also *the inherent ability to achieve specific results prior to manifestation.* Additionally, potential is defined as *unseen power capable of producing continuous outcomes.*

## I. Existing in Possibility

Existing in possibility is the most inclusive and comprehensive definition of potential. It incorporates the true essence of why you have potential and what it can do for you. *"We all have possibilities we don't know about. We can do things we don't even dream we can do,"* according to Dale Carnegie. Do you believe that you possess potential, and you are able to do great things with it? Have you placed your dream behind a locked door because it seems too big or impossible for you to accomplish? Bear in mind that potential and possibility are inseparable. This is an important question that you must ask yourself. Why would God give you TAGs, if He did not intend for you to use them at some point during your lifetime?

The intended outcome of potential is manifested change which occurs because of the unseen and inherent possibilities stored in your seed. A brief look into the process of seeds developing into fruit will help you gain a better understanding of the possibilities associated with potential. Under the right conditions, the inherent capabilities of the seed enable it to produce fruit and seeds on a continuous basis. Although the seed possesses the innate possibilities to transform into fruit, the fruit is not evident when looking at the seed. The seed must undergo transition and development before the intended outcome is manifested. The process requires the seed to transform into a fruit bearing tree. The fruit manifests when the process and development stages are successfully achieved.

Possibilities are within the seed in the form of potential to become, to release and to create change. The relevance of the seed analogy is that your potential can create something valuable that is yet to be seen. When you look at the end result, which is the fruit, the normal response would be to say that it is impossible to get the fruit from a seed. The seed does not look like or taste like the fruit, but it possesses the power to transform into something valuable and beneficial. The same principle applies to your potential. Based on the right conditions, your hidden potential will turn situations that seem improbable or impossible into possibilities.

> **Potential turns perceived impossibilities into possibilities.**

You may have asked the question in your mind, *"How does potential turn impossibilities into possibilities?"* I am glad that you asked the question because the answer is very important to understand. Your potential is a seed full of unseen possibilities, but it waits for the right conditions before the process of manifestation takes place. This means that some degree of change must take place before the end result becomes a possibility.

**Change is a manifested possibility orchestrated by your potential.** What do I mean by this statement? This statement means that potential is filled with power to change people, situations, and circumstances. Whenever you tap into your potential, power is released to turn perceived impossibilities into possibilities. That is why your potential is a key factor in changing your outcomes to line up with the path and passion of your heart. I have listed below, for your review, various outcomes that occur whenever your potential is either released or dormant:

**Released potential create(s)** - *Possibilities that initiate change and make things possible. It creates beneficial outcomes that produce good and helpful results or effects.*

**Dormant potential perpetuate(s)** - *Impossibilities that overshadow possibilities and creates uncertainty. Dormant potential fuels unbeneficial* *and untrue thoughts that limit your possible outcomes. It also perpetuates doubt which makes situations seem impossible to overcome.*

Hopefully, you have a better understanding of the definition *"existing in possibility."* Remember that impossible situations become possible when you release your potential along the path of purpose. You possess the power to create options and opportunities in life. The possibilities related to your specific purpose are unique to you alone. These possibilities can produce beneficial results that will enrich the quality of your life. As you consider your next steps in life, don't forget the fact that potential resting in a dormant state is unbeneficial and unproductive to you.

## II. Dormant Ability

Dormant ability is another popular definition of potential. This definition suggests that there is internal power to create possibilities in your life, but the switch that controls the power rests in an off position. Think for a moment about an electrical light switch. It controls the power and light, but it is not the source. When you turn the switch on, "WOW" light appears. The light represents the outcome of an intended result that was previously dormant.

The next point that I am about to make is very important for you to keep in mind. **You were born to release your internal power because it is designed to give light to the world.** Your power exists within you in the form of potential. The light that you share is the fruit of your released potential. You are the only person that can answer this next question. Perhaps, do you think that the reason why you feel incomplete or as though something is missing in your life is because unreleased power is burning in your heart?

If so, I would like to share with you that the most critical consequence of having dormant ability is the unforeseen impact it has on the quality of your life, career, dreams, and desires of the heart. The impact is significant because the prerequisite for fulfilling purpose is the ability to recognize, harness and release your creative power of potential. Another unfortunate consequence of having unreleased potential is the reality that you will never discover who you are born to be. I realize that this statement may seem difficult to digest. Think about it for a moment, if who you are naturally is never seen or kept locked behind a closed door, then how will you or anyone else know what or who you are supposed to become?

Let's look at the issue of dormant ability from a different perspective. At a certain point in its development, the parents begin to spend more time away from the nest and bring less food to the young bird. During this critical phase, the young bird must draw upon its dormant ability, exercise its wings and practice flying from the comfort of the nest. Whether motivated by the lack of food or by the insistence of its parents, the fledgling must leave the comfort of the nest and fly for the first time.

The bird's purpose is to fly, and its potential enables it to accomplish this objective. Although the potential to fly is innate, it rests in a dormant state until activated. If the bird fails to activate the potential to fly, then it will not be able to fulfill its true purpose and will ultimately become a victim of circumstances. More sadly, it will never resemble or experience the benefits of what it was born to become.

> **Potential is intended to be your inherited investment that yields exponential growth and returns.**

Just as the young bird's potential is linked to its ability to fly, your potential is also linked to certain purpose-oriented results. Dormant ability is not valuable in its unused state. What if you had a certain amount of money deposited on your account in the bank, but you refuse to withdraw it? Although there is money in your account, you must withdraw and use it to enjoy the benefits of having it. Are you starting to sense that there is much more to your potential than you realized? I hope so!!! Let's move on to the next definition.

### III. Inherent ability to manifest specific results

This next definition is an amazing truth about your potential. Has anyone ever told you that inherent ability to manifest specific results is a consequence of having potential? What's amazing is that there are predetermined outcomes already reserved or assigned to you. These outcomes will enrich your life and create unimaginable joy. David confirmed the reality of a predetermined future when he spoke these words about God's plan for his life, *"You saw me before I was born. Every day of my life was recorded in your book. Every moment was laid out before a single day had passed."* Did you know that God has already arranged for you to produce predetermined results?

Keep in mind that the full extent of the things your potential will do for you may not be revealed initially. This is a major reason why you cannot give up on your dreams and the visions that come to point you in a certain direction. Eleanor Roosevelt was correct when she said, *"The future belongs to those who believe in the beauty of their dreams."* **Your purposeful dreams hold beautiful potential realities.** You deserve to enjoy life, achieve success, and bask in the wonderful experience of manifested potential.

During his lifetime, George Washington Carver was an educator, artist, scientist, botanist, chemist, inventor, lecturer, mentor, pianist, and economic advisor, among other things. He was born in the 1860s into slavery as a poor sickly boy. He was also separated from his birth mother when only a week old. His biological father died before he was born, and he left his adopted parents' household at the age of thirteen. Yet, in addition to the skills noted above, Carver's potential allowed him to achieve many other accomplishments. Although the list of accolades, achievements and accomplishments are too many to list, it is noteworthy to mention the following:

- He invented over 300 uses for peanuts.
- He met three American presidents (Theodore Roosevelt, Calvin Coolidge, Franklin D. Roosevelt).
- He was a close friend to Henry Ford (Pioneer of Ford Motor

Company).
- He received a job offer of over $100,000 from Edison Laboratories.
- His portrait appeared on US postage stamps and currency.[4]

Let's take a deeper look into one aspect of Carver's inherent ability, the invention of over 300 uses for peanuts. How did he discover so many different uses from such a small nut? Here is the answer that he reportedly gave during a speech in the summer of 1920, *"Years ago, I went into my laboratory and said, Dear Mr. Creator, please tell me what the universe was made for?"* The great Creator answered, *"You want to know too much for that little mind of yours. Ask for something more your size, little man."* Then he asked, *"Please, Mr. Creator, tell me what man was made for?"* Again, the Creator replied, *"You are still asking for too much. Cut down on the extent and improve on the intent."* So, then he asked, *"Please, Mr. Creator, will you tell me why the peanut was made?"* [5]

Again, let's reflect on my previous comment, when I said, Jesus was saying that if you believe in the power of God and also believe that you possess the potential to do something or become something, then that belief opens the door of possibilities that existed before you started believing. Carver's testimony and accomplishments validate this truth. The various uses of the peanut existed prior to his discoveries, but Carver had to activate his inherent potential to manifest the results. It is obvious that he understood how the power of God works with your potential to manifest or materialize possibilities that were previously invisible, unknown, and unseen. Are you aware of the Apostle Paul's words, *"I can do all things through Christ who strengthens me?"*

Carver began his life as a victim of circumstances with numerous disadvantages and ended it as one of the most impressive American figures of his lifetime. He was a tremendous asset to America and an inspiration to thousands of people, even though he started his life as a poor orphaned black slave. His life and legacy are a testament to the transforming power of potential. Carver's steps in life led him on a path of a very productive and fruitful life. He once said, *"Start where you are, with what you have. Make something of it and never be satisfied."* His words and the life that he led, clearly indicates that he was aware of the power of potential to manifest specific results. If for some reason, you are struggling to believe in your self-worth, I encourage to continue to read because you will discover that there is a direct correlation between your potential, God's plan, and your life's purpose.

> **U**ndeveloped potential is personal wealth waiting to be polished and put on display.

The magnificence of your creation will continue to unravel as you read. Suffice to say, your life is more important than your previous accomplishments or lack thereof. Regardless of how you feel or what others have said or done, your TAGs are not useless or ineffective gifts. *Your abilities are strategic instruments that help to guide you along a specific course in life and fulfill specific objectives.* For these reasons, it is important to understand, recognize and accept your natural abilities. Listed below are 6 classifications of abilities that typically affect your potential:

- Unknown –the innate abilities are neither known nor discovered.
- Known – innate abilities are known and accepted thereby creating possibilities in life.
- Undeveloped – innate abilities are known, but not developed fully.
- Developed – innate abilities are known and refined increasing the possibility of achieving the desired result with distinction.
- Unapplied – innate abilities are known, but unused resulting in underachievement and failure to maximize your potential.
- Applied – innate abilities are known, developed, and applied thereby creating peace of mind and a productive life related to your purpose for living.

When evaluating these categories, it is possible to conclude several important facts. Firstly, there is no significant benefit from having unknown,

Understanding Your Potential

undeveloped, or unapplied abilities. Secondly, unapplied abilities lead to a life of underachievement and failure to maximize your potential. Thirdly, positive outcomes occur whenever your abilities are known, developed, and applied. Fourthly, applied abilities create a productive, fruitful, and rewarding life. The conclusion is that undiscovered and unreleased potential leads to a yearning for relevance. It also leads to uncertainty about your designated course and discontentment with your life's accomplishments. The chart below divides the categories into two groups that highlight these points:

**Unbeneficial**

<u>Unknown</u>  -  <u>Undeveloped</u>  -  <u>Unapplied</u>  =  Uncertain Purpose

**Beneficial**

<u>Known</u>  +  <u>Developed</u>  +  <u>Applied</u>  =  Fruitful Life

---
**Applied potential leads to a fruitful and successful life's journey.**

---

The ability to manifest specific results depends on knowing, developing, and applying your potential. Carver's admonition to *"never be satisfied"* are important words of wisdom. The seeds of potential that you have will enable you to live an effective, productive, and fruitful life from start to finish. These benefits of applied potential will also produce continuous purposeful outcomes and results.

### IV. Unseen power capable of producing continuous outcomes

Have you ever wondered in amazement about the longevity and popularity related to released potential? Let me clarify this point with another question. When you think about your favorite movie star, athlete, performing artist, teacher or any other professional, how long were they producing beneficial outcomes for themselves and others? Without much thought, you would agree that their success lasted much longer than one movie, game, occasion, or event. Their success was or is continuous because of released potential.

Natural springs are visual evidence of an underground water source. The source of the water is a natural phenomenon that requires no intervention from humans. Some springs produce vast quantities of water while others produce small volumes. Nonetheless, all springs have two things in common. Firstly, the water reserve is hidden on the inside of the earth. Secondly, the water flows to the surface on a continuous basis.

As you know, your potential is hidden in your TAGs. The significance of your fruit of potential is always unseen until it manifests, just like a natural spring. It is unnatural for a spring to stop flowing. Likewise, it is unnatural for your potential to stop flowing.

Your potential is meant to flow continuously. If it ceases to flow, then the continuous manifestation of your desired results will cease as well. If this happens, then your potential will be unbeneficial to you and others. I sincerely hope that you agree that it is time to release your natural spring in the form of potential. Your future depends on making the right decision.

## V. The future of something trapped in the present

God said to Jeremiah, *"I knew you before I formed you in your mother's womb. Before you were born I set you apart and appointed you as my prophet to the nations."* Does this mean that Jeremiah's future was trapped in his present? Absolutely, he entered the earth with his potential and purpose already on the inside. The word "appointed" means to be given or to be entrusted. God gave Jeremiah the seeds of potential to yield the fruit of a prophet. In a similar regard, God created you with the materials and tools to match your assigned task or assignment.

The future of something trapped in the present is an exciting and motivating definition because it affirms the belief that your potential is intended to take you to a future designation. ***Potential erupts into manifested power whenever your present meets your destined future.*** Do you recall the comments made about the young bird that we discussed earlier in this chapter? If so, it is important to understand that the day the young bird begins to fly is the day that its present meets its future destiny. At that point, the present life for the bird matches its intended course, because its potential to fly is no longer trapped but released.

This concept applies to your potential as well. The definition that potential is the future of something trapped in the present relates to your predestined path being trapped in dormant potential. At this very moment, your future related to what you would like to become or to do is trapped inside of you waiting to be released. To offset this dilemma, you must understand your potential, identify the path that you are destined to take and be determined to release your power to manifest the desired result.

*"What this power is I cannot say; all I know is that it exists and it becomes available only when a man is in that state of mind in which he knows exactly what he wants and is fully determined not to quit until he finds it."* Those words were spoken by Alexander Graham Bell. I believe that the power that he referred to is potential which is activated once you recognize your TAGs and decide to move in the right direction. Do you know that there are natural characteristics associated with potential that help you to understand it fully?

## The Nature of Potential

Naturally speaking, potential serves as a gateway between the hidden you and the person you are destined to become. It provides you with an opportunity to place your priceless commodity on display for the world to receive and admire. Your willingness to release your potential frees it to follow its natural course. At this stage of reading, there are 5 additional principles about the nature of potential that are important for you to understand:

**Nature #1 - Potential is not worthless, it produces valuable results.**

Do you believe that your life is worthless or valuable? I will answer the question for you, just in case, circumstances or your environment has caused you to question your existence. You are just as valuable as a priceless diamond. A raw diamond comes in many shapes, sizes, and colors. The rough unpolished stone looks nothing like the polished cut stone. To the untrained eye, the raw diamond holds little to no value. However, to a professionally trained jeweler, the true potential of the raw uncut stone is evident at first glimpse.

Although I have never met you, I believe that you possess tremendous value in the form of potential. Unfortunately, your value may not be evident to you and others. Why? Much like the raw diamond, your potential in its raw, unpolished, and unrefined state may seem to be worth very little in possibilities. Don't believe this assessment about your life. The real value of your life is confirmed when your talents, abilities and gifts are polished, refined and displayed for others to see.

Nevertheless, I am not naïve. I realize that there are countless individuals that believe only a few privileged people have potential. Perhaps, their belief derives from the fact that many people exhibit inactive, under-developed or manufactured potential. Nonetheless, the idea that some have potential, and others do not is an erroneous thought. The key to proving the critics wrong is to awaken your sleeping potential and point it in the direction of your destiny.

**Nature #2 - Potential is dormant, it responds to stimulus.**

Have you ever heard the term "sleeping giant?" It is used to refer to someone or thing that possesses significant potential, but it is either unrealized or it has not materialized. The term also means that there is a significant untapped resource resting in a state of dormancy. Guess What? If you have not yet maximized your full potential, then you are a "sleeping giant." By no means is your potential to do great things small. It is capable of enlarging your area of influence and greatly increasing the demand for your talent, ability or gift.

Consider these additional enlightening points when you think about potential. It is stored energy that ignites accomplishments through predetermined actions and abilities. It responds to internal and external stimulus. It sleeps until awakened by some sort of activity. If you are wondering how to awaken your "sleeping giant," then the answer is simple. You can awaken the great power that you possess by taking intentional steps in the direction of purpose and God's will for your life. Today, make a conscious effort to start the ball rolling in the right direction. If you need a little motivation to get started, a glimpse into the life of Benjamin Franklin will help.

> **Inaction is a contradiction to potential.**

Benjamin Franklin was a founding father of the United States of America. At various points during his lifetime, he was also a publisher, writer, politician, scientist, entrepreneur, inventor, and diplomat. During his early years, he was the epitome of a "sleeping giant." Can you imagine one person possessing all those abilities and more? His limited access to formal education did not prevent him from becoming one of America's most impressive historical figures. His zeal to learn and grow as a person stimulated him to achieve successful outcomes.

In his era, many people struggled with the thought of pursuing things that seemed out of their reach for various practical reasons. Unfortunately, this issue still holds true today as people find it hard to believe that hidden within them is the solution to an issue that effects their daily lives. Franklin was stimulated into action by the circumstances that surrounded him. He responded by releasing his potential as a solution to either filling a void or addressing a prevailing need. This quote he once made offers words of wisdom,

*"Hide not your talents. They for use were made. What's a sundial in the shade?"*

> **T**he greatness of your potential is refined as you grow and experience different things in life.

Are you familiar with the story of David and Goliath? Goliath awoke the giant inside of David when he challenged Israel and their God. Listen to David's reply to his challenge, *"What will a man get for killing this Philistine and ending his defiance of Israel? Who is this pagan Philistine anyway, that he is allowed to defy the armies of the living God?"* Although David was much younger than the soldiers in the army and much smaller than Goliath, he did what seemed to everyone, including King Saul, to be impossible.

David's encounter with Goliath is an amazing testament to the awesome power of activated potential. Standing in front of him was a menacing mountain of a man. Goliath was a giant and a skilled warrior. David approached him with a sling and small stones.

As you read the full encounter found in I Samuel 17, can you picture yourself as a spectator watching the events unfold? A young boy picking a fight with the biggest, tallest, strongest, meanest, and most experienced warrior. I am sure that the entire situation seemed crazy to everyone, except David. He did not waver in his belief that activated potential changes situations that seem impossible, at first glance. Goliath did not die when David spoke to him, he died when David activated his developed potential and used it.

The message is that God gives potential to you to be an agent of change, just like David. For this reason, your potential cannot remain in an inactive state. Mountains and giants that attempt to stop you from fulfilling your purpose in life can be removed. Are you willing to free your TAGs from the shackles of complacency, doubt, fear, or hesitation to see what's behind the door of released potential? Goliath stimulated the giant inside of David. Once awakened, David's potential proved to be much greater than the enormous obstacles in front of him. What do you need to motivate you into action?

**Nature #3 - Potential does not mature instantly; it develops over time.**

I understand that we live in an age of instant access to information and things through the worldwide web. Albeit, everything in life is not instant, as some things take time to develop. Your potential is an example of this reality. It is the nature of potential to develop and mature as you continuously use it. Your talent, ability or gift must undergo a process of refining before you are able to fully maximize it. Once this happens, then perhaps you will become as well-known as Michelangelo.

Some regard Michelangelo as one of the greatest artists of all time. For over 500 years, hundreds of thousands of visitors have traveled to Vatican City, Rome for a glimpse of his magnificent work on the Sistine Chapel ceiling and altar wall. Invariably, the visitors leave awe stricken after seeing firsthand the intricate and acute details of his masterpieces. However, these great works were not his only masterpieces.

He completed many paintings and sculptures that continue to receive international acclaim as some of the greatest artistic treasures known to humanity. Despite this tremendous respect, it is important to understand that Michelangelo artistic genius was not instant. At the age of 13, his father sent him to study as an apprentice artist. Subsequent years following his initial training, he had other opportunities to refine his abilities. At each stage of training and development, his confidence and abilities grew stronger. [6]

Potential comes in the form of seeds of possibilities. Just as seeds go through a process of development, potential undergoes a developmental phase before the true value becomes evident. Michelangelo once stated, *"I saw the angel in the marble and carved until I set him free."* His comments suggest that greatness is not in the recognition of one's potential, but more so in the ability to manifest the things seen through the window of the heart.

Therefore, *true greatness comes when your potential develops to the point whereby it is capable of producing an exact replica of the hidden image revealed in the secret crevices of your thoughts and dreams.* Michelangelo discovered his potential at an early age and worked very hard to master his skill for many years. The tremendous skill and beauty of his works are a clear indication that his potential was innate and not manufactured. More importantly, his great masterpieces reveal the amazing possibilities of fully developed and released potential.

**Nature #4 - Potential is discovered not manufactured.**

Did you know that attempting to manufacture potential is a violation of your original nature? Attempting to manufacture potential is a violation of your original nature because it requires you to do something that does not come naturally or to become someone that you are not supposed to be. Although some may have tried, it is not possible to sing the way Whitney Houston sung, play basketball the way Michael Jordon played or influence the world of computer technology the same way Steve Jobs and Bill Gates did.

This doesn't mean that you cannot make your own mark in life, it only means that true success comes when you add your uniqueness and potential to your assigned purpose. Unfortunately, due to a lack of potential to produce the desired or specified results, many people attempt to reach the mark through the manufacturing of results. As an example, each year athletes from around the world resort to cheating to enhance their potential and possibilities of achieving greatness. However, it is important to understand that *true potential is natural and requires no foreign substance to be great.*

Any attempt to manufacture results is a clear indication that either you do not have the natural potential, or it is not developed enough to accomplish the objective. Remember that God made sure that you were perfectly and

*Understanding Your Potential* 35

wonderfully equipped to fulfill the purpose that He assigned to you. By no means am I advocating quitting or giving up on your dreams if you possess the potential, perhaps you will be able to achieve your desired objective through additional hard work, dedication, and perseverance. Nevertheless, ask yourself, "Am I doing this because it is my purpose in life or am I doing this for other reasons?"

**Nature #5 - Potential is not endless, it is subject to time.**

Are you aware that your potential cannot stop the hands of time from moving forward? In other words, you cannot prevent change from occurring in your life. Always remember that your purpose lasts for a lifetime but your potential is subjected to time. Therefore, I encourage you to not make a habit of saying that *"I will pursue my dream tomorrow"* or *"I will follow the path of my heart when I get older."*

An athlete possesses the potential to compete within a particular sport. However, there is a timeframe on the potential that the athlete possesses to play at the highest level. The opportunity is based on their physical and mental ability to compete up to the designated standard. Once they reach a certain age, his or her athletic ability diminishes and the potential to meet the specified standards gradually fades away. At that point, most discover that they have potential to do other things. Are you aware of how this point relates to your potential?

Remember that when the timeframe expires on releasing potential in one area of your life, then the opportunity exists to discover your other hidden seeds of potential. *"Consult not your fears but your hopes and your dreams. Think not about your frustrations, but about your unfulfilled potential. Concern yourself not with what you tried and failed in, but with what it is still possible for you to do."* Those words from Pope John XXIII are encouraging.

Although time brings about physical and natural changes that may negatively affect some aspects of your potential, be encouraged because you have enough seeds of potential to last a lifetime. Therefore, *"Don't let the fear of the time it will take to accomplish something stand in the way of your doing it. The time will pass anyway; we might just as well put that passing time to the best possible use."* Those instructions from Earl Nightingale are excellent advice. What are you going to do with his advice? Are you prepared to move forward in life?

# THE NEXT STEP

There is an Ancient Egyptian proverb that says, *"To know means to record in ones memory, but to understand means to blend with the thing and assimilate it oneself."* You can interpret the saying in several ways. However, in the context of this chapter, it means that when you truly understand your potential, then you should work towards manifesting it. Did you know that your released potential forms your identity in life? This is true because potential changes your exterior environment and circumstances to reflect your internal dreams, desires, and thoughts.

Although released potential is able to win the external fight over your destiny, it is powerless against the internal damage created by an unbelieving heart. Don't let these words of Edgar Allen Poe become your reality, *"Deep into that darkness peering, long I stood there, wondering, fearing, doubting, dreaming dreams no mortal ever dared to dream before."* Instead, listen to God's promise and words of comfort, *"Don't be afraid, for I am with you. Don't be discouraged, for I am your God. I will strengthen you and help you. I will hold you up with my victorious right hand."*

Do you believe that God wants to help you manifest your potential and pursue your purpose in life? If so, don't allow yourself to doubt, don't become discourage and don't be afraid of your future. Hopefully, you will agree with the statements that I have made thus far about the tremendous value of your potential. God promises to help you live a victorious life. At this stage, you must accept the fact that your potential will assist you in achieving things that you thought were impossible to accomplish.

This chapter provided foundational information to help build a basic understanding of the value hidden inside of you in the form of potential. In the next chapter, we will dive deeper into exploring the concepts of potential. As you read along, it is imperative that you remember the definitions, principles, and illustrations, because each succeeding chapter will add more information to what you have already learned. Remember this important point as you move forward, ***Potential is your internal power that's capable of generating unimaginable accomplishments while shattering the barrier of impossibilities.***

> **Quick reference to understanding your potential principles:**

1. Potential will turn your situations that seem improbable or impossible into possibilities.
2. Potential turns perceived impossibilities into possibilities.
3. True potential speaks from within and directs your path towards manifesting possibilities.
4. The prerequisite for fulfilling purpose is the ability to recognize, harness and release your creative power of potential.
5. Inherent ability to manifest specific results is a consequence of having potential.
6. Undeveloped potential is personal wealth waiting to be polished and put on display.
7. Your abilities are strategic instruments that help to guide you along a specific course in life.
8. Applied potential leads to a fruitful and successful life's journey.
9. Your potential is evidence that what others consider to be impossible is possible to or for you.
10. Potential erupts into manifested power whenever your present meets your destined future.
11. Your purpose provides a future destined path intended specifically for you.
12. The nature of potential is expression, and the responsibility of potential is manifestation.
13. Potential power is a universal attribute of all living beings that fuels growth and development.
14. The true nature of potential is the expression and manifestation of the original intent of a thing.
15. Potential provides a gateway between the hidden you and the person you are destined to become.

16. Life is a stage to showcase the greatness of your unique potential.
17. Potential is stored energy that ignites accomplishments through predetermined actions and abilities.
18. The greatness of your potential is refined as you grow and experience different things in life.
19. True potential is natural and requires no foreign substance to be great, only hard work.
20. Potential is your internal power that's capable of generating unimaginable accomplishments while shattering the barrier of impossibilities.

# Chapter Two

## The Purpose of Potential

> *"There is no passion to be found playing small –
> in settling for a life that is less than the one
> you are capable of living."*
> **Nelson Mandela**

On June 8th, 1982, President Ronald Reagan gave a tremendous speech to British members of Parliament at the Palace of Westminster in London. Standing with an air of confidence, resolve and power, he eloquently addressed his viewpoint that totalitarianism and tyranny would fall to the growing outcry for political change. He also spoke on the rise of democracy as the only viable alternative to the human desire for freedom. His thirty-four-minute speech was considered short but captivating and memorable. He prophetically predicted the fall of the Soviet Union and Communism, due to the rise of the human spirit seeking freedom of self-determination and self-expression.

Many will argue that President Reagan's direct opposition and confrontational policies resulted in the collapse of the Soviet Union and the radical shift away from Communism. Contrarily, others will suggest that his military spending and indirect involvement in Soviet military conflicts fueled the Cold War and international political tension. Nevertheless, President Reagan's speech before the British Parliament was also nothing less than a masterful and eloquent viewpoint about the natural destiny of the human spirit.

President Reagan believed that the destiny of the human spirit is not to be controlled and oppressed by a privileged and select few. He stated, *"What I am describing now is a plan and a hope for the long term -- the march of freedom and democracy which will leave Marxism-Leninism on the ash-heap of history as it has left other tyrannies which stifle the freedom and muzzle the self-expression of the people."*[7]

Less than a decade later, the world witnessed an unstoppable tide of change that swept across the Soviet Union and Communist controlled countries. On December 29th, 1991, the Soviet Union collapsed thereby enabling 15 countries and millions of citizens the right to determine their own national and personal destinies. Two years prior to the full and complete collapse of the Soviet Union, major political changes also took place in Poland, Hungary, and East Germany. The infamous Berlin wall fell on November 9th, 1989.[8]

President Reagan's policies were proactive and aggressive. He developed and successfully implemented a strategy to minimize the reign of terror and its assault on the human spirit. As a result, millions of people from former Communist controlled nations joined millions of others in democratic countries in possessing the freedom to discover and express their potential. This statement that he once made sums up what he believed about the inherent value found in every human, *"I know in my heart that man is good. That what is right will always eventually triumph. And there's purpose and worth to each and every life."*

Arthur Ashe, the famed African American tennis player once said, *"My potential is more than can be expressed within the bounds of my race or ethnic identity."* His words epitomize the sentiments of the Ancient Greek philosophers and the viewpoints of Reagan. His words also validate the belief that potential is not limited to ethnic origin or nationality.

Between 500-400 B.C., Ancient Greek civilization popularized short ideas that represented truths and words of wisdom. These ideas were known as tenets. Although, the Greeks were intellectuals with advanced philosophical, cultural, and educational knowledge, the most prevalent topic on the minds of all was the tenet "know thyself." This expression permeated the culture and influenced daily conversations and thoughts. The main sentiment regarding this admonishment related to understanding the value, ability, and purpose of self. In this regard, the phrase "know thyself" had nothing to do with the color of your skin, the neighborhood you came from, your cultural heritage or socio-economic standing.[9]

The architects of the most popular governing system of modern civilization, concluded centuries ago that knowing self is not possible without an understanding of your potential and the purpose for which your potential was given. Aristotle commented, *"Knowing yourself is the beginning of all wisdom."* Like Aristotle and Socrates, Greek citizens believed in the power and virtue of having self-knowledge. Additionally, they believed that it was wise and productive to pursue the right course in life based on the proper understanding about the inherent attribute of self. What's your viewpoint on potential? Do you believe that there is a source of your potential? If so, do you believe that the source has limited or placed boundaries on your potential?

## The Source of Potential

The scriptures are very clear on the fact that God is the source of all creation, with Jesus being His firstborn. Afterwards, Jesus presided over everything else that was created. *"For in him all things were created: things in heaven and on earth, visible and invisible, whether thrones or powers or rulers or authorities; all things have been created through him and for him."* Additionally, John stated that, *"All things were made through Him, and without Him nothing was made that was made."* Do you realize that "all things" referred to in the above scripture includes you, your potential, purpose, and destiny in life?

Now, let's dig deeper into the source of potential. Moses is a central figure in the history of the Jewish people. To some, he is known as a deliver, and to others a law giver. However, before revealing those aspects of his purpose and hidden potential, he had an unforgettable encounter with God. The Angel of the Lord appeared to Moses in a flame of fire coming out of a bush. This incident precipitated a conversation with God about the people of Israel and God's desire for Moses to deliver them. During that encounter, Moses asked God, *"Who should I say sent me?"* God responded by saying, tell them that *"I AM That I AM sent you."*

The first point to the statement clearly indicates that God has full authority over every resource that you need to be successful in your assignment. Whatever you need to accomplish His purpose for you, His response is "I AM" it. The phrase *"I AM That I AM"* also means that God is the source of whatever is right, good, perfect, righteous, or holy. *"Every good and perfect gift is from above, coming down from the Father of the heavenly lights..."* Therefore, "I AM" is the originator of all potential and TAGs. In other words, God is the source of your potential, and He enables it to manifest things from the invisible realm into the visible realm.

## Why Do You Have Potential

In the previous chapter, there were several interesting definitions listed to give you a comprehensive understanding of potential. Now that you have a basic understanding of the word, it is imperative that you build upon that knowledge and look at potential in a broader sense. When considering the true impact of potential, it is critical to note its root meaning. The root meaning adds more perspective on the magnitude and value of your individual potential. ***The word potential derives from the root word "potentia" that means force, power, might, ability, capacity, authority, influence and sway.***[10]

Based on the etymology of potential, it is reasonable to conclude that it equates to having an inherent force, power, might, ability, capacity, and authority to influence change in your life. In other words, *potential is your force, power, might, ability, capacity, authority. It is also the influence that gives life to your TAGs, dreams, and desires of the heart*. Remember, you possess potential because you have an assignment that you were born to complete.

Your potential ensures that you are adequately equipped for the task. In recognition of this information, it is now time to discuss the purpose of your potential.

> **A** great misconception is the belief that life will make room to express potential. The truth is that potential makes room to express life to the fullest.

## The Purpose of Potential

What is the true purpose of your potential? Although the answer to this question is subjective and could vary based on many factors, I believe that there are, at least, 6 good reasons why you possess potential. Firstly, potential identifies the precise area in life wherein your developed abilities will lead to dominion and personal leadership. Secondly, potential points you in the direction of your purpose in life. Thirdly, potential helps to answer the question "Who Am I." Fourthly, potential confirms your uniqueness and your intrinsic value. Fifthly, potential ensures that your impact during life is maximized. Lastly, potential enables you to produce continuous fruit in the form of consistent productive results.

1. **Potential identifies your area of dominion and personal leadership.**

Whitney Houston possessed one of the most amazing singing voices in the world. Her ability was celebrated and enjoyed by millions worldwide. In 2009, she was recognized by The Guinness World Records for being the most awarded female artist of all time and the one artist to chart seven consecutive number one singles on the Billboard Hot 100 Chart. Listen to her comments about potential, *"God gave me a voice to sing with, and when you have that, what other gimmick is there?"* What else do you need to have dominion in your area of gifting or to become a leader in your specialized field of endeavor?

For centuries, the mindset of celebrating and admiring athletes, artists, movie stars, musicians, wealthy people, and politicians has influenced the perception of individual value and self-worth. The celebrated few that fall within these categories tend to get more recognition from the masses for their accomplishments, contributions, and lifestyle. This universal favoritism and worship of a select few causes many people to believe that if you do not fit into a specific category, then you are "nobody."

I recall an occasion when I attended the annual 4th of July celebration at the US Ambassador's home in Nassau, Bahamas. During that event, I happened to meet a nice couple from Atlanta, Georgia. It was a pleasure meeting them, especially since my family and I were planning on relocating to that city sometime during the same year. However, something very perplexing happened to me when the very pleasant lady casually said, *"When you get to Atlanta, call us, because we know everybody who is somebody."*

Although the offer to introduce me to key influencers in Atlanta seemed like a great opportunity, her comment had a subtle undertone that promoted an elitist mentality. I did not know that her, seemingly harmless, suggestion would haunt me for years. Immediately, I thought to myself, *"If a person doesn't fit within her classification of being 'somebody' are they nobody?"* In other words, there are many who believe that some people are valuable, and others are worthless or have no intrinsic value.

Nevertheless, this viewpoint contradicts the concept of potential. Potential is neither selective nor discriminatory. As we discussed, God is the source, and He controls the keys to potential. He has established the unbreakable precedence that every human receives a measure of potential related to their purpose. This is good news!!! Do you recall the words which derive from potential? Your potential confirms your dominion and personal leadership.

Did you know that your area of talent, ability, or gift falls under your rulership? This means that it serves you. You are perfectly equipped to dominate it. The concept of dominion denotes that a person, place, or thing must come under subjection of an authority. For instance, a king's dominion comes from the people and the things under his subjection or control. In like manner, since your TAGs are subject to your control, then you are a leader by nature. This is true because you were created to dominate or master your specific gift related to your purpose in life. When you master it, then your dominance in your area of gifting attracts attention from others and it acknowledges that you are a leader in that specialized area. *"You will never have a greater or lesser dominion than that over self."* Hopefully, the information contained in this book will cause you to concur with those words spoken by Leonardo da Vinci.

Leonardo was born out of wedlock in 1452 to a wealthy father and peasant mother. His social status as an illegitimate child came with significant disadvantages and challenges. However, at an early age, he convinced himself that he could overcome his misfortune by mastering his abilities. He never accepted excuses for under-achieving. He lived his entire life never settling for average but always seeking to do more.[11] He once said, *"Iron rusts from disuse; water loses its purity from stagnation... even so does inaction sap the vigor of the mind."*

Early in life, Leonardo learned the value of potential and the importance of developing it to become a person of influence and dominance. As a result, he became known as one of the greatest artists, painters, inventors, sculptors, and scientist of all time. Billions of people have lived since Leonardo made his mark hundreds of years ago, but very few have come close to matching his dominance in his fields of interest. The power of his potential still has a lasting impact on successive generations. His painting of the "Mona Lisa" which was completed in the 16th century is arguably the most famous painting in the world.

Likewise, your potential is as valuable and great in the areas you were born to dominate. Leonardo took dominion over his TAGs. By doing so, it transformed him into a dominant force during and long after his lifetime. He understood and accepted his purpose in life and realized that it could only happen by maximizing his potential. Are you ready to take your leadership role and expose the tremendous intrinsic value of your potential?

**2. Potential points you in the direction of your assigned purpose.**

Perhaps, your experience differs from mine. Throughout my lifetime, I can honestly say that I have not found many people that are able to articulate their purpose for living. In fact, the majority did not seem to care about the issue. For them, connecting the dotted line between potential and purpose was or is irrelevant. Is it correct to presume that there are millions of people walking around without a clue about their potential or purpose in life? Think about your family members, classmates, friends, or co-workers. What is your assessment? How many do you suspect fall into the category of either not knowing their purpose or not caring about discovering it?

Based on my experience, many people believe that they have no purpose and that their lives have no significant meaning. This belief contradicts how it should be when it comes to purpose. When looking at nature, it is abundantly clear that each animal seems to carry out its purpose daily as a matter of routine. Instinctively, animals embody purpose in everything that they do and in everything that they become. A dog instinctively pursues its purpose of being a dog. The same applies to cats, birds, fishes, and so on.

Are humans different from other creatures when it comes to having purpose in life? In addition, is it reasonable to suggest that some people are born with purpose while others are destined to wonder haphazardly in the vast wilderness of uncertainty? The answer to both questions is "NO." The main difference is that some use their potential to discover and fulfill purpose while others elect not to use their potential and live a life of uncertainty.

Are your daily actions pointing you in the direction of purpose and creating opportunities for you to maximize your potential? Furthermore, do you realize that an action precedes the manifestation of your potential? Associated with every TAG is a corresponding action. The action forms the basis of a

*The Purpose of Potential* 49

designated path or specific path. In other words, the gift of singing corresponds with the act of singing. The talent to draw corresponds with the act of drawing. The ability to run corresponds with the act of running.

The point is that your potential is associated with a path in life. When you put action to your dormant potential, then you begin to develop a glimpse of who you really are and what you can achieve. Was Thomas Jefferson correct when he said, *"Do you want to know who you are? Don't ask. Act! Action will delineate and define you?"* I believe that he was correct. The discovery of purpose and the confidence to pursue it comes when you put action to your potential. In later chapters, we will discuss the issue of purpose in more detail. There is more good news!!! You will discover a wealth of knowledge and understanding about purpose that I am sure will point you in the right direction.

**3. Potential helps you answer the question, "Who Am I?"**

*"There is no planet, sun or star could hold you if you but knew what you are."* That perspective on self-knowledge from Ralph Waldo Emerson is very interesting. His view coincides with the belief that there is more to you than you know. When you are guided by your potential, then your passion to reveal your inner self will assist you in staying focused. Eventually, your passion will cause the doors to open which will allow you to expose your true identity to the world and yourself. Stay tuned, we will discuss the question "Who Am I" in more detail in later chapters.

**4. Potential confirms your uniqueness and inherent value.**

Hopefully, you have not modeled your life based on a desire to be someone that you are not. Scientists confirm that the DNA of each person is different. This means that the natural cells that makes us human ensures that there are no exact copies. There are similarities but no perfect matches without any differences. The same truth applies to your potential. Your potential forms the original blueprint. Others may copy your released potential, but they will never be able to duplicate it exactly.

Potential is equivalent to a piece of a jigsaw puzzle. Some pieces may look similar, but each has a designated position in the world that matches its design. Attempts to force pieces to match the wrong slot are to no avail. Your potential is uniquely designed to fit perfectly with your assigned purpose in life. Therefore, you are destined to be successful in life pursuing your own purpose and utilizing your own potential. You are the perfect "You." There is nobody else in the entire world capable of being 100% like you.

Years ago, there was a popular commercial that centered around the theme, *"Like Mike, If I Could Be Like Mike."* The commercial spawned a generation of young basketball players attempting to play like Michael Jordan. They purchased Jordan sneakers, wore his number on their jerseys and attempted to play with a swagger, like the original. The reality is that out of the thousands that tried, none were successful in playing like him. In the same regard, the best Elvis Presley impersonator can never match the greatness of "The King of Rock 'n' Roll." Why? This statement is true because potential is a perfect match for a specific and predesignated path in life. For this reason, your potential carries the same value and power to enable you to make your own significant mark on this earth.

### 5. Potential confirms that you were born to have a positive impact on your surrounding.

Everyone is similar in one regard. Each person is perfectly equipped to change or impact their environment in a positive way. The impact is intended to come when you release and maximize your full potential along the path of purpose. Therefore, the true measure of your success is not in how much potential you have, but what you do with what you have.

For this reason, it is not good to compare what you have done with what others have done or what others are doing. Whether or not your potential is

# The Purpose of Potential

considered great or small, it is still valuable to you and others. Listen to Mae Jemison's words of advice, *"It's your place in the world; it's your life. Go on and do all you can with it and make it the life you want to live."* True potential only competes with itself. Therefore, I believe that the greatest threat to releasing your full potential is having low standards related to your career or assignment in life.

Remember that if you have the physical capabilities, then maximizing your potential is necessary to complete your life's journey. Hopefully, you are not and will not become one of the persons described in this statement by Dr. Ben Carson. *"A lot of people simply don't realize their potential because they're just so risk adverse. They just don't want to take the risk."* I understand that the risk of stepping outside of your comfort zone is intimidating. However, have you ever weighed the risk of inaction related to releasing your full potential?

**6. Potential produces continuous results from continuous effort.**

Ask yourself this question, "What do I have that positions me to generate consistent returns every time I use it or do it?" Another way to phrase the question is to ask, "What do I have naturally that enables me to be unique, and it also allows me to be fruitful?" In my search for answers to the issues of potential and purpose, I discovered that one of the most significant aspects of potential is its ability to produce continuous productive results.

Potential is not disposable, use it once then you throw it away. This is reassuring for you to know because your potential is capable of duplicating successes on a consistent basis. *"Continuous effort - not strength or intelligence - is the key to unlocking our potential,"* according to Winston Churchill. Potential requires effort to manifest it from the unseen realm into the seen realm. Whenever effort is applied continuously, then results are produced continuously.

A key reason why God gave you potential is for the continuous and unabated production of fruitful outcomes. Fruitful outcomes mean that you were born to generate beneficial results for the good of yourself and the well-being of humanity. Simply speaking, God wants and expects you to produce fruit consistently. What is your fruit? Your fruit is stored in your seeds of potential.

Your potential comes in the form of seeds of talents, abilities, and gifts. These natural attributes are not intended to stay undeveloped in seed form only. Your TAGs are destined to be developed to the point whereby you are able to produce fruitful results on a consistent basis. Listen to these words of admonition spoken through Apostle Peter, *"As each has received a gift, use it to serve one another, as good stewards of God's varied grace."* With these thoughts in mind, let's take a closer look at the concept of TAGs to ensure that you have the right foundation to produce fruitful results along the path of purpose.

## Your Gift

Unfortunately, TAGs are not widely discussed as tools to help discover purpose during the formative years. However, thousands of years ago, Plato gave this advice and conclusion about TAGs holding the secret to discovering purpose. *"Do not train a child to learn by force or harshness; but direct them to it by what amuses their minds, so that you may be better able to discover with accuracy the peculiar bent of the genius of each."* His theory on finding purpose was accurate, as TAGs preoccupy your mind and constantly prompt you to act or move in a certain direction. Since your TAGs are the foundation of potential, they are also the perfect source to identify your area of focus in life.

I hope that you believe a simple and fundamental truth. That truth is, "You were born for a purpose, filled with potential and equipped for a very important assignment." ***Destiny calls from the depths of your heart to gently nudge and steer you towards the path of purpose.*** Once you are on the right path, then you must overcome opposition and release your TAGs.

Do you know your identification tag? Again, I would like to dismiss the belief that only a select few people possess TAGs. This is not true, everyone is born with, at least, one talent, ability, or gift. Your identification tag consists of three commonly known elements. These elements are your talents, abilities, or gifts. It is widely accepted to associate these elements together, as they are used interchangeably in the same context. Often, the word "gift" is used interchangeably for natural talent and ability. In other words, your potential in the form of your TAG is commonly known as your "gift."

## Understanding the Value of Your Gift

In my junior year of college, I switched majors from Accounting to English. Ironically, the motivation behind switching from one major to another was not due to my knowledge of potential, but my desire to become well-rounded. I really enjoyed taking accounting classes, but I had an extreme fear of English. Nevertheless, the thought of living my life with a fear of writing was too overwhelming.

It did not take long after switching majors to realize that I had a natural gift and interest for writing. That interest was not clear before, because I never explored my full potential. Changing majors required me to give my complete attention to the new subject. As it turns out, writing was an ability that came naturally, but it was not acknowledged previously. So why did I have a fear? The fear was established based on past negative experiences and a lack of understanding.

It is correct to say that I stumbled my way into having a better appreciation for my writing potential and purpose. In my career, I have written numerous successful business plans to create opportunities for myself and others. In addition, this is the second book that I have written. Early in life, I did not understand my gift related to writing. As a result, there was a lack of acknowledgment, a willingness to starve it and a failure to release it fully. Years later, I am completely happy with my decision to change majors because it introduced me to an aspect of myself that I did not know existed.

That experience and many others taught me that gifts initiate the expression of self and exposes its true value. Therefore, if your gift is used in the wrong way, then you are not reflecting the image you were designed to portray. In other words, if the pure and uncontaminated state of your gift is corrupted this will prevent you from producing your destined results and reflecting the right image. Referring once again to the wisdom of Plato, he commented, *"All things will be produced in superior quantity and quality, and with greater ease, when each man works at a single occupation, in accordance with his natural gifts, and at the right moment, without meddling with anything else."*

Do you believe those words of Plato? I believe that if his advice is followed, then life would not seem as confusing and purpose so mysterious. Have you discovered your gift? Perhaps, the starting point begins with the proper understanding of the word. Therefore, for the purpose of this chapter, **a gift is the inherent capacity to fulfill a function that addresses a specific need in the world.**

*"When you start using your gifts and talents to earn a living, you naturally gravitate towards work you are naturally great at and can excel at. It's kind of fun to do the impossible."* Are you open to believing those exciting words from Walt Disney? Do you think that Disney, the visionary behind Walt Disney World, knew something about the power associated with your gift? Always remember that your gift is something that you show signs of excelling at. It is also something that you enjoy, and it comes natural to you.

Did you know, *"A gift opens the way and ushers the giver into the presence of the great?"* In this quote, King Solomon is referring to a gift that you give to someone as a present. During his lifetime, the type and quality of the gift would bring recognition to the giver. If the gift was significant, then the giver would be given access to great things and people. In other words, whenever you refine your personal gift and make it valuable, then the world comes knocking at your door wanting to receive it. Has your gift created opportunities for you?

Let's pause for a moment because I need to ask you a serious question. Why would you have a gift to do something or solve some problem, if it wasn't necessary or needed in the world? Based on the information that you have read thus far, it is my hope that you are prepared to acknowledge that there is a reason, requirement, responsibility, and recognition associated with your gift. For additional clarification, I have listed the following points for you to understand about your TAGs.

## Reason, Requirement, Responsibility, Recognition and Recurring Successes

**Point #1** – There is a **reason** why you have life, TAGs, potential and purpose. The reason is made clearer over time through your reoccurring thoughts, dreams, and visions. *"The dreams and passions stored within hearts are powerful keys which can unlock a wealth of potential,"* according to John Maxwell. Although sometimes life seems unfair, challenging, and unpredictable, your purpose is confirmation of your appointment with destiny. Remember that your TAGs ensure that you have the capacity, authorization, and abilities to fulfill your specific assignment.

**Point #2** – There is a very important **requirement** associated with your TAGs. Manifestation is the objective of every seed. What the seed can transform into is already determined. Therefore, the ability of the seed to transform into the predetermined or specific image is inherent. In other words, the future image of an orange seed is an orange tree. This designation or image is locked inside of the seed. It cannot successfully produce any other future image.

Recurring thoughts about utilizing your TAGs are common. These are planted in your mind because there is a predetermined manifestation that your purpose leads you to becoming. Your TAGs are necessary for you to transform into that predetermined person. If you fail, for some reason, to transform into the designated image, then the TAGs that you possess become unproductive. Remember that the image or likeness that you transform into must line up with the predetermined manifestation associated with your purpose for living.

**Point #3** – There is a **responsibility** associated with life, TAGs, potential and purpose. The first responsibility that you have is to recognize who you are. Afterwards, it is important that you accept who you are and refuse to be led astray by your friends, culture, or social environment. *You were born to be an original not a copy of someone else.* Your purpose in life determines the type of gift that you possess.

After you discover your gift, it is important that you develop, refine, and release it to the world. Did you know that *"The greatest gift is a portion of yourself,"* according to Ralph Waldo Emerson? This means that the greatest gift you can give yourself and the world is the portion of yourself stored in your seeds of potential. Can you imagine the consequences of your failure to manifest who you are through your potential? The information that you are learning will prevent you from experiencing the consequences that came to mind. Are you motivated to explore, discover, refine, and release your potential?

**Point #4** – There is **recognition** associated with your life, TAGs, potential and purpose. Remember that your gift can usher you before great people. This statement also means that your gift will cause people to respect you and seek out what you have to offer. Listen to the comments from John Maxwell, *"Talent grips us. We are overtaken by the beauty of Michelangelo's sculpture, riveted by Mariah Carey's angelic voice, doubled over in laughter by the comedy of Robin Williams, and captivated by the on screen performances of Denzel Washington."*

Maxwell's sentiments are universal. People gravitate to individuals that master their gifts and place them on display for the world to enjoy. Your gift

*The Purpose of Potential* 57

is no less valuable than the individuals celebrated in your country or community. People may not like you personally for numerous reasons, but they will learn to respect, recognize, and seek after the value of your TAGs. As you will discover, there is a target audience waiting to enjoy the fruits of your potential.

**Point #5** – **Recurring** success is the destiny reserved for your life, TAGs, potential and purpose. The objective of the seed is to produce fruit. As you know, fruit carry seeds inside. This reality ensures that the seed reproduces fruit on a continuous basis. Similarly, your TAGs are seeds of potential that are inherently capable of generating fruit on a continuous basis. For this reason, comfort zones should be foreign because they are detrimental to releasing your full potential. By nature, comfort zones don't add or increase the value of something, as they promote stagnation and inactivity.

> **Gifts possess the capacity to reproduce fruitful outcomes.**

You cannot say to the seed, *"Stop producing now or only give me a small harvest."* Why? It is predetermined that if you create the right environment for the seed, then it will do what it is designed to do. Furthermore, it will produce continuous outcomes that are beneficial, productive, and valuable. The same concept applies to your TAGs. Recurring successes are expected and are stored on the inside of your TAGs. Create the right environment and you will reap the rewards of continuous success.

Let's examine an important point that is typically overlooked when considering the success of others. When you examine the life of individuals that are successful in releasing their gifts, common patterns are revealed. Firstly, the gift was inside of the individual but needed to undergo a process of development. Secondly, at some point during their lives, they received attention because of the gift. Thirdly, their notoriety and popularity grew because they pursued the same path over time. After years of consistently producing the same results, people began to associate their name with the gift. As an example, when you think of the king of pop music, Michael Jackson comes to mind. Creating music was Michael's gift and he used it to create continuous productive outcomes.

Let's pause for a moment to reflect on several key points. You have learned that purpose is fulfilled through the releasing of your potential in the form of your TAGs. As you know, the perpetual releasing of your natural potential creates a continuous cycle of fruitful results. Therefore, **released potential ensures that purpose is fueled by a source that regenerates and produces designated results.**

In other words, your gift comes with the inherent capacity to reproduce and achieve predetermined consistent outcomes. The power to reproduce and achieve consistent outcomes is possible because the destined result is contained in the gift from the beginning. However, beware of the self-imposed enemies of your potential. These enemies present obstacles to the discovery of your gift and the releasing of your full potential.

## Enemies of Your Gift

Years ago, Andrew Carnegie made this interesting statement, *"The average person puts only 25% of his energy and ability into his work. The world takes off its hat to those who put in more than 50% of their capacity and stands on its head for those few and far between souls who devote 100%."* What do you think about the words of Carnegie? There are some obvious thoughts about his comments but there are also some valuable points that are not as obvious. The point that less than maximum effort is an abuse of potential is noteworthy. Additionally, when you give less than maximum effort related to releasing your full potential, then you rob yourself of notoriety and self-worth.

One of the costliest mistakes that you can make in life is to underestimate the value of your hidden potential. Although your potential is a valuable natural resource, it is often used too little, under-appreciated and misunderstood. Dr. Myles Munroe once said, *"Whenever purpose is unknown then abuse is inevitable."* This leads to a very important question. Is it possible to abuse your potential because of ignorance concerning its true purpose? Unfortunately, the answer to that question is "YES." This is the reason why underestimating your potential is a costly mistake.

Regrettably, there are additional consequences that you are susceptible to experiencing if you possess the wrong viewpoint concerning the purpose of potential. If you have the wrong views about potential, then you are susceptible to developing the wrong mindset towards maximizing it. Listed below are 5 consequences of having the wrong attitude towards your gift that inhibits full development, expression, and manifestation:

- **Lack of acknowledgment** – Sadly to say, a major obstacle to releasing your potential and discovering your gift is a lack of acknowledgment. Low self-esteem is the likely culprit causing this dilemma. Hopefully, you now believe that you possess, at least, one gift from God. Thereby, reducing the likelihood that you will fall victim to this negative attitude.

- **Subject it to the wrong environment** – What is considered the wrong environment for you and your gift? Well, the answer to that question is debatable. Surely, if you are exposed to individuals or things that offer no value to enhancing it or they become major distractions in the process of releasing your potential, then you should evaluate the benefit of having the relationship. Subjecting yourself and your potential to the wrong environment could have a negative effect on your purpose in life.

- **Starve it** - This occurs when you neglect to develop or nourish your gift through the development and refining of your natural abilities. Once you plant your seed of potential and it starts to sprout, then it is necessary to nourish it in order to experience continuous growth.

Starving your potential means that you are denying yourself opportunities to accomplish successful outcomes in the future.

- **Failure to release it fully** - This means that you are comfortable with your accomplishments and have decided that it is not necessary to release your potential on a continuous basis. Failure to maximize your potential leads to living beneath your assigned position in life. Did you know that one of the greatest threats to releasing your full potential is your last success?

- **Improper Usage** - This occurs when your gift is used for the wrong reasons such as illegal purposes, criminal intent, and dominance over other human beings. The misappropriation of your potential leads to either the abuse of your abilities or the abuse of others for your personal gain and gratification. If you are suppressing your gift in a way described above, then the time is now for you to reconsider your approach.

Now, this is a good point to pause. We have discussed the purpose of your potential and understanding the value of your gift. In addition, you have just reviewed enemies of your gift. At this point, do you think that it is a good time to do some real soul searching? Think for a moment about your life and what is it that you would like to accomplish.

*"Focusing your life solely on making a buck shows a certain poverty of ambition. It asks too little of yourself. Because it's only when you hitch your wagon to something larger than yourself that you realize your true potential,"* according to President Barak Obama. Are you focusing solely on making money in life? Have you concluded that there is a purpose for having potential and it is bigger than what you have accomplish thus far? For the remaining pages, we will discuss key reasons why it is necessary to pursue your full potential. Are you excited about your potential?

## The P.O.I.S.E.D. Concept

When I moved to the Bahamas years ago, I worked for a subsidiary of a large foreign insurance company. The senior leaders of this company were British expatriates and the other employees were Bahamians. I was the only American. Additionally, I was newly married and faced with adjusting to a new and uniquely different culture.

After several unsettling months of employment, the CEO expressed to a mutual friend that he was not happy with our relationship. He stated that I was different from the other Bahamian employees. The main issue centered on my reluctance to take advantage of his open-door policy. It was customary for individuals to sit with him and gossip or have dialogue regarding work related issues.

Upon hearing about his concern, I went to him to discuss this matter. He started the conversation by saying, *"John the problem you have with me is that you don't cater to me."* He went on to say, *"Everyone else comes into my office to socialize but you just don't seem interested in being a part of this family."* His comments were accurate. I was an outsider with a different mindset. I did not want to compromise my moral standards to win the approval of the CEO. Nevertheless, there was one major issue that I needed to resolve. How could I bridge the gap without compromising my values? As CEO, I realized that his ultimate concern related to generating revenue and making a profit.

With that knowledge in mind, I developed an independent strategy to use my insurance underwriting abilities to target new commercial clients for the company. Soon thereafter, I created an Excel spreadsheet of potential clients. I drove around Nassau in my car recording the names of businesses and companies. Additionally, I spent time searching through the yellow pages and writing down the names of companies that I thought would be interested in receiving an insurance quote.

After creating my spreadsheet, I went back to the CEO and asked for his input on adding information and contact details. Over the next several weeks and months, we worked very closely together on my strategy of underwriting new commercial business. Thankfully, I was successful in acquiring several new large commercial accounts and marketing the company's products.

At the end of the year, the CEO called me into his office to review my Christmas bonus. I will never forget his statement, *"John, please don't tell anyone, but your bonus is larger than everyone else and you deserve it."* I used my potential to turn a negative situation into a positive experience for me and for others. I saved my commercial clients thousands of dollars. More importantly, I created a new revenue stream and changed the CEO's opinion of my potential, without losing my dignity.

My colleagues thought that I was crazy driving around town recording information and going through the business directory. Not to mention the insane ideas of creating a potential client list and cold calling company executives. However, that situation confirmed my belief that released potential has life changing properties that lead to personal success, peace of mind and happiness.

*"Desire is the starting point of all achievement, not a hope, not a wish, but a keen pulsating desire which transcends everything."* Napoleon Hill was a successful American author and advisor to two presidents. He spoke those words. The keen pulsating desire which transcends everything is defining the word, passion. Let's review another personal story that adds value to understanding the purpose of potential.

There is a very important point about potential and purpose that you should be aware of. It is necessary for you to understand that when you travel along the path of purpose, then perceived setbacks are opportunities to move closer to the designated mark. Years ago, when I served as the General Manager of a small insurance agency, I experienced a perceived setback. I was hired by one of the directors after the company's tumultuous first year of operation. It was in a very bad position. It had debt, a net loss and all employees had resigned.

The outlook was bleak, but the opportunity was a perfect match for my potential. I hired new employees, brought in several large commercial accounts, and called a CPA friend to assist in cleaning up the financial records. After several weeks of long hours and hard work, the company was finally moving in the right direction. Our sales increased and we started to see a profit.

Nevertheless, I was not aware that the shareholders secretly wanted to add another executive team member because of a desire to have a person of a different race be the face of the company. To make matters worse, they wanted to bring in an unproven individual, and pay him more money and offer benefits that were never given to me. I saved the company from disaster, improved its image, made a profit each year, but because of the color of my skin, future opportunities looked bleak. When I approached the board of directors regarding the issue, I was directed to make room for the new person as the decision was made and it was non-negotiable. Eventually, I decided to leave that company, but I took my potential with me.

Did I duplicate the success elsewhere? Absolutely, that experience was merely a stepping-stone to prepare me for greater successes. My potential opened the door of opportunity for me to pursue the passion of my heart. Additionally, I was able to positively impact that company for a designated season. The position also exposed my gifts to many others and provided direction for future career pursuits.

Based on personal experiences, I developed a concept that suggests that potential causes other key things to happen in your life to assist you in fulfilling your purpose. The P.O.I.S.E.D. concept is an acronym that highlights the characteristics positively impacted when you have a strong desire to release your potential. Your potential is equivalent to an arrow, as it is the natural component that you use to hit the mark or your assigned purpose. Whenever you release your potential, it ensures that you travel along a straight path towards your destiny. My theory suggests that passion leads the way to attracting the other components of the P.O.I.S.E.D. concept which are shown below:

## P.O.I.S.E.D.

(**P**assion – **O**pportunity – **I**nfluence – **S**eason of Impact - **E**xposure – **D**irection).

| Direction | Exposure | Season of Impact | Influence | Opportunity | **Passion** |

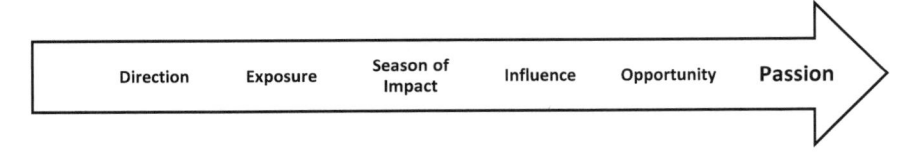

**Passion**

Passion is the head of the arrow that ensures you hit your assigned mark in life with pinpoint accuracy. Howard Thurman, noted American author, educator, and philosopher, was very passionate about releasing his full potential for the good of all humanity. Listen to his advice, *"Don't ask yourself what the world needs; ask yourself what makes you come alive. And then go and do that. Because what the world needs is people who have come alive."* Would you say that your potential and purpose have come alive? If not, do not be dismayed your awakening moment is approaching soon.

Thurman's conclusion regarding the impact of passion on your life and the lives of others is valid because passion drives you to achieve and succeed. Your passion leads the way and causes your potential to open the doors of opportunity, influence, seasons of change and exposure. Passion also serves to invigorate your potential while pointing you in the direction of the most rewarding path to complete your assignment.

What are you passionate about in life? Are you passionate about the clothes you wear, the car you drive, spending time with friends or making more money? Or, is it true that you have not discovered a passion in life?

According to Zig Ziglar, *"When you catch a glimpse of your potential, that's when passion is born."* In both personal stories, I caught a glimpse of my potential and passion was born that spearheaded my successful purposeful outcomes.

Therefore, I strongly agree with Ziglar's assertion. He asserts that an awareness of your potential gives birth to passion in life. This is true because passion is born from the womb of potential. When you really accept the true value and significance of your potential, then passion is born from love, joy, and respect for your assignment. These elements provide the fuel that ignites a fire of passion for pursuing your assigned purpose and the maximization of your potential.

Tiger Woods requires no introduction. In fact, the mention of his first name alone is synonymous with PGA greatness. Tiger's professional golf statistics and accolades are beyond impressive. He once said, *"I love to play golf, and that's my arena. And you can characterize it and describe it however you want, but I have a love and a passion for getting that ball in the hole and beating those guys."* Do you believe that Tiger would have been as successful in the sport of golf if he lacked passion? Furthermore, do you think that his potential and passion opened the doors of opportunity for him to influence the game that he loves?

## Opportunity

*"Life is a gift, and it offers us the privilege, opportunity, and responsibility to give something back by becoming more."* Accordingly, as indicated by that Tony Robbins' quote, your life is a gift and presents an opportunity to share yourself with the rest of the world. As others glimpse the passion sparks radiating from your potential, then doors of opportunities will open so that you are able to set the world on fire.

Before Abraham Lincoln became the 16th President of the United States, he once said, *"I will prepare and one day my chance will come."* Being prepared for an opportunity means that you have acknowledged and developed your potential. Once you are confident that your potential is primed for success, your passion should drive you to prepare, ask, seek, and knock.

Are you aware that Jesus said, *"Ask and it will be given to you; seek and you will find; knock and the door will be opened to you?" "For everyone who asks receives, the one who seeks finds; and to the one who knocks, the door will be opened."* Are you asking God to open the doors of opportunity, seeking His will for your life, and knocking at the door of wisdom? Equally as important, have you prepared yourself to take advantage of the opportunities to maximize your potential?

Lincoln believed that he possessed the ability to lead America through its most difficult era. His passion for political leadership was clear for all to see. He possessed a "Don't Quit" attitude. Did you know that he lost several Illinois state elections prior to his accession to national notoriety? Nevertheless, each failure was an opportunity for him to prepare for leadership, ask for political support, seek political positions, and to keep knocking at the door of fulfillment of purpose and potential. Although Lincoln lost two consecutive bids to become a U.S. Senator prior to becoming President, his influence grew stronger with each opportunity. Remember these words of Thomas Edison, *"Opportunity is missed by most people because it is dressed in overalls and looks like work."*

## Influence

We live in an era whereby social media dominates. In fact, popular social media influencers have tremendous power. The concept of rallying a group of followers to support individuals is not new, but the way that it is happening is certainly new. It is new because of the platform used to communicate and increase the followers. If the influencers can find followers, then you can as well. Is your potential influencing the lives of others in a positive way?

Booker T. Washington was the founder of Tuskegee University. Although he was born into slavery, his life was a testament to the power of potential to elevate your life and that of others. He persevered through the difficult periods riding on the wave of his passion, which eventually opened the doors of opportunity and influence. *"There is no power on earth that can neutralize the influence of a high, simple and useful life."* Washington made that statement when opportunities were very limited, and life was extremely challenging for African Americans.

Although it is popular to become an influencer using means that lower your personal standards, character, or values, that approach should not be the preferred way to reach the spotlight. The preferred approach to success should follow the advice of Washington. I agree with his sentiments. Likewise, I believe that maintaining high morals or high ethical standards, as well as a simple and productive life adds value to your released potential. Washington also said, *"Character is power."* Imagine this, if potential is power and character is power, what happens when you add the two forces together? The answer is that these ingredients will erupt into an explosion of influence.

Worldwide, released potential has proven to be one of the most effective ways to garner local and national influence. In fact, people from various occupations have used success in their chosen fields of endeavor to influence their way of life and the lives of others. This is evident when you observe the impact that celebrities, athletes, and successful business leaders have on their surroundings. The common thread is that their released potential ignited a sensation in the hearts of others and caused their influence to grow.

*"Never underestimate the power of dreams and the influence of the human spirit. We are all the same in this notion. The potential for greatness lives within each of us."* That advice came from Wilma Rudolph. She elevated women's track and field in the United States after earning three gold medals in the 1960 Olympics in Rome.

Her potential for greatness in sports changed her life and created a platform to influence others in a positive way. During the highlight of her career, she was the fastest woman in the world. Her comments regarding the power of potential are noteworthy particularly since she overcame childhood illness and wore a brace on her leg and foot until the age of nine. Rudolph's life and success highlights the reality that potential leads the way to a season of impact related to your purpose.

**Season of Impact**

*"There is a time for everything, and a season for every activity under heaven..."* The thought that time and seasons impact everything and every activity is still a valid observation. For instance, the color of leaves on certain trees change from green to shades of white, red, yellow, and brown depending on the season of the year. Change occurs because of changes in the environment. Therefore, the tree and leaves are subject to the season because it determines the outcome, However, the season is not subject to the tree and leaves. This means that the tree and leaves do not determine when, why, where, and how the season changes, it happens automatically.

Let me explain my statement about the tree is subject to the season, but the change in season is not subject to the tree. Before reading this book, did you know that there is an appropriate season to release your potential and pursue purpose? The season is destined to come automatically at some point during your lifetime. In the context of these statements, you are considered the tree. Your season to release your potential will come automatically, as it is controlled by God. Those individuals that meditate on and pursue His purpose for their lives, *"They are trees planted along the riverbank, bearing fruit each season. Their lives never whither, and they prosper in all they do."*

*"A man's worth has its season, like fruit."* Many years ago, Francois de la Rochefoucauld made that observation. His statement suggests that life is subjected to seasons which determine when your fruit of potential is ripe enough to take advantage of opportunities. There is an Ancient Egyptian

proverb which says, *"Every man must act in the rhythm of his time... such is wisdom."* In other words, there is a season associated with your time on earth and the wise person discovers it.

Nestled deep inside of the heart of all humans are seeds of potential waiting for the right environment to grow and release fruit. Every fruit tree has a defined season when it produces its fruit. Therefore, the full impact and benefit from having the tree comes when its potential materializes. Whenever the tree produces fruit, it is fulfilling its destiny at the appropriate time. In the same regard, the existence of your potential ensures that you will have a season of impact, but you must be successful in developing it first. When you release your developed potential at the appropriate time, then you are influencing your environment at the right time.

Destiny calls to the person holding the potential prompting them to make a positive impact on earth by leaving an indelible mark that is impossible to erase from either history or the hearts of mankind. What this means is that if you have life and the physical abilities, then you can experience a season of impact. You are destined to experience your moment in the spotlight whereby everything comes together and works according to the dream in your heart. Your potential has the power to create positive change. When this happens, you will receive the proper exposure that you deserve, and life will take on a new and wonderful meaning.

*"We each were endowed at birth with a unique gift, something we were born to do or become that no one else can achieve the way we can. God's purpose is that we bear abundant fruit and release the blessings of our gift and potential to the world,"* according to Dr. Myles Munroe. Do you believe that the world awaits the gift of your released potential?

## Exposure

There are two important aspects of exposure relevant to potential. The first point is the exposure related to your family, peers, or centers of influence.

The people that you socialize with or consider to be your closet friends tend to have an impact on your life. Sometimes the impact that others have on your life is positive, or sometimes it is negative. For this reason, in the context of potential and purpose, it is wise to follow these instructions from Warren Buffett, *"It's better to hang out with people better than you. Pick out associates whose behavior is better than yours and you'll drift in that direction."*

At some point in life, your passion, opportunity, influence, and season of impact will catapult you into purposeful stardom. Purposeful stardom is a phrase that I use to emphasize the point that refined or developed potential will launch you into the spotlight. Your moment of recognition will come at the appropriate time and season. Perhaps, it will come before you finish reading this book. Do you believe that it is possible?

The second important aspect about exposure is the automatic response to released potential once it is activated. Potential attracts the attention of the host. After the host releases it, then it influences the surrounding environment in a positive way. The exposure that you receive from releasing your potential will open doors of opportunities and make you a person of influence. However, always remember these words spoken by John Wooten, *"Talent is God given. Be humble. Fame is man-given. Be grateful. Conceit is self-given. Be careful."* Is the P.O.I.S.E.D. concept giving you a new appreciation for releasing your potential?

**Direction**

*"If one advances confidently in the direction of his dreams, and endeavors to live the life which he has imagined, he will meet with a success unexpected in common hours,"* according to Henry David Thoreau. I agree with Thoreau's conclusion, if your dreams coincide with your natural potential and purpose in life, then success is inevitable. <u>*Success awaits you because potential is the lighthouse on the shores of your heart that provides direction to escape the perils of uncertainty*</u>.

Since your potential is identified through your dreams and TAGs, then following it is the safest option when considering your purpose and the right path to take. Following the potential path ensures that you will enjoy what you are doing while making a positive contribution in life. You can also think of your potential as your internal compass. Therefore, *if potential knocks at the door of your heart, open the door and let its awesomeness permeate your future.*

## THE NEXT STEP

*"If you take responsibility for yourself, you will develop a hunger to accomplish your dreams."* Do you agree with that statement from Les Brown? Either way, the reality is that the responsibility for your potential is in your hands. Therefore, give the world a glimpse of your splendor and majesty.

In doing so, you will fulfill your purpose for living and have a rewarding life for yourself and others. I have given you a lot of information about potential thus far. What do you think about the information? I realize that some of the content may require that you read it more than once to fully understand what I am attempting to convey. That is fine. Take your time and digest this life changing information.

In the next chapter, you will discover secrets to managing the responsibility associated with receiving potential. The knowledge that you receive will ensure that you get the most value from your intrinsic asset, and that you find peace with your chosen life's path. Although there are no monetary charges levied against you when you receive your potential, you should be aware that it comes with a cost. *"There are no extra pieces in the universe. Everyone is here because he or she has a place to fill, and every piece must fit itself into the big jigsaw puzzle."* Those words of Deepak Chopra provide the best summary and introduction for the next chapter. Let's move forward towards understanding the responsibility of your potential.

> **Quick reference to the purpose of potential principles:**

1. God is the source of potential.
2. Potential provides the inherent force, power, might, ability, capacity, and authority to influence change in your life.
3. A great misconception is the belief that life will make room to express potential. The truth is that potential makes room to express life to the fullest.
4. Potential identifies your area of dominion and personal leadership.
5. Potential points you in the direction of your assigned purpose.
6. Potential helps you answer the question, "Who Am I."
7. Potential confirms that you were born to have a positive impact on your surroundings.
8. Potential produces continuous results from continuous effort.
9. Destiny calls from the depths of your heart to gently nudge and steer you towards the path of purpose.
10. A gift is the inherent capacity to fulfill a function that addresses a specific need in the world.
11. Gifts possess the capacity to reproduce fruitful outcomes.
12. Potential ensures that purpose is fueled by a source that regenerates and produces designated results.
13. Your potential is the lighthouse on the shores of your heart that provides an escape from the perils of uncertainty.

# CHAPTER THREE

## THE RESPONSIBILITY OF POTENTIAL

> *"Every right implies a responsibility;*
> *Every opportunity, an obligation,*
> *Every possession, a duty."*
> **John D Rockefeller**

Suffering under the stifling circumstances surrounding segregation, social injustice and racial discrimination, tensions in America reached a boiling point in the late 1950s. The extreme social and economic inequities for millions of African Americans gave birth to the Civil Rights Movement. This movement represented an unwavering, and unrelenting non-violent campaign to uproot the systematic oppression perpetrated by the white majority against the black minority. The momentum from widespread protests against inequality led to the Civil Rights Act of 1964. This iconic legislation outlawed discrimination based on race, sex, color, religion, or national origin and sealed the legacy of America's greatest civil rights leader.

*"When a person gets to know his Creator, and finally comes to know himself, then his leadership is born,"* according to Dr. Myles Munroe. Often, great leaders rise to prominence not because of a desire for recognition, but a sense of responsibility or obligation to spearhead change. America's greatest civil rights leader epitomized the statement "lead by example." His charismatic persona radiated as a bright star during the height of unrest. The fire of his non-violent leadership against social inequities ignited a global following

of the young and old, black and white, rich and poor, educated and uneducated.

To some, he was a fearless shepherd willing to give his life for his flock, and to others, he was a powerful lion boldly advancing towards confrontation with the entrenched promoters of racial and civil discrimination. Arguably, one of the most profound characteristics of all was his willingness to accept the heavy responsibility of releasing his full potential for the good of his people and all humanity. Dr. Martin Luther King Jr. said, *"I knew that I could never again raise my voice against the violence of the oppressed in the ghettos without having first spoken clearly to the greatest purveyor of violence in the world today – my own government."*

What would America look like today without the extreme sacrifice and unfaltering commitment of Dr. Martin Luther King Jr.? During his famous speech "I've Been To The Mountaintop," he masterfully articulated the universal responsibility associated with individual potential. After discussing the mindset of the Good Samaritan and his view on the plight of the Memphis sanitation workers. He stated, *"The question is not, if I stop to help this man in need, what will happen to me? The question is, if I don't stop to help the sanitation workers, what will happen to them? That is the question."* The day following his memorable speech, he was assassinated.

Although he died at the age of 39, his legacy continues to shine as a beacon of hope and assurance that all things are possible to them that believe. Dr. King embraced the responsibility associated with having the ability to initiate personal and corporate change. The opening quote from Rockefeller is worth repeating, it says *"Every right implies a responsibility; Every opportunity, an obligation, Every possession, a duty."* Perhaps, this explains Dr. King's motivation to lead the movement for social change, because attached to every TAG is a corresponding responsibility, obligation, and duty. Again, I ask, *"Have you ever considered why you possess the talent, ability, or gift?"* It was given to you without your request and irrespective of your opinion. Have you also considered how your life would be different if you found a way to free your gift from the invisible cage of dormancy?

Dr. King's life exemplified the responsibility associated with possessing the power to create change. The cry of his heart was *"Use me, God. Show me how to take who I am, who I want to be, and what I can do, and use it for a purpose greater than myself."* This world is a better place because of Dr. King's commitment to addressing the difficult issues of injustice and racial discrimination. It was a hard struggle and one that eventually cost him his life. I am convinced that he understood the responsibility associated with releasing his full potential. Although he encountered very dangerous, powerful, and ruthless opposition, he stood courageously and proclaimed, *"The time is always right to do what is right."*

Sometimes, the responsibility of potential requires unrelenting sacrifice and dedication. As you are now aware, attached to your potential is a purpose that directs you to travel along a specific path. That path is the path of destiny. Therefore, your destiny is impacted by how responsible you are with the potential that you are given. *"For we are each responsible for our own conduct,"* particularly our attitude towards freely releasing our gift. Perhaps, John Maxwell was correct when he said, *"The greatest day in your life and mine is when we take total responsibility for our attitudes. That's the day we truly grow up."*

## Responsibility / Obligation / Duty

According to historical records, before Jesus was crucified by the Jewish leaders, they arrested him and brought false claims against him. He was presented to Pilate, the Roman governor over Judea, for him to approve his execution. During the conversation, Pilate asked Jesus, *"Are you the king of the Jews?"* After a short exchange of words, Jesus replied, ***"You say that I am a king. In fact, the reason I was born and came into the world is to testify to the truth. Everyone on the side of truth listens to me."***

What truth was Jesus referring to? Before answering that question, it is important to note that on a separate occasion, Jesus said to his disciples, *"I am the way, the truth and the life..."* Now that you have a proper foundation, we can answer the question about truth. The answer is that Jesus came to testify and give truthful answers about everything related to life. He possessed the truth about everything, and it was his responsibility, obligation, and duty to share this information with those that would listen. In fact, he clearly states that he is the conduit to finding your path *(way / course / assignment)*, the truth about God's will and the life that you are predetermined to live.

Based on this information, you have the assurance in knowing that Jesus holds the key to understanding the truth about your potential, and he is eager to assist you so that you can bear much fruit. Listen to his words. *"Remain in me, and I will remain in you. For a branch cannot produce fruit if it is severed from the vine, and you cannot be fruitful unless you remain in me. Yes, I am the vine, you are the branches. Those who remain in me, and I in them, will produce much fruit. For apart from me you can do nothing."*

What is the truth about your potential? The truth is that you have a responsibility, obligation, and duty to be fruitful. Do you recall the following words spoken by Dr Munroe in the previous chapter: *"We each were endowed at birth with a unique gift, something we were born to do or become that no one else can achieve the way we can. God's purpose is that we bear abundant fruit and release the blessings of our gift and potential to the world."*

Why would a bird have the innate potential to fly, if flight was not associated with its destiny? Alternatively, why would the fruit seed possess the natural ability to become a tree that produces fruit, if fruit did not represent the fulfillment of the seed's potential? Now, the next point is very important for you to understand. The question is why would you have potential to do something or be someone, if you were not supposed to do it or become it? Do you agree that this would be a contradiction or a waste of resources? In other words, there is importance and significance associated with your potential.

Ultimately, this means that the recipient of the potential is responsible for its utilization.

I was the first person that Dr. Myles Munroe considered as an official personal assistant. In fact, in the Dedication section of this book, I inserted two short notes that I received from him. While the title of personal assistant to a world-renowned person would seem like a dream come true for many, the role came with great responsibility, obligation, duty, and sacrifice. First and foremost, I volunteered my time and abilities. Furthermore, the role required me to spend countless hours away from my wife and kids on a weekly basis. Nevertheless, through it all, the experience, and memories that I received working with him for approximately 10 years are now priceless.

I recall having many conversations regarding potential, purpose, and leadership. Some of my greatest learning experiences would come after he arrived back in town from an international trip. Some trips were to countries that required many hours of exhausting travel. Not to mention the fact that while in those countries, he would speak on numerous occasions, greet hundreds and sometimes thousands of people.

Upon arriving back, sometimes he would travel straight from the airport to the local service. In the 20 years that I knew him, I never once heard him complain or say, *"I'm too tired, I can't do it right now or I need a break."* Instead, on every occasion, he was always energized, highly passionate and exceptionally prepared. Furthermore, he was always eager to teach as though the audience consisted of foreign diplomats, corporate executives, political leaders, or influential students.

Frequently, he would say *"John, I am here doing my part. It does not matter if it is one person or a thousand in attendance, I will always give the best that I have."* In addition to delivering a profound, inspirational, motivational, and transformational message, he would also remain after the service to greet people, give advice and to answer questions. Often, those informal sessions would last for over an hour. As I stood by his side and watched family and friends leave to enjoy Sunday dinner, I would always reflect on the significance of my responsibility, obligation, and duty to remain faithful.

Dr. Munroe had an acute understanding and in-depth knowledge regarding many subjects. In fact, he became the walking embodiment and a subject matter expert in the areas of potential, purpose, and leadership, to name a few. Every facet of his life was centered on these issues. In other words, he lived to maximize his potential, pursue his purpose, and transform followers into leaders. Now, the mantle is transferred to me to give you vital information about potential, purpose, and your leadership role. Are you prepared and ready to be responsible for your potential? Additionally, are you ready to transform into a leader in your area of gifting?

## Potential Prepares You

Good News!!! Your potential prepares you for the responsibility, obligation, or duty that God has assigned to your life. In other words, potential is more than a talent, gift, or ability, it is the power source from God that is responsible for transforming the invisible into visible. When you link your potential to God's power source, you should be able to, *"... call into being things that were not."* For these reasons, remember that your ***potential is the greatest and most powerful transformational tool known to mankind***.

God expects you to become a leader. That's one of the reasons why your potential comes loaded with the power to deliver vital information, direct your thoughts, build your confidence, influence your attitude, prepare you for the future and to spark a fire of motivation. Therefore, maximizing your potential should consume your thoughts, as this is the driving force to ensure that your confidence, attitude, preparation, and motivation are always at the highest level. I am here to encourage you to start the journey towards maximizing your potential. The first step in this journey begins with information.

**Information**

*"Information is the oxygen of the modern age. It seeps through the walls topped by barbed wire, it wafts across the electrified borders,"* according to President Ronald Reagan. Information is also the gateway to knowledge and understanding about your purpose in life. Although the information that you receive about your purpose may come from various sources, it is critical that you weigh it against your potential. This means that you evaluate whether the information is consistent, right, or accurate based on your passion and TAGs.

> **The responsibility of potential requires that you evaluate your present circumstances and make the right decisions based on the information that you gather.**

Your potential is not a mystery because either you have it in a certain area, or you do not have it. These words spoken by Robert Kennedy Jr. are noteworthy, *"There were a lot of years that I was trying to do things that other people wanted me to do. But you have to follow your heart. Believe that you have a unique group of talents and abilities that are going to allow you to accomplish something in an area that interest you."* Kennedy is not the exception. Everyone receives information about careers or jobs from social media, family, friends, teachers, and the list go on. Sometimes this information directs you to make choices or decisions in your life based on factors outside of your natural potential.

Understanding your potential is vital because it gives you a glimpse into what you can do and who you can become in life. For example, before becoming a world-famous painter, a person receives information through the window of released potential that motivates them to pursue the path of drawing and painting. In other words, it is the responsibility of your potential to reveal to you your TAGs and purpose. **Whenever you discover and release your potential, it reveals who you are**. On the other hand, whenever you shut the door of your potential, then nobody knows your true identity, including yourself. The more you release your potential, the more information you will receive about your capabilities and your path of destiny. *"Be sure you put your feet in the right places, then stand firm."*

Those words were spoken by President Abraham Lincoln. Putting your feet in the right places means that you have pointed your feet in the direction of your potential, and you are not turning back. When this happens, it is your responsibility to be a good steward and work diligently at producing fruitful returns. For these reasons, it is important that you constantly find time to think about your potential and fill your mind with information about the path that your heart reveals to you.

## Thoughts

*"For as he thinks within himself, so is he."* Throughout the years, this popular scripture has been used to explain the correlation between thoughts and actions. In simple terms, this statement suggests that thoughts dictate or determine how you feel about yourself and how you respond to the issues of life. Continuous and unrelenting thoughts about your potential in life are the sparks that are intended to light a blaze of passion in your heart.

The advice of Henry David Thoreau regarding this issue holds true. He commented that, *"A single footstep will not make a path on the earth, so a single thought will not make a pathway in the mind. To make a deep physical path, we walk again and again. To make a deep mental path, we must think over and over the kind of thoughts we wish to dominate our lives."* Thoreau's words of wisdom related to the power of thoughts is key to understanding why you have a persistent natural beacon. These thoughts filter through your mind automatically without your prompting, opinion, or permission.

*"Nothing in this world can take the place of persistence. Talent will not: nothing is more common than unsuccessful men with talent. Genius will not; unrewarded genius is almost a proverb. Education will not: the world is full*

*of educated derelicts. Persistence and determination alone are omnipotent."* Those words from President Calvin Coolidge are still relevant and very insightful. Your TAGs, knowledge and education mean little related to having sustained peace of mind, if you fail to release your full potential. However, remember that your potential carries responsibilities as well. Your potential spearheads persistent and determined thoughts.

Do you know why you have persistent and determined thoughts related to releasing your TAGs? It is because your potential cries to be released from the confines of your mind. Your seeds of potential want to grow and become fruitful. Dismissing the value of your potential will not remove the thoughts because your persistent thoughts are the seeds that fuel your dreams and desires.

Again, the objective of this chapter is to understand the responsibility associated with potential. Allowing your mind to race with thoughts that limit or contradicts your potential is counterproductive. *Thoughts lead to ideas that form the basis of your belief system about your potential and purpose in life.* Be mindful that your ideas about the potential that you possess will dictate your actions.

Dr. Mae Jamison, a former astronaut, commented on the power of ideas when she said, *"I think of ideas as potential energy. They're wonderful, but nothing will happen until we risk putting them to action."* Although her words are true, if you think that you possess no potential, then you will stumble around idle with no sense of meaning. Contrarily, if you have potential centered thoughts, then you should begin to develop and release them.

*"Strong minds discuss ideas, average minds discuss events, weak minds discuss people,"* according to Socrates. What ideas do you frequently think about related to your potential and purpose in life? A better question to ask is, "Do you have any ideas about your future that you think about?" Are you spending most of your life discussing events in your life or people? These

questions are important to ask because it is popular to live in the moment and not think about the importance of self-actualization.

Socrates' comment adds to the notion that self-evaluation of your thoughts about potential leads to healthy conversations and a purposeful life. Exploring the ideas in your mind about your natural TAGs begins the process of self-discovery, releasing your potential and identifying the path of purpose. According to Napoleon Hill, *"Any idea, plan, or purpose may be placed in the mind through repetition of thought."* Having intentional and deliberate thoughts about the path you want to take is critical to living a focused and successful life.

There is a popular short story surrounding a conversation that Walt Disney had with a young eight- year-old boy. The young boy asked the question that millions are still pondering in their hearts. His question was, *"…I would like to know the secret of life."* Disney's answer was interesting because it centered around the concept of thinking, believing, and acting on your personal potential. Paraphrasing his answer, he suggested to the young boy that the answer involves thinking about how you want to live your life, believing in yourself, dreaming about your abilities, and daring to release your stored potential.[12]

Walt Disney was the founder of the greatest and most popular theme park in the world. Annually, Walt Disney World attracts millions of guests from around the world. The founder of this world-renowned conglomerate of media and entertainment empire concluded that the secret to your life rests inside of you. The responsibility associated with having potential requires that you spend time understanding who you are related to your TAGs and dreams. Hopefully, honest introspection will awaken your thoughts to the unlimited possibilities stored within your seeds of potential. As you gain more knowledge and understanding about your potential, it is my desire that your confidence grows in the area of your purpose in life.

> **L**ack of confidence diminishes the power of your potential to orchestrate significant change in your life.

**Confidence**

*"This is the confidence we have in approaching God: that if we ask anything according to his will, he hears us."* Hopefully, you are starting to believe that it is God's will for you to accomplish great things using the natural attributes that He gave to you. Do you believe that God hears the cry and yearning of your heart to be fulfilled in life? He knows that you have a need and desire to release the hidden you, because it is a natural response or reaction to dormant potential. Fortunately, when potential is dormant, warning bells ring internally sounding an alarm and a call for action.

Honestly speaking, do you have confidence in your ability to maximize your potential? If so, that is very good. If not, have you considered the outcome if you continue to doubt the core value that you possess in the form of potential? Norman Vincent Peale also said, *"Believe in yourself! Have faith in your abilities! Without a humble but reasonable confidence in your own powers you cannot be successful or happy."*

Peale suggested that belief and faith are prerequisites for establishing confidence in yourself and releasing your internal power. What is faith? *"Faith is the confidence that what we hope for will actually happen; it gives us assurance about things we cannot see."* Perhaps, you did not know that confidence is a side effect of having faith. Therefore, the more you have faith in your potential, then the more your confidence will grow. Do you hope for the opportunity to release your full potential? If so, what steps are you taking to make it happen? Let me answer that question for you. Reading this book is the right start to ensure continual growth and development.

What are your thoughts about these simple words from Peale, *"What you can image, you will be, in the long run?"* His words emphasize the point that the core essentials of who you are and who you can become centers on your natural abilities, faith, and confidence. Therefore, is it possible to believe in yourself without believing in the potential inside of you? Another way to look at this point is to say, **"Whenever you doubt your natural abilities you are doubting who you are and who you are supposed to become in life."**

Having faith in God's word and plan for your life is necessary to combat negative thoughts and attitudes. He does not make mistakes. Listen to these words from Dr. Ben Carson, *"The most important thing for me is having a relationship with God. To know that the owner, the creator of the universe loves you, sent His Son to die for your sins; that's very empowering. Knowing Him and knowing that He loves me gives me encouragement and confidence to move forward."*

Please be aware that my next statement is not an attempt to patronize you, it is a true statement. **<u>You are not an accident or meaningless person destined to be relegated to a life of obscurity</u>**. God has a plan for your life. He has equipped you with the tools to succeed. From this point forward, it is critical that you build your confidence level by acquiring more information about your purpose and thinking positively about your potential. Again, reflecting on the advice of Peale, it is important to *"Try, really try. Think, really think. Believe, really believe."* Your attitude towards your potential will determine what happens moving forward in life.

## Attitude

*"You cannot tailor-make the situations in life, but you can tailor-make the attitudes to fit those situations."* That comment from Zig Ziglar is correct. Do you have the mindset of a winner or loser? Winners tend to have an attitude that leads to successful outcomes, while losers tend to have an attitude that leads to failure. I realize that sometimes unintended results occur even

though you give your best effort. Nonetheless, have you allowed your negative experiences to dictate your attitude about maximizing your potential?

*"A great attitude does much more than turn on the lights in our worlds; it seems to magically connect us to all sorts of serendipitous opportunities that were somehow absent before the change."* Do you believe those words from Earl Nightingale? An optimistic attitude or positive thoughts about your potential will give you hope of a brighter future and outlook on life. Do you remember Nelson Mandela's experience? He experienced unthinkable hardships and challenges. Nonetheless, his legacy speaks to the value of a positive attitude and the power of potential to orchestrate change against the greatest opposition. Listen to his advice regarding the issue of releasing your full potential, *"There is no passion to be found playing small – in settling for a life that is less than the one you are capable of living."*

Mandela's comment speaks against an attitude of mediocrity, complacency, and average living. Remember, you are destined to excel and achieve greatness. Settling for less than what your potential is capable of achieving is not a viable option. It is not viable because it leads to having the wrong attitude and experiencing a marginal life.

I agree with this observation also spoken by Zig Ziglar, *"Your attitude, not your aptitude, will determine your altitude."* Hopefully, you agree that the right attitude is a prerequisite for maximizing your potential and fulfilling your purpose for living. Why? Let these words spoken by Thomas Jefferson answer the question, *"Nothing can stop the man with the right mental attitude from achieving his goal; nothing on earth can help the man with the wrong mental attitude."* The conclusion is that both individuals are prepared. One is prepared for success and the other is prepared for failure.

*"If you are going to achieve excellence in big things, you develop the habit in little matters. Excellence is not an exception; it is a prevailing attitude."* Colin Powell, former Secretary of State and military general gave that advice. His sentiments revert to the issue of your attitude being a determining

factor in what happens in life. In other words, there are always challenges and opposition to releasing your full potential. Nevertheless, whether fair or not, the responsibility of maximizing your potential falls on your shoulder. Would you agree that it is time to prepare to move in the direction of maximizing your potential?

**Preparation**

What do you think about these words of Confucius, *"Success depends upon previous preparation, and without such preparation there is sure to be failure?"* Destiny awaits the prepared and unprepared person. The prepared person capitalizes on the moment and advances towards their assigned purpose. Whereas, the unprepared person misses the opportunity and lives with the thought of *"what could have happened if ..."*

The thought of being unprepared in life should invoke a sense of urgency. Your potential will ensure that you are ready to seize the moment, but you must allow it to work for you. What is a good reason for you to ensure that your potential matures properly? Listen to the words of Arthur Ashe, *"One important key to success is self-confidence. An important key to self-confidence is preparation."*

***The person that is prepared to fulfill their destiny acts and sounds different from others because they have a glimpse of the brightness of their future.*** As they get closer to maximizing their potential, they begin to take on a new nature. Their new nature personifies self-confidence not arrogance. Are you a self-confident person because you are prepared to release your potential, or do you feel less confident because you are unprepared? When you think about your response, remember that self-confidence is a by-product of preparation.

Each moment that you spend enhancing and developing your potential is time well spent towards maximizing it. *"There is no shortcut to achievement. Life requires thorough preparation – veneer isn't worth anything,"* according to George Washington Carver. Veneer is a deception of reality because the material underneath the outer covering is not made of solid substance and is susceptible to crumbling under the pressures and tests of life. In other words, it is an imitation of the original version.

As you process Carver's comment about preparation, remember that you are not an imitation or copy. You are an original specimen sent to earth with the power of potential to change the world. Developing your potential through consistent use and refinement ensures that you are properly prepared to withstand the weight of life's challenges. Equally as important, your preparation will lead to motivation to pursue, achieve, and manifest your dreams. Have I given you enough information to become decisive about your potential? If you need additional help, listen to the advice given by Napoleon Hill, *"The way to develop decisiveness is to start right where you are, with the very next question you face."* Are you motivated to start moving in the direction of maximizing your full potential?

**Motivation**

*"The secret of getting ahead is getting started."* What is the significance of that statement from Mark Twain? Simply speaking, getting ahead means that you are moving in a positive direction beyond the point where you are currently. The existence of your potential is a clear and undeniable guarantee that your future is achievable. *"Accept the challenges so that you can feel the exhilaration of victory."* Do you accept that comment from General George Patton as a personal challenge?

Unfortunately, I have discovered that there are people motivated to accept the challenge and there are unmotivated people that run away from the challenge. Amazingly, the reality and impact of this human dilemma is often overlooked. Think for a moment. There are people that are truly motivated to do what is right and there are people unmotivated to do right. There are people motivated to work and there are people unmotivated to work. There are people motivated to achieve and there are people unmotivated to achieve. As you will agree, the list of things that separate the motivated person from the unmotivated person is too great to record them all.

If you agree with these words of Earl Nightingale, then *"Your problem is to bridge the gap which exists between where you are now and the goal you intend to reach."* The motivated person believes in a brighter future, but the unmotivated person accepts the routine life. The motivated person overcomes the challenges of life, and the unmotivated person settles for blaming others. The motivated person looks for opportunities to achieve and succeed, but the unmotivated person looks for chances to receive and take by any means necessary. The motivated basks in the refreshing confidence of self-value and purpose for existence. Whereas, the unmotivated drowns in the turbulent seas of doubt tossed by swirling winds of uncertainty.

Do you desire to become a motivated person related to releasing your potential? *"Desire is the key to motivation, but it's determination and commitment to an unrelenting pursuit of your goal – a commitment to excellence – that will enable you to attain the success you seek,"* according to famed American car racing driver, Mario Andretti. He identifies desire, determination, and commitment as the underpinning characteristics necessary to sustain your motivation when pursuing goals. These characteristics are also essential ingredients in building and sustaining your motivation to release your potential. As you will discover or already know, motivation is easier to sustain when you experience successes in fulfilling your dreams.

Be mindful not to forget Andretti's statement about *"commitment to excellence."* The success that you desire to experience in life requires the correct attitude, preparation, and motivation to produce excellence. Please be aware that there are always challenges and oppositions to releasing your full potential. It is your birthright to be a winner. Remember that with God's help you will prevail over every opposition.

## Opposition to Potential

In addressing the issue of opposition to potential, I fully appreciate that there are varying levels of freedoms, privileges and opportunities which may differ from country to country. I hope that you live in a country that doesn't limit the releasing of your potential or prevent you from pursuing your purpose in life. Although some of the remaining information may or may not apply to you, the message is still the same. You have a responsibility related to your potential which requires some form of action, whether its prayer, faith or agreeing to make deliberate steps as you move forward.

Perhaps, you realize that one of the greatest internal struggles is the fight between the desire to release your potential and the confining barriers imposed by society, political oppression, or economic disenfranchisement. Sometimes you may face considerable opposition to pursuing your purpose stemming from these sources of conflict. How do you handle it when your potential is prompting you to manifest the hidden person, but your environment is limiting your progression? This opposition is real and presents moments of confusion, fear, reluctance, and a lack of clarity.

I also realize that sometimes in life there are unpreventable obstacles that cause emotional, mental, physical, and financial setbacks or challenges. If you find yourself experiencing one of these setbacks, then the Spirit of God is waiting to assist you. God's word says, *"...not by might nor by power, but by my Spirit, says the LORD Almighty."* In other words, what you are uncapable of achieving through your might or power, He can turn things around for your good. Also remember that *"The eyes of the LORD watch over those who do right; his ears are open to their cries for help."* Furthermore, *"...the eyes of the LORD range throughout the earth to strengthen those whose hearts are fully committed to him."*

*"Success is to be measured not so much by the position that one has reached in life as by the obstacles which he has overcome,"* according to Brooker T. Washington. Do you believe that sometimes opposition comes to

test your commitment to fulfilling your dream or the will of God? Regardless of how you feel, it is imperative that you prove the opposition wrong. Listed below are 3 prevalent obstacles that you must contend with in your quest to free your potential:

- Environment
- National Conflict
- Culture

**Environment**

Social factors are formidable challenges in the quest to release your potential. Each year, many fall victims to the pressures that emanate from their environment. However, *"You see, it's never the environment; it's never the events of our lives, but the meaning we attach to the events – how we interpret them – that shapes who we are today and who we'll become tomorrow."* To some extent, I agree with those sentiments from Tony Robbin's related to the issues of potential and purpose. How you process the events surrounding your desire to maximize your potential and fulfill your purpose shapes your attitude towards moving forward.

In every society, there are various opinions and thoughts about who you are and what you can do. Likewise, sometimes there are limiting or tough conditions such as poverty, discrimination, war, and the list goes on. One of the issues is whether you will allow the environment to change the path that God has assigned to you, or will you have enough faith to believe that He will help you achieve a successful outcome. Preferably, you will choose not to be held back and decide to express yourself through releasing your potential.

There was an occasion when Jesus and his disciples were crossing a lake in a boat. *"Suddenly, a fierce storm struck the lake, with waves breaking into the boat. But Jesus was sleeping."* The change in weather presented real dangers and concerns to everyone but Jesus. *"The disciples went and woke him up, shouting, Lord, save us! We're going to drown!"* Let's pause for a moment. Do you think that God would have let them drown or do you believe that it was a learning lesson on how to become an overcomer? Jesus answers the question with this response, *"Why are you afraid? You have so little faith! Then he got up and rebuked the wind and waves, and suddenly there was a great calm."*

That experience was a lesson on overcoming the opposition that may surface from your environment. It doesn't matter whether the challenge is physical or mental, the conclusion is still the same. God's response is don't be dismayed or afraid, have faith. If He needs to tell the winds or waves blowing in your life to *"cease and be still,"* then you must believe that He can make it happen. Therefore, don't wait for the perfect environment without any challenges or obstacles. *"If you can't fly, then run, if you can't run, then walk if you can't walk, then crawl but whatever you do, keep moving."* Dr. Martin Luther King Jr spoke those words of admonition.

The difficulty that some environments present in your life should not be underestimated. Notwithstanding this reality, please remember that you deserve the opportunity to explore and develop your potential irrespective of the external factors. During the heightened political and social tensions in America, Dr. King made that statement encouraging his followers to keep moving forward in the best way possible. Likewise, the message to you is the same. Irrespective of the challenges that your environment presents, you must *"press to reach the end of the race and receive the prize…"*

## National Conflict

National conflict is a serious detriment and a restraining factor in the pursuit of purpose through the releasing of potential. Unfortunately, an inordinate number of people around the world are subjected to the harsh realities of living in failed or failing conditions. In the same regard, the world is full of dictators and tyrants that feel as though their country and citizens are their personal possessions. They strip the country of its natural and economic resources for the pleasure of themselves and a hand full of privileged insiders.

The end result is a world with millions of desperate people fleeing hardship, war and systematic corruption.

National and political conflict are also dilemmas affecting people in stable and progressive countries, as well. Adding to the global problems is the fact that racial and socioeconomic divisions are increasing and causing significant national turmoil. Unfortunately, with the rise of national conflict there seems to be a decrease in viable solutions and visionary political leadership. Nevertheless, I have good news for you. The good news is that the smothering effects of national conflict are not the end of the road.

Whenever the calamity and discomfort surpasses the threshold of tolerance, it becomes necessary to rely on a proven option to find solutions. The words of George W. Bush, the 43$^{rd}$ President of the United States gives insight into the best alternative for solutions. During one of America's most difficult periods, he said, *"The course of this conflict is not known, yet its outcome is certain. Freedom and fear, justice and cruelty, have always been at war, and we know that God is not neutral between them."* Although conflict tends to cause uncertainty, fear, despair and doubt, there is a solution.

According to President Bush, God is not neutral between the destructive forces and freedom. In fact, if you really believe that He will bring you through successfully, then it will happen. Have faith in God and His words. *"The Lord hears His people when they call to Him for help. He rescues them from all their troubles."* More importantly, are you aware that God has established an invisible domain on earth that operates inside of every country and on each continent. His domain comes with its own governmental systems designed to meet the needs of each citizen. When you live within the parameter of His domain, then everything you need will be provided.

What is this invisible domain? God's domain is called the Kingdom of God. Listen to His promise to grant you access, *"...don't be afraid...For it gives your Father great happiness to give you the Kingdom."* Now that the Kingdom of God is accessible to you, guess what else is available as well?

The answer is *"... God will meet all your needs according to the riches of his glory in Christ Jesus."* Therefore, I encourage you to *"Seek the Kingdom of God above all else, and live righteously, and he will give you everything you need."*

Are you encouraged by the news of the Kingdom of God? *"Until John the Baptist, the law of Moses and the messages of the prophets were your guides. But now the Good News of the Kingdom of God is preached, and everyone is eager to get in."* These are the words spoken by Jesus about God's alternative to your country. Is your name on the list of individuals that are eager to get citizenship into His Kingdom or are you already a resident? Listed below are the prerequisites for you to enter into God's Kingdom:

- *"The time promised by God has come at last!" he announced. "The Kingdom of God is near! Repent of your sins and believe the Good News!"*
- *Jesus replied, "Very truly I tell you, no one can see the kingdom of God unless they are born again."*
- *Jesus answered, "Very truly I tell you, no one can enter the kingdom of God unless they are born of water and the Spirit."*

I would recommend that you review Dr. Myles Munroe's books on the Kingdom of God for a more comprehensive overview on kingdom living. The introduction of the Kingdom of God adds to the removal of excuses as to why it is not possible to fulfill God's mandate for your life. With God, all things are possible. Remember that your potential was given to you for a reason and all things are possible with God. It was given to you for your purpose and assignment in life. Falling victim to national conflict and cultural barriers is not an option. These obstacles do not determine who you are and what you can become with God's help. Now is a good time for you to repeat the quote, *"I am a possibility creator and an impossibility destroyer."*

## Culture

In the UN report titled "Our Creative World," it states that, *"Culture is the whole complex of distinctive spiritual, material, intellectual and emotional features that characterizes a society or a group. It includes creative expressions, community practices and material or built forms."* This comprehensive definition of culture is thorough and very detailed. From it, you can ascertain that your culture influences every area of your life.[13]

Nevertheless, let your potential define you and not the expectations of your culture. Bear in mind that your potential flows through the window of the heart, but opinions of others flow through the tides of culture. To break through the opinions of others, comfort zones and cultural norms, you must have an unwavering commitment to releasing your potential and an unrelenting passion for the fulfillment of your purpose.

Rags to riches true stories are a testament to the power of potential to break through the cultural imposed barriers. Oprah Winfrey was born into poverty in the Deep South to a poor unwed teenage mother. Searching for a better life, her mother relocated with Oprah to the inner city of a Midwest city when she was 6 years old. By her own admission, she was a victim of sexual abuse, teenage pregnancy, and drugs. All of which, were rampant in her culture and social environment.

Her story has a magnificent ending because she discovered her gift for speaking and communicating at an early age. After spending years developing her potential, she was given an opportunity to host her own television show and the rest is history. The Oprah Winfrey Show captivated audiences and grew to become the top-rated talk show in America. Oprah used her potential to overcome her childhood misfortune and become the world's first known woman billionaire.[14]

Listen to her advice regarding overcoming opposition, *"It isn't until you come to a spiritual understanding of who you are – not necessarily a religious feeling, but deep down, the spirit within – that you can begin to take control."* Once you take control over your life-defeating cultural influences and barriers, then as she states, you must *"Understand that the right to choose your own path is a sacred privilege. Use it. Dwell in possibility."* Oprah's sentiments fall in line with the view that potential opens the doors of possibility to accomplish things beyond your expectations.

## THE NEXT STEP

I commend you for continuing the journey towards maximizing your potential. This chapter contained valuable information about your responsibility to discover and release your potential. Regardless of what you have experienced in your life thus far, releasing your potential must take precedence in your mind. The world is waiting to receive it and you deserve to receive the benefits associated with having it.

*"In dreams begin responsibilities,"* according to William Butler Yates. Is it possible to stop purposeful dreams from entering your mind? Furthermore, is it possible to remove your potential from your heart? If you answered "NO" to either question, then it goes without saying that you bear some degree of responsibility for the outcome. Believe it or not, I had to accept my responsibility to write this book. There were two questions that I had to consider in making my decision. The questions were "What will happen to me if I don't do it and What will happen to your potential and purpose, if I don't do it?" Are you glad that I accepted the extremely difficult challenge of bridging the gap between understanding potential and pursuing your purpose for living?

*"It doesn't matter if you come from the inner city. People who fail in life are people who find lots of excuses. It's never too late for a person to recognize that they have potential in themselves."* Do you concur with those words spoken by Dr. Ben Carson? Remember that releasing your hidden potential will open doors of opportunity for you. The opportunities will lead to a rewarding and fulfilling life. Additional benefits of released potential are included in the next chapter. As you continue to read, focus on what it will take for you to release your natural potential.

One of the most rewarding feelings in life comes when you are maximizing your potential. Reason being, maximizing your potential leads to self-actualization which is the highest form of personal expression. Before moving on to the next chapter, it is important that you accept your responsibility and prepare yourself mentally to move to the next step. The next step in your progression is to begin the process of releasing your potential. Continue reading and remember the statement, *"I am a possibility creator and an impossibility destroyer,"* as you proceed to the next chapter.

### Quick reference to the responsibility of potential principles:

1. Your potential prepares you for the responsibility, obligation, or duty that God has assigned to your life.
2. The responsibility of potential requires that you evaluate your present circumstances and make the right decisions based on the information that you gather.
3. Understanding your potential is vital because it gives you a glimpse of what you can do and who you can become in life.
4. Whenever you discover and release your potential, it reveals who you are
5. Continuous and unrelenting thoughts about your potential in life are the sparks that are intended to light a blaze of passion in your heart.
6. Lack of confidence diminishes the power of your potential to orchestrate significant change in your life.
7. You are not an accident or meaningless person destined to be relegated to a life of obscurity.
8. The person that is prepared to fulfill their destiny, acts and sounds different from others because they have a glimpse of the brightness of their future.
9. The motivated person believes in a brighter future, but the unmotivated person accepts the darkness of defeat.

# Chapter Four

## Releasing Your Potential

*"Know, first, who you are,
and then adorn yourself accordingly."*
**Epictetus**

The greatest societal contributions since the foundation of the world continues to come from individuals that find ways to release their seeds of potential, against all odds. As mentioned in earlier chapters, everything that manifested in the seen realm existed invisibly in the form of potential before it materialized. **Released potential serves as a crystalized snapshot of your internal TAGs that pre-existed prior to manifestation.** This is true because every materialization is a product of its creator and a glimpse of the secrets hidden in the creator's heart. Therefore, the process of releasing your hidden treasures impact your life's purpose and exposes your true identity.

In the introductory quote, Epictetus suggested that once self-knowledge is known, then you should adorn yourself accordingly. His use of the word adorn has symbolic meaning. Adorn means *to decorate or beautify*. Therefore, Epictetus' statement provides encouragement to enhance your life with the beauty of your potential and purpose. In other words, your life is made valuable when you expose the world to the jewels hidden inside of you.

Self-knowledge relates to understanding the tools that you have on the inside. The action component of the interpretation means that you should construct your self-image using the natural tools that you were born with. Therefore, another way to interpret his thought is to suggest that the splendor of your self-image is more attractive when it reflects the greatness of your unique innate attributes. Adorning yourself with your potential attributes establishes clarity regarding your life's purpose and identifies you as a reservoir that quenches the thirst for solutions.

The life and experiences of Steve Jobs is a good example of these truths. Early in life, Jobs recognized his keen interest and talent in the area of electronics. His passion and potential were driving factors in understanding the mechanics surrounding electronic consumer products. As his knowledge and skills grew, his ability to comprehend the dynamics of electronics exceeded that of his peers.

However, in other areas of his educational experience, he underachieved. In fact, his college tenure was unimpressive, as he dropped out after two years. Eventually, Jobs focused his attention back on his first love and decided to become an entrepreneur in the field of electronics. This venture into electronics provided the opportunity to pursue a path suitable for his potential and to expose the world to his innovativeness. At the young age of 21, Jobs co-founded Apple Computers. [15]

The pursuit of his potential produced unimaginable results and catapulted him into world-renowned legendary status. Riding on the success of Jobs' creative and visionary products, Apple rose to the enviable position of the world's largest technology company. Although he died from cancer in 2011, Apple continues to benefit from his initiatives and pioneering products. In 2019, the company generated over $250 billion in gross sales and revenue.[16] Jobs gave the world one of the secrets to Apple's international success when he stated, *"What is Apple, after all? Apple is about people who think 'outside of the box' people who want computers to help them change the world..."*

He made history for himself and Apple with his passion for electronics, innovative mind, and visionary leadership. He also revolutionized the electronic industry as the CEO of Apple and helped to raise it to the supreme position that it currently occupies. Listen to a comment that he once made, *"I want to put a ding in the universe."* To the benefit of all, Jobs accomplished his objective to *"put a ding in the universe"* of consumer technology.

For his efforts, his name is now synonymous with Apple, the world of smartphones and the greatness associated with being one of the best innovators ever. As a young kid, he explored his natural abilities that led to an understanding of his true potential and passion of the heart. He also discovered that when you focus seeds of potential on hitting the mark of excellence, the impact made along the way will change your environment forever.

Thankfully, Jobs left his signature on this earth and changed the world in the process. In speaking with his employees, he once commented, *"...We are aware that we are doing something significant. We're here at the beginning of it and we're able to shape how it goes. Everyone here has the sense that right now is one of those moments when we are influencing the future."* Did Jobs' released potential leave an indelible mark on humanity?

## RELEASED POTENTIAL

What would life be like without the many fantastic innovations and products produced by Apple over the years? Now, if you are a user of Apple products like the iPhone, iPad, or Macintosh computer, what would your life be like without it? It is correct to say that Jobs' released potential changed the world that we live in. I hope that you believe that your released potential is valuable to yourself and the world, as well. Let's go back to the seed concept to illustrate this point.

Again, the process of a seed developing into a fruit-bearing tree is a good illustration of the practical application of potential. Production of fruit is the main objective for planting a fruit seed, but it must first develop into a tree or plant. At each stage in the process, the potential exists to reach the next stage so that the fruit or continuous beneficial outcome is achieved. In this illustration, the seed has potential, the tree has potential, and the fruit has potential.

If the potential remains in seed form only, then the tree will never exist. If the tree fails to exist, then the fruit will never exist.

Likewise, if the tree fails to yield fruit, then there will be no additional seeds. The conclusion to this illustration is the fact that you have a responsibility to expose your potential to the right environment in order to produce continuous positive outcomes. Furthermore, the manifestation of potential requires the active expression of your TAGs. As you know, the initial deposit of potential must be refined and released in order to receive its fruit. Therefore, the prerequisite for the manifestation of dreams, desires and goals is the expression and manifestation of your inherent potential.

> **Limited ability to express potential will lead to limited personal development and growth.**

When you look at a caterpillar, what do you think? Perhaps, you are thinking that it is an unattractive creature that provides little or no benefit. If you came to that conclusion, I am sure that you are not alone. Nevertheless, a more in-depth study of a caterpillar reveals its amazing value.

There are two very important points about the caterpillar. The first point is that the caterpillar possesses the potential to become something that does not resemble the original state. This unique potential leads it through various stages of development until it transforms into the splendor of its original intent. Before the metamorphosis takes place, the caterpillar has no resemblance of its final image. However, when the developmental process is complete, the caterpillar transforms into a butterfly, which exemplifies magnificence, splendor, and excellence.

The second very important point is that the butterfly is a pollinator, just as the honeybee and the hummingbird. This means that it performs a critical role in the well-being of plants, animals, and human beings. The butterfly ensures that we have a continuous source of food, beautiful plants, and flowers to enjoy. Keep in mind that its value did not begin when it transformed but at the beginning of life.

What started the process of transformation that led into the caterpillar becoming a butterfly? The answer is released potential started the process of conversion into an image of beauty. What enables the butterfly to become an effective pollinator? Again, the answer is its potential. Similarly, your released potential enables you to fill a void in society, transform into a leader, become a person of influence and a valuable contributor to the well-being of others.

Therefore, failure to release your potential would result in an inferior quality of life for everyone involved. Another issue with failure to release potential is that it doesn't make practical sense to have potential and not use it in some way to do something positive or productive. Jesus stated it a better way, *"Would anyone light a lamp and then put it under a basket or under a bed? Of course not! A lamp is placed on a stand, where its light will shine."*

Although God's words about you confirms your value and the greatness of your future, it is still up to you to release your potential and become what He intends. Are you starting to sense that transformation is taking place in your mind regarding releasing your potential? Like the caterpillar and butterfly, your potential can transform your current state into something different and rewarding, as well. This is true because the objective of released potential is the activation of dormant ability capable of changing your circumstances and situations.

Because of released potential, a person born into poverty can transform into an inspirational, motivational, and international leader. It happened for Dr. Myles Munroe. He became an international political advisor, business consultant and motivational speaker. Because of released potential, a person with limited formal education can blossom into a business leader, public official, and an international diplomat. It happened for Benjamin Franklin. He became a founding father of the United States, a diplomat, and an inventor. Because of released potential, a person born under a repressive political regime can break the shackles of oppression and lead a nation into unprecedented change. It happened for Nelson Mandela. He became the President of South Africa.

Furthermore, because of released potential, a person of mixed culture and race can rewrite history and become the leader of the most influential democracy on earth. It happened for President Barack Obama. He became the first person of African descent to become the President of the United States. Because of released potential, a poor person living in the slums of Calcutta could feed and clothe thousands of poverty-stricken individuals and win the Noble Peace prize. It happened for Mother Teresa who became an international symbol of humility and servitude. The transformation was possible in the lives of these great individuals because released potential changes circumstances, even when it seems impossible.

## Benefits of Released Potential

What would South Africa be like today without Nelson Mandela and his released potential? *"We know what we are, but not what we may be,"* according to William Shakespeare. His statement indicates that there is uncertainty about a person's future destiny. Uncertainty exists because of a lack of understanding about the inherent value of potential and a lack of knowledge about God's plan or will for your life. Nevertheless, uncertainty is not in your future, because you are learning about the importance of releasing your potential.

> Released potential produces specific and beneficial results.

It is my sincere hope that you are beginning to understand the tremendous value you have resting on the inside of you. Before something happens, the potential to make it happen already exists. Before a boy turns into a man, the potential to become a man exists inside of the boy. Before a fish swims for the first time, the potential to swim exists inside of the fish. Before a seed transforms into a fruit-bearing tree, the potential to bear fruit exists within the seed. *"Your existence is evidence that this generation needs something that your life contains,"* according to Dr. Myles Munroe. The "something" that he referred to in the quote is your potential.

At this point, I am not going to ask whether you believe that the existence of your potential is evidence that this generation needs you to release it. Hopefully, you have accepted the fact that you possess the natural potential to positively impact your life and others. I would like to emphasize the other benefits of released potential. The chart below highlights the fact that it defines, dictates, determines, directs, and delivers you to an appointed destination:

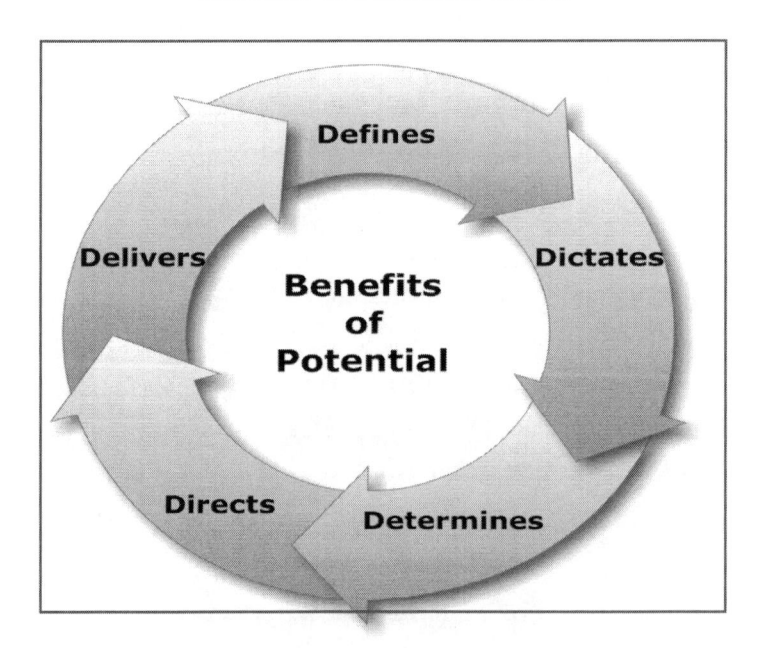

## Benefits of Potential Chart

The benefits of potential chart suggests the following:

- Potential **defines** who you are.

- Potential **dictates** what you are capable of doing.
- Potential **determines** when you should do something.
- Potential **directs** the path that you should take in life.
- Potential **delivers** you to your desired destination in life.

Take a moment and meditate on these points. In secret, you may have yearned for basic answers about your existence. Perhaps, you have felt as though there is more to life than to work to pay bills and struggle to make ends meet. Maybe you have accomplished things, but still feel as though there is something else missing or yet to be accomplished. I encourage you to stay alert and active because your life was never intended to be a mystery. You were created to sow your potential along the path of purpose.

## **Sowing Released Potential**

According to John Maxwell, *"Success is knowing your purpose in life, growing to reach your maximum potential and sowing seeds that benefit others."* Therefore, based on his assessment, true success is determined by purpose, reaching maximum potential and sowing seeds for the good of others. His definition of success contradicts societal norms because it does not include wealth, power, or money. Contrary to popular belief, released potential makes you a wealthy person, it gives you personal power and it enables you to make money doing something that you love. Furthermore, when you release your potential, you are sowing seeds that grow to produce fruitful outcomes for you and others. This premise coincides with Ralph Waldo Emerson's statement, *"The creation of a thousand forests is in one acorn."* Can you envision the benefits of this principle regarding your released potential?

In 2015, American Pharoah became the first thoroughbred in 37 years to win the coveted Triple Crown in horseracing. He is the great grandson of Unbridled, a Kentucky Derby and Breeders' Cup winner. Although Unbridled never won the Triple Crown, his winning characteristics and physical traits made him extremely valuable as a stud horse. He was successful in siring 482 foals during his lifetime. Unbridled died in 2001, but his winning bloodline continues in the genes passed on to his living offspring.

If Unbridled died without siring any offspring, then the potential that he possessed would have died as well. However, American Pharoah inherited ability through his outstanding pedigree. His horse racing success and achievements validate the fact that released potential is not diminished by time.[17] It continues to live and evolve through the generations.

Whenever released potential is sown it creates residual effects. The residual effects have a positive impact on you and others. Mary Anderson's talent and abilities were another example of this truth. Many years ago, Anderson was riding in a streetcar and the driver's vision was impaired by inclement weather. She thought to herself that it would be safer and beneficial if the windshield of the streetcar could be cleaned as it is driven. While sitting in it, she sketched a window cleaning device that would later be known as the windshield wiper.[18]

## Wasted Potential

The benefits of Anderson's invention are innumerable and unquestionable. In fact, the number of vehicles worldwide that went into production, and continue to be produced with windshield wipers is incalculable. To finalize the point about the continuous effect of released potential, let's move back to Emerson's suggestion *"...a thousand forests in one acorn."* I agree with his conclusion. Have you accepted that sleeping inside of you is a seed of potential that possesses the power to create an incalculable harvest? Sadly, if that potential is wasted, then it would be a tragedy.

> **W**asted potential is one of the greatest threats to success in life.

Without doubt, there is overwhelming proof that Mary Anderson's potential to conceive and manifest the first prototype windshield wiper was invaluable to her and humanity. However, what is the conclusion regarding those individuals that have failed to release their potential during their lifetime? *"Every human life contains a potential, if the potential is not fulfilled, then that life was wasted."* Is that statement made by Carl Jung a noted psychoanalyst true? Unfortunately, his assessment is still correct. Throughout the ages, countless individuals have died and carried to the grave unreleased potential and dormant abilities.

If an apple tree dies without producing fruit, then the value of that tree is lost forever. If the tree produced fruit during its lifetime, then value extends beyond the life of the tree through its fruit. Thus, if the tree dies after producing seeds, then the value of the tree lives on through the seeds that possess the possibility of bearing fruit. The conclusion is that unreleased potential is only valuable if the possibility exists to either extract or release it in the future.

> **Unreleased potential results in failure to express your true nature.**

Unfortunately, there are millions of people from around the world that fall victim to social conditions and circumstances that force them to focus solely on satisfying their basic survival needs. Abraham Maslow developed a psychological theory surrounding the priority of human needs. His theory is known as, "Hierarchy of Needs." His popular assertion suggested that humans desire to express themselves in the form of self-actualization; however, the fulfillment of critical basic survival needs take precedence. Maslow's assessment about basic survival needs is an unfortunate reality that still exists today.

Focusing on basic survival needs cannot replace the need to release your potential or pursue your purpose for living. You may be a teenager and haven't put much thought into planning your future. You may be in your twenties and unsure about what direction to take in life. You may be in your thirties and confused and frustrated with the career path that you have taken. You may be in your forties and feeling as though your life is a waste. You may have reached fifty and now fear that you are unprepared for the future. You may be sixty and worried about the lack of financial security.

This is a good point to pause, take a moment to meditate on your life and what you desire to achieve. Whether or not you fall into one of these categories, it is important to understand that potential is alive within you and capable of changing your circumstances. The process of change begins with an approach that centers on your potential and the power it possesses to initiate a different series of life events.

## Who Am I

For centuries people have grappled with the concept of defining self. Answering the question "Who Am I" has proven to be very difficult to do in a world that is full of restrictions, external influences, and significant personal struggles. Confusion surrounding the proper way to approach the issue has led many to answer the question by giving a response that either includes their nationality, ethnicity, name, socioeconomic status, skin color or age. However, these types of responses are merely descriptions of external features, or social, physical, and economic characteristics.

> **E**xpressed potential is a catalyst that initiates a cycle of key events that have a profound impact on what happens in a person's life.

Whenever you seek to define yourself, it is important to take into consideration factors such as internal nature, talents, abilities, and gifts. This statement means that your answer to the question should articulate your potential or the expression of your potential. For instance, if a person understands his artistic abilities and accepts this as his or her purpose in life, then the answer to the question should be *"I am an aspiring artist."* This response addresses their potential, gives meaning to purpose, and determines their career path.

Ultimately, these things will lead to focused objectives, accomplishments, self-actualization, and a successful life.

On one occasion, Jesus asked his disciples, *"...Who do you say I am? Peter answered, You are the Messiah."* This name means that Jesus possessed the potential to be the anointed one from God. Did you notice that Peter did not say that Jesus was the son of Joseph and Mary or a Jew from Nazareth or Bethlehem? Jesus followed the same approached when he spoke of his inherent potential. These statements made by him are examples of this truth, *"I am the good shepherd or I am the bread of life."* There are many other expressions of Jesus' potential that he used to answer the question, "Who Am I?" Regardless of the response that he gave, it always pointed back to his potential.

Defining one's self based on an awareness of the internal factors that make you unique and special inspires self-confidence, promotes self-awareness, and initiates a pursuit of purpose. However, it requires that you also have an understanding of the purpose linked to your potential. If your response is based on external descriptions, classifications, and physical characteristics, then you may be susceptible to believing the corresponding presupposed barriers, stereotypes, prejudices, and limitations associated with these factors. However, potential is colorless, it has no nationality, no race, no social status and is full of possibilities not limitations. In addition, it effects each person uniquely by defining their life's path.

## The Potential Effect

The Potential Effect on life is a belief that key elements of an effective life rotate around an axis of potential. It asserts that potential is the main link that initiates an understanding of your purpose, finding your career path, achieving the right milestones, reaching the level of self-actualization, and experiencing true success in life. In other words, your life is destined to evolve around a potential axis that takes you from one stop to another. Therefore, the discovery of potential is critical to understanding your life's path and processes. Potential is also the basis for discovering self and the course in life that will yield your most productive fruit.

The Potential Effect also identifies the elements impacted when your life's plan coincides with God's path. These elements are mutually dependent on potential and each of the other elements circling the axis. It is important to note that if potential remains dormant, then it will have a detrimental effect on each aspect in life. The diagram below identifies the elements that revolve around the potential axis:

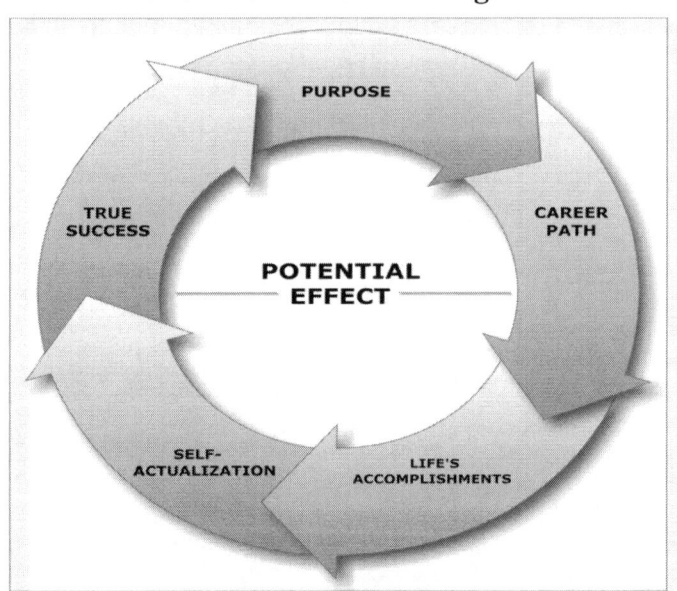

**The Potential Effect Diagram**

## The Potential Effect Application

The Potential Effect suggests that effective living follows a circular journey initiated by potential and is activated when you pursue your purpose for living. Released potential starts the wheel turning towards a path that leads to understanding who you are and what you are capable of accomplishing in life. As the wheel turns, you will find that the preceding category impacts the next.

In other words, your purpose in life should determine your career path. Your career path is intended to be the launching pad for life accomplishments that lead to self-actualization.

As mentioned, the Potential Effect takes into consideration the premise that potential is a major factor in life and requires serious consideration when making life decisions. Have you notice that *"Successful and unsuccessful people do not* vary *greatly in their abilities, they vary in their desires to reach their potential?"* John Maxwell, a successful American author and leadership advisor, made that observation based on his experience. Similarly, having a passion to release your full potential in life is essential because the quest for fulfillment leads to answers for key life questions.

I recall an occasion when knowledge of my potential played a key role in my journey as an insurance professional. Years ago, I was a claims adjuster on the catastrophe team of a large insurance company. Following a major earthquake in California, I was given the order a day after the event to travel there and stay for an extended period. At the time of the earthquake, my tenure with the company was only one year.

Shortly after reporting to my assigned catastrophe office, my manager gave me a supervisory position even though I appeared to be the least qualified person on the team. During our initial conversation, he advised me that I would be his team leader responsible for overseeing the handling of all claims and the supervision of 6 claims adjusters. This decision was surprising because I was the shortest tenured member with the least amount of technical field experience. Additionally, my experience level on paper did not show my hidden potential to be an effective claims adjuster and team leader.

Naturally, I asked why he chose me over those that had years of experience. His response was, *"I believe in your abilities."* From our brief interview, he was able to ascertain that I possessed confidence, passion, and the natural potential to excel over my colleagues. For ten months, I held the position of team leader responsible for processing over $2 million dollars in claim payments and managing numerous claim adjusters. His assessment was correct, throughout my tenure our team ranked first in closed claims and satisfied customers, compared to the other teams in our district.

Based on my experience, I believe that true success is a by-product of living a self-actualized life. For clarification, a self-actualized person fulfills his or her purpose by maximizing their potential routinely. Self-actualization is the final phase of released potential. This position in life brings perpetual joy, satisfaction, and peace of mind in your chosen careers. These things are possible because of the following:

- Potential determines your purpose for living.
- Potential and purpose dictate the right career path for you to take in life.
- Potential, purpose, and career path lead to rewarding life accomplishments.
- Potential, purpose, career path and life accomplishments provide the confidence to continue until you reach the very highest level of expressing your full potential. This means that you have found your place in the SPOTLIGHT and you are shining brightly.
- Potential, purpose, career path, life accomplishment and self-actualization all merge to ensure a successful life.

*"The value of life is not in its duration, but in its donation. You are not important because of how long you live, you are important because of how effective you live,"* according to Dr. Myles Munroe. Therefore, the Potential Effect model supports the belief that your definition of true success must include the releasing of your full potential and the pursuit of your purpose for living. At the end of the day, your potential and purpose will define you and expose your contribution to humanity. As Dr. Munroe concluded, the value of your life will be measured not by duration but donation. The gift that you are supposed to donate to the world is also known as your signature.

## Released Potential Is Your Signature

Do you have a hand-written signature that you are known by? Hopefully, the answer is "YES." If so, then understanding this point becomes more relevant. The point is that your released potential is equivalent to a statement or mark of identity. As you continue to use it, it becomes what you are known by. Jesus once said, *"Every tree is known by its own fruit."* What did he mean? The interpretation is that your released potential is the fruit that you will be known by and the mark of your signature.

> **R**eleased potential is an instinctual reaction to natural ability that results in the manifestation of an original signature.

Are you starting to sense that released potential is the greatest expression of self-identification? *"Each warrior wants to leave the mark of his will, his signature, on the important acts that he touches. This is not the voice of ego but of the human spirit, rising up and declaring that it has something to contribute to the solution of the hardest problems, no matter how vexing!"* That statement from Pat Riley indicates that a certain group of individuals are passionate about leaving an indelible mark or signature through the expression of their potential. Do you believe that your signature is the solution to a problem or issue?

As you know, the signature is a personal mark used as a form of authentication and acknowledgment. In ancient times, the king used the mark from a signet ring as a seal of approval or representation of his signature. Artists etch marks and names on their masterpieces to authenticate and acknowledge their works of art. People from all cultures and backgrounds create and use their personal image in the form of a signature. In this regard, the signature is now the most widely used expressed mark of identification and authentication.

Unfortunately, most people only associate a signature with the mark written on paper. Having this limited definition of a signature is a problem as it fails to recognize the powerful effects associated with potential. It is important to understand that ***there is a trademark signature attached to every released gift of potential that validates your self-worth and identifies you as a world changer***. In other words, released potential is the secret to changing your current circumstances, finding true contentment with your life's pursuits, discovering the value of self, and leaving an indelible mark in life. Therefore, learning the secrets to developing your "personal signature" and leaving your mark in life are essential.

*"I am here for a purpose and that purpose is to grow into a mountain, not to shrink to a grain of sand. Henceforth will I apply ALL my efforts to become the highest mountain of all and I will strain my potential until it cries for mercy."* In my opinion, that personal statement from Og Mandino should become everyone's motto in life. Please read it again and think about, as Walt Disney admonished the young boy, the values you would like to live by.

Becoming the highest mountain in life is the same as establishing your mark and becoming a passionate person of authority in your area of purpose. The process for achieving this success requires instinctual reactions to your potential in order to reach the highest level of accomplishment. Having instinctual reactions to your potential is the same as saying that your thoughts, desires, and actions are in sync with your abilities. This also means that your instinctual reaction to life centers on the fulfillment of your innermost desires associated with your life's purpose.

STOP!!! We have discussed many concepts and principles in this chapter related to releasing your potential. Although there is more to come, you must take a break to think and meditate on the information that you are learning. Afterwards, you may wish to read over certain sections again before moving forward. I am sure that you never realized that there is so much information about potential and purpose. Most, if not all, of these concepts will be or have been new to you. Therefore, patience is the key to digesting the information and allowing it to enrich your thoughts and life. Now, are you ready to make the final push to complete this chapter? Let's discuss more of the benefits of released potential.

## Released Potential Reveals Your Value

Just in case you still need more convincing, let's look at a good example to validate the points about originality verses imitation. Can you guess who was one of the most well-liked musical artist of the 20th century that blazed a masterful and unique trail of success? During the 1980's, Michael Jackson's idolization and fame reached an unprecedented level. Born into a musical family, he showed tremendous potential and amazing talent at a young age. He reached the level of international stardom appeal with an incredible gift for singing, dancing, and performing. His fandom totaled tens of millions from all cultures, races, genders, and ages. By far, Michael was the most popular and imitated singer during that era.

Jackson's amazing voice, mesmerizing dance moves and popularity spawned thousands of "wannabes." As his popularity soared, the number of young people imitating him increased as well. They wore one white glove, became experts at moonwalking and masters at lip-syncing his songs. Nevertheless, Michael was an original. He understood the value of his potential to form self-identity and determine his path in life. People recognized his artistic musical genius, but few knew of his keen awareness of potential. He once stated, *"The meaning of life is contained in every single expression of life. It is present in the infinity of forms and phenomena that exist in all of creation."* Your released potential is intended to be your expression of life.

Did you know that one of the greatest mysteries surrounding human existence is the subjective nature of potential? What happens with the potential that an individual possesses depends entirely on what the individual decides to do with it? There is no automatic mechanism to activate or release potential at a certain point in a person's life. Imitators have a limited understanding of their own potential and its importance in defining their path of purpose. Do you know when potential starts to impact your life?

> **P**otential is the prerequisite for understanding purpose. Purpose is the prerequisite for understanding your path of destiny.

Potential begins its impact at the beginning of life and finishes at the end. It is a natural component designed to determine your direction in life, provide the tools to fulfill your purpose and reveal your path of destiny. Without potential, purpose would have no substance and destiny no relevance. Furthermore, for purpose and destiny to meet in life, potential must exist, and produce its destined fruit.

In simple terms, one of the most overlooked tragedies in life is the disregard for the gift of potential. Countless people search for the meaning of life and the definition of self without realizing or accepting the answers revealed by their potential. *"At the end of the day, the circumstances of your life-- what you look like, where you come from, how much money you have, what you've got going on at home--none of that is an excuse... where you are right now doesn't have to determine where you'll end up. No ones writthen your destiny for you, because here in America, you write your own destiny. You make your own future."*

Think for a moment about those words from President Barack Obama. Where does the accountability related to your life rest? Although he directed his comments towards the benefits of American citizenship, the substance of his conclusion about life should be relevant to all people. His statement is true because the path of destiny is carved out by purposeful actions that are fueled by passion and potential.

Barack Obama made history when he became the 44th President of the United States of America. Most people never imagined that they would live

*Releasing your Potential* 119

to see a person of African descent occupy this admirable position. His election for two consecutive terms sent shock waves around the world and validated the value of his potential. Regardless of political affiliation, it is important to recognize and celebrate the greatness of his accomplishments.

President Obama's potential brought clarity to his purpose for living and ordered his steps of destiny. At some point in life, he recognized the value of his potential to change his personal circumstances, determine his future and influence his surroundings. His accomplishments should provide inspiration and the impetus to put action to your dormant potential. As proven by his victorious election for two terms as President, purpose prevails regardless of your racial background or financial circumstances.

*"Change will not come if we wait for some other person or some other time. We are the ones we've been waiting for. We are the change that we seek."* Those additional comments from President Obama suggest that there is power hidden on the inside of each person that is capable of causing the change that we secretly desire. This power that he is referring to is your natural potential. Once activated, potential starts the process of impacting your life. Initially the impact begins with reoccurring thoughts, dreams, and desires of the heart to be something or pursue a certain path. Are you aware that it is the source of creativity that authenticates your uniqueness?

## Released Potential is the Source of Creativity

Every day, the thoughts and actions of others impact the world that we live in. Think for a moment about the numerous things that we are accustomed to enjoying and taking advantage of that make our lives more convenient; things such as cellphones, cars, planes, microwaves, ovens, etc. Everything that came to mind was the result of someone putting action to their thoughts and potential.

This leads to the next important point about the impact potential has on life. Potential paves the way for self-actualization. According to dictionary.com, self-actualization is *"the achievement of one's full potential through creativity, independence, spontaneity, and a grasp of the real world."*[19] Since self-actualization is the ultimate destiny of released potential, failure to release potential results in a life of discontent and a lack of creativity.

Bill Gates' name is synonymous with Microsoft and operating systems for personal computers. Along with Paul Allen, Gates founded the company in 1975 and served in the roles of CEO, Chairman and Chief Software Architect. His contributions to the world of personal computers is unfathomable. Under his leadership, Microsoft became the world's largest technology company. Gates used his natural potential to lay the foundation of success in the computer operating system industry for years to come.[20] Although Gates is no longer the head of Microsoft, the 2020 revenue for the company was over $140 billion dollars. One of his most inspirational quotes is *"Don't compare yourself with anyone in this world. If you do so, you are insulting yourself."*

## Released Potential Creates Possibilities

Recently, Australian researchers discovered the secret to inducing the mango tree into producing fruit out of season. Researchers found a way to stimulate the trees into yielding fruit over and above traditional expectations. With the help of fertilizers and ripening gas, the researchers were able to cause the trees to flower and produce fruit twice within a one-year period. Excitement about this experiment is spreading throughout the farming industry because generating fruit on a more frequent basis provides a dual benefit. Firstly, producing mangoes out of season enhances the farmer's return on investment and maximizes the mango tree's potential. Secondly, getting Australian mango trees to produce when trees in regional countries are out of season creates new opportunities to capitalize on markets previously inaccessible for Australia.[21]

> **I**mpossibilities are glass ceilings that are susceptible to shattering under the weight of your potential and the power of your belief.

Prior to the Australian project, proof that mango trees possessed the ability to exceed normal production expectations did not exist. Although the inherent ability to produce fruit out of the typical season existed, it was hidden in a dormant state. The successful experiment confirms that unreleased potential holds the secrets to inconceivable possibilities that defy conventional thinking.

For centuries, farmers from around the world never knew that it was possible to produce mangoes twice a year. They formed their expectations based on their limited knowledge about the tree's known potential. The results reinforce the position that unreleased potential creates low expectations whereas released potential creates high expectations. Furthermore, released potential provides the creative power to turn impossibilities into possibilities.

> **I**mpossibilities are possibilities prevented from materializing because of suppressed potential.

Because something has not been done, does not mean that it cannot be done. Because something has not been achieved, does not mean that you cannot achieve it. Because it has not been accomplished before, does not mean that you cannot accomplish it. What am I attempting to say? Years ago, Vince Lombardi had the perfect response to my statements. He said, *"We would accomplish many more things if we did not think of them as impossible."*

Sometimes a lack of confidence in your abilities gives birth to the belief that dreams, and desires of the heart are not possible to achieve. If that is the case, note the words of Thomas Carlyle, *"Every noble work is at first impossible."* Activating your potential in the area of your talents and gifts will create a positive atmosphere full of possibilities. You will be amazed at the possibilities that your released potential will create for you. When the doors open, your potential will also initiate confidence, hope, satisfaction, freedom, and purpose.

## Released Potential Builds Confidence

How confident are you about your potential? *"Have no fear of moving into the unknown. Simply step out fearlessly knowing that I am with you, therefore no harm can befall you; all is very, very well. Do this in complete faith and confidence."* Pope John Paul II admonished believers to move forward in confidence when fear surfaces. His sentiments relate to having confidence in God's promise to guide you through your comfort zones. In fact, the scripture says that *"Those who know your name trust in you, for you, LORD, have never forsaken those who seek you."*

Defeating areas in your life that seem impossible to overcome requires that you display faith in God's promises and confidence in your potential. Sometimes barriers that seem impossible are self-imposed limitations created as a reaction to either low self-esteem or extremely difficult situations. Typically, mental barriers form after information passes through the natural senses and a conscious evaluation is rendered. Seeing the intimidating mountain in your life is enough to influence your thought process to render an opinion that the situation is impossible to overcome. Furthermore, constantly hearing from others that it will never be done can impact your belief system and perpetuate a pessimistic mindset.

When your potential is given an opportunity to flourish, then the next step is to have confidence and believe that you can do it. Norman Vincent Peale was quoted as saying, *"Believe in Yourself! Have faith in your abilities! Without a humble but reasonable confidence in your own powers you cannot be successful or happy."* In the same regard, President Theodore Roosevelt once said, *"Believe you can and you're halfway there."*

I strongly believe that faith and belief are interchangeable and necessary attributes for effective living. *"Faith shows the reality of what we hope for; it is the evidence of things we cannot see."* Having faith in your potential shows the reality of what you hope for, and it is the evidence of things to come. Failure to make the connection between your potential and self-worth will handicap your ability to believe in your power to turn the impossible situation into a possibility. Although God promises to work out the situation, it is your responsibility and requirement to move forward in faith and confidence.

If you find yourself wavering about the power of your innate potential, then remember that confidence is a by-product of action. Confidence comes after you have successfully completed a task or after gaining experience doing something. Remember that *"Inaction breeds doubt and fear. Action breeds confidence and courage. If you want to conquer fear, do not sit home and think about it. Go out and get busy,"* according to Dale Carnegie. Therefore, successfully releasing your potential is one of the best ways to have sustained confidence and hope in life.

## Released Potential Brings Hope

According to Merriam-Webster online dictionary, hope is defined as, *"to expect with confidence."*[22] Hope gives you the confidence to pursue your purpose for living. Are you a believer in these words of Helen Keller, *"Optimism is the faith that leads to achievement. Nothing can be done without hope and confidence?"* Accordingly, potential impacts your faith, beliefs, confidence, and hope in life. It is also safe to say that potential precedes the ability to achieve and succeed in life.

Millions of people around the world lack hope in their ability to change their personal circumstances. Perhaps, this feeling of hopelessness persists due to a lack of the right companionship. Associating yourself with focused and motivated individuals makes a tremendous difference whenever you plan to act on your potential. More importantly, *"...those who hope in the LORD will renew their strength. They will soar on wings like eagles; they will run and not grow weary, they will walk and not be faint."*

Once you decide to act on your potential, the fire grows and consumes your life. The consuming fire that burns within and promotes unrelenting effort is known as passion. *"Passion is energy. Feel the power that comes from focusing on what excites you."* That sentiment from Oprah Winfrey is good advice.

Along the way, watch the intense fire fueled by your potential engulf and burn away doubt, complacency, and negativity. The result is a clear path leading in the direction of your purpose for living. Therefore, as Norman Vincent Peale instructed, *"Formulate and stamp indelibly on your mind a mental picture of yourself as succeeding. Hold this picture tenaciously. Never permit it to fade. Your mind will seek to develop the picture… Do not build up obstacles in your imagination."*

## THE NEXT STEP

WOW!!! There was a lot of valuable information covered in this chapter. Whenever you release your potential in the right way, then you are fulfilling your purpose in life. It is also important to understand that released potential has the greatest impact on selecting your career path and fulfilling your purpose for living. Remember that potential is obvious, but purpose is discovered.

For this reason, potential is the best tool to use when seeking to discover your purpose in life. Under the right circumstances, potential identifies your designated career path and leads to understanding your purpose for living. Remember these words from President John F. Kennedy in the context of your potential, *"There are risks and costs to action. But they are far less than the long-range risks of comfortable inaction."*

> **Quick reference guide to releasing your potential principles:**

1. Released potential serves as a crystalized snapshot of your internal TAGs that pre-existed prior to manifestation.
2. Limited ability to express potential will lead to limited personal development and growth.
3. Released potential produces specific and beneficial results.
4. Potential **defines** who you are.
5. Potential **dictates** what you are capable of doing.
6. Potential **determines** when you should do something.
7. Potential **directs** the path that you should take in life.
8. Potential **delivers** you to your desired destination in life.
9. Wasted potential is one of the greatest threats to success in life.
10. Unreleased potential results in failure to express your true nature.
11. Expressed potential is a catalyst that initiates a cycle of key events that have a profound impact on what happens in a person's life.
12. Released potential is an instinctual reaction to natural ability that results in the manifestation of an original signature.
13. There is a trademark signature attached to every released gift of potential that validates your self-worth and identifies you as a world changer.
14. Potential is the prerequisite for understanding purpose. Purpose is the prerequisite for understanding your path of destiny.
15. Released potential is the source of creativity.
16. Impossibilities are glass ceilings that are susceptible to shattering under the weight of your potential and the power of your belief.
17. Impossibilities are possibilities prevented from materializing because of suppressed potential.
18. Released potential builds confidence.
19. Released potential brings hope.

# Chapter Five

## Understanding Purpose – Part I

> *"Your job is your skill that they can fire.*
> *But your work is your gift. No one can*
> *take that from you."*
> **Myles Munroe**

Sitting next to me in the conference room of a major Lloyds of London insurance brokerage firm, Paul reached over and said, *"John, they don't understand. This is our life. This is who we are and a reflection of what's on the inside."* He was correct, pursuing the path of insurance was our purpose and the source of our passion.

I was in London to consummate a deal that took months of negotiations, fulfilling requirements, analyzing projections, and drafting business plans. Paul was the acting underwriter for a Lloyds of London syndicate. In this executive position, he was responsible for his company's distribution of casualty insurance products worldwide. At that time, I was the vice president of an insurance agency in the Bahamas.

I leaned over to Paul and said, *"You are correct, this is purpose and destiny being fulfilled."* Prior to the end of the meeting, Paul announced to his senior employees that he would extend his company's underwriting authority to me. As a result, the company that I worked for would become a Coverholder of Lloyds of London and I would serve as the authorized representative.

The process of becoming a Coverholder began as a thought in my mind. It was a thought that few believed would ever happen. Reason being, this prestigious distinction is very difficult to achieve and typically takes years to complete the process. Nevertheless, I believed in the possibility and worked diligently until it finally happened. More importantly, I considered achieving the Coverholder status as my purpose in life. In this regard, I released my potential, pursued destiny, and achieved success.

For thousands of years, people have struggled with the issue of defining self and finding true meaning in life. Often, the quest to understand life leads to unanswered questions about purpose and opens the door to unproductive pursuits. The conclusion to this dilemma is that most people are consumed or preoccupied with the "how" in life. How am I going to buy this thing? How am I going to get this job or attend this college? How am I going to accomplish this objective? How am I going to become associated with this person or group? As you would agree, your personal lists and thoughts related to "how" to achieve set goals are endless.

Understanding how to achieve your goals and accomplish your plans is necessary, but it is not the first step in the process of you understanding purpose. The first step in the process of self-discovery is to understand "why." Why are you doing what you are doing? Why do you desire to become something? Why do you want to go to a certain college or major in a certain subject?

Why did I pursue the painstaking process of becoming a Coverholder of Lloyds of London? In the very beginning, I realized that I was the solution to a major problem and the answer to the company's needs. The cost of medical malpractice insurance for certain doctors with high risk specialties was outrageous. Although there are several insurance brokers and insurance companies in the Bahamas that sell malpractice insurance, none were able to offer a premium concession. Furthermore, the company I worked for needed a vision for the future, a new revenue stream and a new identity.

When I evaluated the situation, I understood that I possessed the potential to change the circumstances. I also realized that it was my purpose in life to make it happen. On many occasions, I would hear these words of wisdom from Dr. Myles Munroe ringing in my ears, *"Circumstances and crisis are tools to move you into your purpose and the maximizing of your potential."* Even though the process was lengthy and mentally challenging, I was determined to achieve a successful result. For these reasons, I remained focused and was certain that change would happen.

According to Pablo Picasso, *"The meaning of life is to find your gift. The purpose of life is to give it away."* It is interesting that his conclusion coincides with the scripture, *"As each one has received a gift, minister it to one another, as good stewards of the manifold grace of God."* Hopefully at this stage of reading, you are not questioning whether you have a gift. If so, please refute that erroneous and misleading thought. The truth is that you possess a gift from God, and it can and will benefit you and others. *"Don't ever make the mistake of telling God that you have nothing to offer. That simply is not true. God does not create any junk."* Dr. Munroe was correct when he spoke that truth. Your life has value, your gift has value and your purpose in life has value.

Now, let's move back to understanding your purpose and the "why" question. As Aristotle stated, *"we do not have knowledge of a thing until we have grasped its why, that is to say, its cause."* This great philosopher held on to the belief that the first question to ask when seeking to understand something is to ask why it exists. Additionally, the introductory quote from Mark Twain reaffirms the value of knowing "why" as the priority for successful living. For these reasons, this chapter will give you a glimpse of the big picture about your life. Are you ready?

## What Is Purpose

Merriam-Webster's online dictionary defines purpose as: *"That which a person sets before himself as an object to be reached or accomplished; the end or aim to which the view is directed in any plan, measure, or exertion;*

*view; aim; design; intention; plan.*"[23] Another way to define purpose is to say that it is the reason something exists or the original intent of the creator of a thing. This means that everything created is enabled inherently with the design, features, and attributes to operate as intended by its originator.

Based on those definitions, the quest to define self and discover the correct path to follow comes from understanding self from the originator's perspective. However, when you paraphrase the definitions and merge into one concise meaning, a full picture about purpose is revealed. Accordingly, purpose is the life plan or course of action designated for you based on the original intention for your existence.

> **The path of purpose begins on the destiny highway.**

Did you know that purpose carves a predetermined path that leads along the highway of destiny? Let's examine this issue. When a baby turtle is born, it possesses the instinct and abilities to find the ocean's shore. Once it reaches saltwater, it lives its entire life in the ocean wondering from location to location. There is one very interesting fact, when it's time to give birth, the female turtle returns to the place of her birth to lay her eggs. Therefore, certain aspects of her life are predetermined, and it also means that a certain aspect of the baby turtle's life is predetermined.

> **Purpose is fulfilled through the successful completion of assignments.**

In this example, the mother returns to her birthplace because her life is programmed to follow a certain path. All her life, she travels a path of purpose that leads to her destiny. In a similar regard, the baby turtles' birthplace is predetermined and the path that it must follow to give birth in the future is predetermined. In like fashion, the existence of your potential ensures that there is a predetermined place and time designated for you to give life to your dreams. It may seem as though you are roaming from circumstance to circumstance and from situation to situation. If this is the case, be assured that there is a predetermined point whereby your potential will explode into a manifested reality.

## Predestined Future Result

It is also important to understand that purpose is the reason you have a destiny, assignment, and time. I am sure that you can answer this question, but I need to ask anyway, "When did you receive your potential?" You received it at the beginning of life, right!!! *"Your future is not ahead of you, its trapped within you,"* according to Dr. Myles Munroe.

Have you ever had someone tell you that *"your future is trapped within you?"* That statement made by Dr. Munroe is fascinating because I am sure that you were told or taught to search for your purpose in many other ways. *"If you would know yourself, take yourself as starting point and go back to its source; your beginning will disclose your end,"* as concluded by the Ancient Egyptians.

This statement means that knowing yourself requires that you also know your source, which is God. This statement also means that the starting point to discovering yourself is the beginning of life. Remember that you inherited your TAGs at the beginning of life. Therefore, your potential given to you at the beginning defines who you should become in life, not your environment, situations, or circumstances that occur afterwards.

Once you know God and yourself, then your purpose will be revealed at the point that you become aware of who you are. In other words, your predestined future is determined by God and revealed to you. God seeks to introduce you to the person He destined you to become. Alcmaeon, a little known Ancient Greek philosopher and scholar stated, *"Men perish because they cannot join the beginning with the end."* This statement is directly related to the reason why you possess potential and purpose in life. You must be able to see your predestined future at the beginning of the journey. Another way to paraphrase Alcmaeon's statement is to emphasize the importance of connecting the beginning of your life or journey to the end destination or goal.

> **You are expected and capable of achieving a predestined future end-result.**

Every living thing progresses in stages towards a predestined future end-result. Your predetermined end is your future trapped inside of you now. Your predetermined future is also the image and likeness that you are destined to become as your potential is developed. The following points provide additional clarification regarding the concept of a predestined future:

- **The predestined future looks different from the beginning, but the beginning is confirmation of the end.** Do you remember discussing the caterpillar and butterfly in a previous chapter? That example teaches the importance of not "judging a book by its cover." In other words, the person that you are destined to become is already on the inside. Do you believe that you already contain the plan for your life?

- **The predestined end is the future of a thing captured inside of its beginning.** This means that what you are born to become was placed inside of you at the beginning of life. You do not have to create the path to follow, it's already inside of you. Likewise, you do not have to create your purpose, it's already inside of you. The expected outcome of your TAGs is locked inside of you.

- **The predestined future determines what is included in the beginning in order to reach the end.** It is my hope that you accept that you came to the planet with the TAGs needed to fulfill your purpose and destiny. Your destiny is the reason for having your TAGs. They were given to you without charge. You did not acquire your TAGs through educational pursuits or from family and friends. Be mindful that education refines your TAGs, it does not give them to you. Evidence that your TAGs exist is proof that you possess the capacity to fulfill your purpose.

- **The predestined future is never reached without having a beginning.** Unfortunately, you cannot fulfill your purpose if you fail to pursue or release your potential. Failure to develop and maximize your TAGs also jeopardizes your ability to manifest self. It is my intention to help you enjoy the benefits of the predestined life that you deserve to experience and enjoy. Commit to releasing your TAGs to start the process. The process begins with acceptance, information, understanding, wisdom, education, knowledge, and application.

- **The value associated with your predestined future is never seen in the beginning**. The true importance and value of your personal TAGs is hidden in the gift. The value remains inside of the TAG until you release it. Glimpses of the magnificence of your TAGs are released to you in the form of dreams, thoughts, and visions over a period. Dreaming leads to seeing and seeing leads to believing. To add to this point, understand that believing leads to becoming and becoming leads to manifestation.

## Benefits of Purpose

Hopefully, you are glad to know that you have a path of purpose that creates the best environment for maximizing potential, understanding self-identity and finding career satisfaction. **Purpose directs your path towards the perfect platform for showcasing your potential**. It also provides the direction you need for important life changing decisions. Remember, *"They who have no central purpose in their life fall an easy prey to petty worries, fears, troubles, and self-pityings, all of which are indications of weakness,* *which lead, just as surely as deliberately planned sins, to failure, unhappyness, and loss, for weakness cannot persist in a power-evolving universe,"* according to James Allen.

Having a central purpose perspective on life also ensures that you do not attempt to become something that you are not equipped or supposed to become. Additional benefits of choosing to live your life according to a central purpose are:

- Life has significant meaning.
- Everything you need to succeed is along the path of purpose.
- You attract the attention of others.
- Mountains seem smaller.
- Your assignment brings joy and fulfillment.
- Confidence of knowing that you are doing the right thing.
- Time becomes an asset.
- Material & financial wealth do not define you. These assets become conveniences to help fulfill your purpose.
- Decisions become easier to make.
- Your career path is rewarding.

At some point, have you struggled to find true and sustaining meaning in life? If so, then understanding your central purpose in life will help you establish personal objectives, goals, milestones, plans and choose the correct career path. Discovering your purposeful journey should begin as soon as possible. Knowledge regarding why you exist is critical in the process of choosing the right career path. The next statement is a simple point, but is important for you to meditate on. ***Your purpose coincides with the things that your potential will help you to achieve.***

## Purpose is Your GPS in Life

The Global Positioning System (GPS) has forever changed the way we locate, identify, and plot a course to a predetermined destination. Prior to the

# Understanding Purpose - Part I 135

GPS, getting consistent and precise directions from one point to another was very challenging. Maps were a good source of routes and paths if the information was current. However, sometimes the information was outdated and did not reflect changes made to improve or alter driving paths.

Getting directions from others was also popular, but sometimes their directions were confusing and lacked key details. I am sure that you would agree, nobody wants to go back to the days prior to the GPS. Nowadays, navigational systems are in cars and accessible through smartphones. This implementation and advancement greatly simplified the process of getting from one point to another.

The benefits of this directional technology to individuals, corporations, countries, and travel are endless. An obvious benefit is the confidence to travel from one location to another without the fear of getting lost. In addition, unimaginable sums of monies are saved on gas expense because people can get to the designated point without unnecessary detours. Furthermore, corporations are now able to save on operational expenses by being able to monitor shipments, deliveries, and employees. Overall, the GPS has proven to be an invaluable and transformational tool for getting directions and plotting courses.

> **P**urpose isn't a meaningless pursuit into the unknown but a guided journey along the path of destiny.

There are three essential objectives of purpose that you should recognize. Purpose is your **G**uide, **P**ath and **S**traight line to fulfilling your destiny. It is your natural and innate GPS that is always accurate. Having insight into the GPS capability of purpose will help map a plan for your life and begin the process of answering some of your *"Why"* questions. Years ago, President John F. Kennedy said, *"Efforts and courage are not enough without purpose and direction."* Putting forth effort and having the courage to address the hard questions of life is good, but not good enough for you. You must be able to link the responses to a purpose and confirm the correct path to follow. If you are unable to connect the dots, then you will likely think that your life is a haphazard journey that leads to no specific destination.

The first thing that must happen is for you to accept the fact that your purpose is a guide and/or plan designated for you only. As you recall, one of the definitions of purpose is original intent. This means that it serves as an original guide that leads to fulfilling your destiny. Are you glad to know that you have an internal gift in the form of potential that reveals the original path for your life?

The next important consequence of purpose to understand is that it comes with a path and/or destination. The key element of this point is the fact that purpose works best when you follow the path that enables you to develop and maximize your potential. By taking this approach, you can visualize reaching the destination before you arrive. When you visualize living your assigned purpose, your thoughts are positive and unwavering.

Having positive thoughts lead to passion to become yourself and the passion leads to determination. Your determination will lead to confidence and the confidence will lead to acceptance of your true identity. Making the statement that *"I was born to do this"* is simply acknowledging your acceptance of the path in life that matches your talents, abilities, gifts, and career aspirations. In addition to accepting your purpose, it is equally important to understand that it is your destiny. The words of Seneca, the Roman philosopher are worth noting. Seneca said, *"The willing, Destiny guides them. The unwilling, Destiny drags them."*

> **S**traight is the path that leads to a fruitful life.

One of the greatest misconceptions about life is the fact that many people believe that having a lucrative career, living the American Dream and being financially independent will guarantee peace of mind. Maya Angelou, a popular American poet and writer, disagreed with that belief. Listen to her testimony, *"I've learned that making a 'living' is not the same as 'making a life'."* Having an appreciation for the significant impact that purpose has on your thought process, attitude and life is essential. Pursuing a good path in life that is wrong for you will do little to offset the natural tendency to feel as though something is missing.

Do you believe that there are substitutes for the internal voids created by unfulfilled purpose? I challenge the belief that people, places or things are sustaining substitutes for replacing the pursuit of purpose. If you are born with the TAGs to be a painter, but you elect to become a doctor because of social influences, then is it not possible to surgically remove the natural reoccurring thoughts regarding becoming a painter? Once you discover who you are naturally born to be, then you also begin to realize that your purposeful thoughts of becoming what you dream about are not manufactured by external influences.

It is critical that you consider purpose as your GPS because of its ability to navigate a straight life's path. Being able to know what to do in life and why you should do it is essential. This information is helpful in choosing careers, making life decisions, or finding peace of mind. **Purpose charts a straight line from your thought of becoming something to the point of self-actualizing your potential.**

This internal GPS enhances the quality of your life by providing a straight path to follow to reach your ideal destination. Remember that you were born perfectly suited to become the person that you see through the window of your heart. *"Never has a man reached his destination by persistence in deviation from the straight path."* Those are true words once spoken by Mahatma Gandhi. In that regard, your purpose charts a straight path to the destination that matches your innate potential.

Benjamin Franklin lived a very fruitful life because he recognized the value of releasing his full potential in the pursuit of fulfilling purpose. More importantly, he accomplished many things by not wavering to the left or right. He used his time wisely to self-educate and to put action to his many extraordinary talents. Over 200 years ago he wrote in Poor Richard's Almanac, *"It would be thought a hard Government that should tax its People one tenth Part of their Time to be employed in its Service. But Idleness taxes many of us much more, if we reckon all that is spent in idle Employments or Amusements, that amount to nothing..."*

> **D**iscovery of purpose leads to an intentional career pursuit.

During Franklin's lifetime, he observed that the pursuit of idle employments, as a substitute for a purpose driven career, was a major problem. In a similar regard, Abraham Maslow, the 20th century psychologist, commented, *"Where the average individuals often have not the slightest idea of what they are, of what they want, of what their own opinions are, self-actualizing individuals have superior awareness of their own impulses, desires, opinions, and subjective reactions in general."* Although Franklin and Maslow lived in vastly different time periods, the same problems related to purpose was evident.

## **Purpose and Your Career**

A recent job satisfaction survey conducted by The Conference Board in 2018 revealed that only 51% of Americans are satisfied with their jobs.[24] America is the land of freedom and opportunity, yet many are discontent with their job or career choices. If this survey is accurate, then it would also mean that millions of Americans spend most of their lives doing something that they are not happy doing, working at a place they do not want to be at and surrounded by individuals they do not want to be with. Unfortunately, America does not stand alone when it comes to individuals feeling unhappy about their career life.

According to an international survey conducted by Kelly Services in 2013, 48% of the respondents were unhappy with their jobs.[25] Like the Americans, many worldwide are feeling discontentment with the direction their career life has taken. I believe that one of the major reasons why the global issue of job dissatisfaction persists is the tendency to select careers in an unintentional manner. *Pursuit of purpose must be intentional based on the knowledge that you have about your potential.*

Albert Einstein once made this interesting but true statement. *"Everyone is a genius but if you judge a fish on its ability to climb a tree, it will live its whole life believing it is stupid."* The underlying message in his comment is that there is an intentional and purposeful course that supports your potential. His comment also alludes to the fact that negative feelings are associated with daily tasks that are inconsistent with your purpose. Understanding and pursuing your purpose in life will offset feeling worthless or invaluable.

Let's pause and take a breath. I realize that we have been running fast or lifting heavy material. I feel as though I need to slow down a little because these are concepts which require considerable thought and meditation. Before moving forward, you may wish to take time to think about what you have read thus far. Perhaps you may need to re-read some sections to properly digest the information. Take your time. Whenever you are ready, let's move forward together.

Now, in the context of purpose, be mindful that the world is not a chaotic, haphazard and an insignificant array of people, places, and things. The moon, stars, sun, rain, water, dog, cat, bee, and every other thing including you, have an assigned purpose to fulfill. The moon cannot successfully fulfill the role of the sun. The dog cannot fulfill the role of a lion and you cannot fulfill the role of some other person.

Everything and everyone have its assigned purpose to match the inherent potential. Can you imagine what the world would be like without diversity of purpose and potential? It would be a world of clones and copy-cats. This would lead to chaos, unfulfilled needs, and voids. Would you like to live in a world like that?

Think for a moment, can you imagine what your family, community, state, and country would be like if each person discovered their individual purpose and pursued it with a passion? Although the answer to the question is not Utopia, the world around you would look and feel like a better place because of the fulfillment of preassigned assignments. Perhaps, for these reasons, Brian Tracy stated, *"Every single moment shapes our future. Be intentional. Live on Purpose!"*

Tracy suggests that your life is shaped by intentional decisions that cause purposeful events to occur. Therefore, if your decisions are intentional and aligned with your purpose for living, then your career path will be aligned. In other words, discovering career satisfaction requires that you evaluate every moment, opportunity, and decision through the window of your purpose and potential. What a wonderful world it would be if everyone pursued their purpose!!!

---

**P**urpose is the reason why it is necessary to pursue the right career path.

---

*"What is the recipe for successful achievement? To my mind there are just four essential ingredients: Choose a career you love, give it the best there is in you, seize the opportunities, and be a member of a team."* Many years ago, Benjamin Franklin gave those words of wisdom. Unfortunately, there is a widespread misconception about the true meaning and definition of career. The lack of knowledge about purpose and career path continues to plague generations. Solving this problem begins with establishing a definition of career that includes the concept of purpose. This is important because your career and purpose go hand in hand. In other words, your career should relate to your passion in life and your passion should relate to your purpose for living.

*"Choose a job you love and you will never have to work a day of your life,"* according to Confucius. When you break it down, he addresses several key points. Firstly, you must select the right career path. Secondly, you must possess the abilities to perform the assignment. Being able to release your potential creates a love for the job, career, or assignment because your purpose is something that you do to express yourself and experience peace of mind. This means that your purpose is an expression of self and therefore, not an idle employment. Lastly, it is important that you consider your career as a lifetime pursuit in order to have sustained peace of mind.

> **P**ursuit of the wrong career path equates to pursuing the wrong purpose in life.

Choosing the wrong career path has a direct and substantial impact on your purpose and satisfaction in life. One of the easiest ways to get sidetracked in life is settling indefinitely for a job or career that does not match your potential. Furthermore, ***choosing the wrong path ensures that your purpose is sacrificed on an altar built by excuses and comfort zones***. Hopefully, the information contained in this book will prevent you from selecting the wrong career path or settling for less than you are destined to become. Instead,

I hope that you beat the odds and become a victor that rides the waves of career satisfaction by choosing the right path.

Let's take a moment to discuss the components associated with the right career path. I believe that a career should be defined *as a consistent pursuit of a path, course or assignment related to your purpose for living.* Another definition of career is the consistent and intentional pursuit of a central purpose. The following 5 principles are also key to establishing the right perspective and understanding regarding your career:

- The right career path is not a shallow pursuit of appeasement; it is a lasting opportunity to express yourself.
- The right career path is discovered through deep soul-searching, understanding the value of self and a desire to release your natural abilities.
- The right career path is an enjoyable opportunity to fulfill your purpose and share your potential.
- The right career path is an intentional and deliberate action that expresses your natural TAGs.
- The right career path is revealed by analyzing your reoccurring dreams and desires.
- The right career path exposes the original intent for your life.

Since career path and purpose are inseparable, it is important to recognize that the right choices bring order to your career selection and life. Whenever you match your career selection with your natural potential and your passion, then your purpose for living unfolds before your eyes. Furthermore, when these things happen, the foundation for your life is built with the necessary components to ensure peace of mind and satisfaction.

## Purpose Brings Order

# Understanding Purpose - Part I

Okay, let's pause again and take a moment to digest these concepts regarding the connection between purpose and your career. Hopefully, you will not become overwhelmed by the information because it will assist you in making a life changing career decision. I have over 25 years of experience in the same career field. I believe that I was born to do it, but I also love what I do because it brings a degree of order to my life.

In my opinion, without order, the world would be in chaos. Simply speaking, every living creature must adhere to the law of order to function properly or as intended based on the inherent design specifications. Think for a moment, what if every bird decided to cease acting on its natural instincts and adopted the ways of a dog. Over a short period, birds would cease to exist in their designed function and the world would be overloaded with dogs and birds that attempt to copy dogs. This example is humorous because birds do not look like dogs and do not possess the natural qualifications to be successful dogs. Similarly, do you know anyone who is attempting to do things that they are not qualified to do or be someone that they are not naturally? The end-result is that their life is out of order.

> **P**urpose establishes order and potential provides structure. Both are essential to establishing a successful foundation in life.

A lack of order results from the failure to operate based on the original intent specified at the beginning of life. Failure to live within the framework of your designed specification and attributes promotes chaos and a lack of clear direction. Furthermore, it would also suggest that the person, is disregarding vital attributes given to them to ensure their success in life. Purpose establishes order and guarantees that you will be successful being the perfect "you."

*"Order is needed by the ignorant but it takes a genius to master chaos."* What did Albert Einstein mean? Most people would probably take exception

to his use of the word ignorant. However, the basic definition of ignorant is a lack of knowledge. A paraphrase of his statement would read, *"Those without knowledge about purpose need the protection that the right environment affords because succeeding in this confusing world requires the right foundation and exceptional knowledge."* Unfortunately, chaos is a part of many of our lives. Therefore, as Einstein concluded, it takes a genius to put order to it. The process of establishing order begins and ends with a purpose driven life.

*"You are not here merely to make a living. You are here in order to enable the world to live more amply, with greater vision, with a finer spirit of hope and achievement. You are here to enrich the world, and you impoverish yourself if you forget the errand,"* according to President Woodard Wilson.

Wilson's comments help to shed light on considerable disadvantage of oppressing the expression of individual purpose because doing so creates a lack of diversity and voids. Diversity is the natural order of creation. To everything that possess life, there is a meaning, order, and purpose. For this reason, order cannot exist without the expression of purpose. Make a commitment that you will not become a victim of disorder and career chaos. Accept the fact that you were born to provide the solutions to some issues that exist in your family, society, country, or the world.

## Purpose Brings Success

John D. Rockefeller and James Allen joined the list of noted individuals that confirmed the value associated with one's purpose. *"Singleness of purpose is one of the chief essentials for success in life, no matter what maybe one's aim,"* according to Rockefeller. Based on his assessment, success awaits people that have singleness of purpose because your assignment in life is reserved for you alone. Although it is popular to believe that success is designated for a select few, you must be mindful that purpose is indiscriminate and unconditional.

In the 1960's, Mary Kay Ash grew a small startup cosmetic operation into a worldwide business organization. She did this during an era in American history wherein business opportunities were dominated by men. Her natural ability to connect with people and genuine interest in career development for women inspired a cosmetic revolution that spread from Texas to around the world. One of her most memorable quotes was, *"Do you know that within your power lies every step you ever dreamed of stepping, and within your power lies every joy you ever dreamed of seeing? Within yourself lies everything you ever dreamed of being."* Today, with over a million sales representatives worldwide and revenue, exceeding $3 billion, Mary Kay, is a true success story and inspiration.[26]

*"Having conceived of his purpose, a man should mentally mark out a straight pathway to its achievement, looking neither to the right or left."* Those comments from James Allen highlight the pathway to achieving success in your purpose in life. He noted that once your purpose comes alive in your heart, you must set your thoughts on mapping a straight course. Although success is inevitable when you live your purpose, it is important to stay on course. This means that you must be mindful of the things that tend to influence your willingness to continue along the straight path.

## THE NEXT STEP

Hopefully, you will agree that this chapter provided answers to some of the common questions about purpose. One of the biggest misconceptions about purpose is the issue of predestination or predetermination. This means that you have a path to success designated exclusively for you and it matches your TAGs. Remember, your life's path was prearranged to showcase your TAGs. Do you believe that for every purpose there is corresponding moment in time whereby all things work together for your good?

*"You must decide if you are going to rob the world or bless it with the rich, valuable, potent, untapped resources locked away within you."* Those words were spoken by Dr. Myles Munroe. Are you prepared to release your full and unlimited potential along the path of purpose? I hope that you are energized and motivated to pursue your purpose for living. As you now know, it is your path to greatness, wealth, recognition, and self-identification. *"Your destiny is too great, your assignment too important, your time too valuable. Do not let fear intimidate you."* Do you believe that conclusion from Joel Osteen?

I concur with the sentiments of Osteen. Your future is too great, your role in the world too important and your time is too valuable to waste. I will continue to give you information that will assist you in bridging the gap between understanding your purpose and pursuing your purpose. In fact, the next chapter will serve as a continuation dealing with the subject of understanding your purpose.

## Quick reference to understanding purpose principles:

1. The path of purpose begins on the destiny highway.
2. Purpose is fulfilled through the successful completion of assignments.
3. Potential without an awareness of purpose is a tragedy.
4. Your personal dominion on earth is associated with your purpose for living.
5. Purpose gives meaning to the question, "Why am I here?"
6. You are expected and capable of achieving a predestined future end-result.
7. The predestined future looks different from the beginning, but the beginning is confirmation of the end.
8. The predestined end is the future of a thing captured inside of its beginning.
9. The predestined future determines what is included in the beginning in order to reach the end.
10. The predestined future is never reached without having a beginning.
11. The value associated with your predestined future is never seen in the beginning.
12. Your purpose coincides with the things your potential will help you to achieve.
13. Purpose isn't a meaningless pursuit into the unknown but a guided journey along the path of destiny.
14. Straight is the path that leads to a fruitful life.
15. Purpose charts a straight line from your thought of becoming something to the point of self-actualizing your potential.
16. Discovery of purpose leads to an intentional career pursuit.
17. Purpose is the reason why it is necessary to pursue the right career path.

18. Pursuit of the wrong career path equates to pursuing the wrong purpose in life.
19. Purpose establishes order and potential provides structure.
20. Your value in life is of equal importance as the famous, wealthy, or most popular individuals in society.

# Chapter Six

## Understanding Purpose - Part II

> *"The two most important days in your life are the day you are born and the day you find out why."*
> **Mark Twain**

Little is known about Albert Durer, other than the widely circulated short story about his famous brother, Albrecht. Both brothers grew up in the early 15th century in a family of eighteen children. According to the story, both possessed a passion for art and wanted to pursue it. However, their father was a goldsmith by trade and was not able to send them away to study as art apprentices. A lack of financial resources didn't stop them from dreaming and developing a plan.

They agreed that one would stay home and work to support the other's training. Once the training completed, the brother that underwent the training would come home and work to send the other off. Supposedly, the brothers flipped a coin and Albrecht won the toss and Albert went to work in the mines to help support his brother's art apprenticeship. Albrecht excelled in his training and began to receive recognition for his exceptional talent and works of art.

After successfully completing the apprenticeship, he returned home to thank his brother and was excited to repay the favor by sending him away to pursue his passion for art. During a family dinner, Albrecht made the announcement that it was now Albert's turn to follow his dream. As Albrecht admonished his faithful brother to accept his well- earned repayment, tears streamed down Albert's worn face. Albert stood, wiped the tears from his face and held his battered hands up for all to see. After 4 years of working in the mines, all of Albert's fingers were severely damaged. The extent of the injuries prevented him from being able to hold a paint brush steadily to paint works of art.[27]

Albrecht Durer became one of the most recognized German artists of the Renaissance period. His fame spread across Europe, while still in his twenties. Today, a number of his great pieces are still on display today. It is reported that Albrecht's famous painting *Praying Hands* was dedicated to Albert. But what happened to Albert and his potential?

Do you think that anyone was concerned about what happened to his potential and purpose in life? Nothing else was written about Albert and his dream. Circumstances prevented him from releasing his artistic potential and pursuing his dream of becoming a painter and sculptor. He did an admirable thing by helping his brother. Unfortunately, due to circumstances, his time and season for becoming an artist passed.

## Time and Seasons

Years ago, I remember attending a high school basketball game in my hometown of St. Petersburg, Florida. There was much excitement about the local rivalry between two schools with great basketball teams. However, there was even more excitement centered on one player with unbelievable talent and skills. He was crowned as the greatest all around basketball player in the city and without doubt, one the best in the State of Florida, at that time. In fact, he already had a full scholarship to a Division I university with a rich basketball history and legendary coach.

Having played basketball for much of my young life, I understood the game. Instantly, I realized that I was watching someone that was destined for the professional ranks. That night, his performance was mesmerizing. I recall him rebounding the ball on the defensive side of the court, dribbling down the

## Understanding Purpose - Part II

court making incredible moves and passing defenders on his way to dunking on the other end. As the crowd erupted in exuberance, I said to myself, *"At his age, he is the best player that I have ever seen."* He was tall, possessed exceptional ball handling skills, a great shooter and had a mature understanding of the game of basketball.

Unfortunately, the story does not have a happy ending. To the shock of all, he was accused of committing a serious crime before his high school graduation. As a result, he lost his scholarship and opportunity to pursue the path of becoming a professional basketball player. Did he possess the talent, abilities, and gifts? The answer is "YES." Did he develop his skills? The answer is "YES." However, errors in judgement derailed his future. His criminal behavior ruined his basketball career and caused him to miss his season.

*"To everything there is a season, a time for every purpose under heaven."* This statement suggests that there is a timeframe and season to fulfill your purpose in life. It also suggests that at the right time in your life, the things needed to fulfill your purpose will meet you along your designated path. To everything, there is an ideal time to start and an expected time to finish. Since life begins at conception, then the purpose for each life also begins at conception.

After conception, purpose continues until the end of life. The reality of this statement is that each day, minute, hour and second represents a moment in time that you have to advance towards your destiny. That is the reason why it is necessary to pray, *"Teach me to realize the brevity of life, so that I may grow in wisdom."* Whether we understand it or not, we have a timeframe to accomplish our purpose in life and reach our destination.

**Time is an asset that supports the pursuit of purpose**. In fact, purpose waits on the fullness of time to reveal the blessings hidden along the path to assist you with achieving your objectives. The reality of this truth was revealed during the Civil Rights Movement in America. Millions of people were waiting for the right leader to spearhead the advancement of their civil rights.

At the right time in history, countless individuals joined together with Dr. Martin Luther King Jr. in the nonviolent movement to fight against social injustice and racial segregation. Do you remember his words, *"The time is always right to do what is right?"*

Associated with your purpose are certain decisions that you must make and there are experiences that you must encounter to prepare you for the journey. Sometimes, when certain things are happening in your life, it is difficult to understand why life seems so challenging or why you are experiencing uncomfortable situations. Have you ever experienced a situation that you did not understand when it was happening but over the course of time, you received a revelation about the importance of going through it? For Dr. King and many others, time and destiny met together at the right moment in history to catapult them to prominence, but they had to make the right decisions at the right time.

Are you aware that there are lessons to learn and blessings to attract that will help you progress towards releasing the fruit of your purpose into the world? Therefore, finding your path of purpose is essential because it directs you towards situations that will help you understand, develop, mature, and release your natural fruit. Along the way, it is important to recognize the season of purpose and how it impacts your ability to bear the right fruit. Do you know what season of purpose you are currently in?

## Understanding the Seasons of Purpose

I believe that there are three seasons of your life that come to help you understand your purpose. Potential is easy to recognize, but this is not the case when it comes to understanding your path of purpose. Purpose is discovered over time. Since there are some subtle and obvious situations that add value to your purpose for living, it is important to understand that information about purpose comes in seasons.

The relevant seasons related to your purpose are referred to as the pre-conceptualization, awakening and transformational seasons. Understanding the seasons of purpose is vital to building confidence and realistic expectations surrounding your reason for living. If you recognize the season that you are in, then it will also help you understand where you are and what you need to do to fulfill your destiny. The journey to discovering your purpose begins in the pre-conceptualization season.

**Phase I – Pre-conceptualization Season**

The pre-conceptualization season is the timeframe in life before you fully understand your purpose. It is also the phase when events and circumstances happen in your life that add significant value to identifying your assignment. Things such as dreams, desires and reoccurring thoughts come to introduce you to your purpose. The pre-conceptualization season is also the timeframe when you get acquainted with matching your natural TAGs with a path in life. This means that you must understand and explore your meaning of self, and your natural potential.

Furthermore, this season is the preliminary stage in life wherein you connect the dots that motivate and direct your decisions toward becoming who you were born to be. Obtaining the proper understanding about your purpose and potential requires that you spend quality time thinking about your passion and natural abilities. Afterwards, it is necessary that you accept the fact that your purpose must be fulfilled in life. Benjamin Disraeli said, *"I have brought myself, by long meditation, to the conviction that a human being with a settled purpose must accomplish it, and that nothing can resist a will which will stake even existence upon its fulfillment."* Have you come to the same conviction?

Is it possible to have an indication about your purpose at an early age? The answer is "YES." Age is not a factor when it comes to connecting the dots between your dreams, potential, passion in life and the preoccupation that consumes your thoughts. More importantly, age is not a determining factor when it comes to understanding the voice of your heart directing you towards a specific path. The primary objective of the pre-conceptualization season is to direct you towards an awakening of your purpose for living through information overload. If you are successful in understanding the signals, then your journey will lead you into a season of awakening. Remember, *"God has made everything beautiful for its own time."*

**Phase II – Awakening Season**

*"God knows what's best for you, He knows where you are going and He has a plan to get you there,"* according to Bishop T.D. Jakes. However, His plan requires that you awaken your dormant internal talents, abilities, and gifts. Once your TAGs are awakened, then you must activate your dreams by taking intentional steps along the right path. The awakening season begins the moment your mind identifies and persuades you to pursue a course in life that coincides with your natural potential. *"The vision that you glorify in your mind, the ideal that you enthrone in your heart – this will build your life by, and this you will become."* Do you believe that statement from James Allen? His comments suggest that persistent thoughts about becoming something are critical to directing your path in life.

The awakening season in your life occurs when your hidden power begins to erupt into manifested reality. It is also the moment whereby you truly accept and fall in love with your individualism. This means that you accept the singleness and individuality of your destiny. This concept does not mean that you disregard the contributions and importance of others.

In simple terms, I am suggesting that you accept the fact that your purpose is associated with your heart's desire. *"Your vision will only become clear when you can look into your own heart. Who looks outside, dreams; who looks inside awakens,"* according to Carl Jung. In other words, when you look inside your heart to validate your purpose and you pursue the path it reveals, then you are in your personal awakening season. The awakening season automatically leads to transformation into the person that you were born to be.

## Phase III – Transformational Season

If this observation from Peter Drucker is correct, then *"There is a point at which a transformation has to take place."* I believe that Drucker's statement is correct because the transformational season is the culmination of the other seasons. After you understand the importance of manifesting self, then there is a point at which a transformation must take place. The season of transformation ushers in the change from the inside out. Changing from the inside out results in a transformation of your actions and plans as well.

*"First comes thought, then organization of the thought, into ideas and plans; then transformation of those plans into reality. The beginning, as you will observe, is in your imagination,"* as Napoleon Hill noted. His comments provide insight into the mental process that takes place on the inside prior to your transformation on the outside. Remember that transformation cannot happen if your thoughts don't line up with your purpose in life.

According to Earl Nightingale, *"All you need is the plan, the road map, and the courage to press on to your destination."* It is critical for you to understand that a thought always precede actions, ideas, plans and your transformation. The transformation that God desires for your life cannot happen if your actions don't line up with His words. Unfortunately, if your actions don't line up, then it is possible that your ideas, plans and transformation won't line up either.

A good example of this truth is found in God's word. There was an occasion when Jesus and his disciples were travelling on their way to Bethany. Along the way, Jesus became hungry. He saw a fig tree at a distance, and they proceeded to walk towards it. When they arrived at the tree, there were no figs on it, so Jesus cursed it and it withered away. The writer of the scripture said that figs were not in season which is why there was no fruit. This encounter is found in Mark 11:12-14.

Why did Jesus curse a healthy tree? Particularly, since it was stated that figs were not in season. Do you believe that Jesus knew that it wasn't time for the fig tree to bear its fruit before he walked towards it? Surely, the Son of God would have known this fact, right? Think along the lines of potential, purpose, and transformation.

What is the significance of this event and the transformational season? Do you remember the statement, *"Potential turns perceived impossibilities into possibilities?"* Clearly, based on Jesus' actions, the tree possessed the potential to produce fruit out of season. In fact, it was its purpose to feed Jesus and his disciples at that moment in time. However, for some reason, the tree failed to transform into its predetermined image at the right time for the right reasons. The conclusion is that whenever God gives you potential nothing is impossible if you are walking in the purpose that He assigned for your life.

*"The greatest achievement was at first and for a time a dream. The oak sleeps in the acorn, the bird waits in the egg, and in the highest vision of the soul a waking angel stirs. Dreams are the seedlings of realities."* Do you understand that statement from James Allen? The purpose of the acorn is to turn into an oak tree. Likewise, the purpose of an egg is to turn into a bird. In the same regard, the purpose of your life is to transform into the complete manifestation of the image created by your potential and God's will.

The season of transformation is the time when you transform into the visual manifestation of who you are on the inside. The visual manifestation is the expressed image of who are naturally. Merriam Webster's online dictionary defines image as *"a visual representation of something."*[28] When you consider the power of purpose, you must recognize its ability to transform you into that image that you see through the window of your heart.

## Transformation Initiates Change

*"It may be hard for an egg to turn into a bird: it would be a jolly sight harder for it to learn to fly while remaining an egg. We are like eggs at*

*present. And you cannot go on indefinitely being just an ordinary decent egg. We must hatch or go bad,"* according to C.S. Lewis. A deeper look into Lewis' comments reveal a few natural truths.

First, an egg cannot transform into a bird without undergoing a process of change. Even though the egg contains the ingredients necessary to transform into a bird, it cannot happen without change. Likewise, the bird possesses the potential to fly but flight comes as a process of change. The bird grows wings, feathers, and the confidence to launch out from the safety of the nest. Again, the entire process requires change at each level for the bird to realize its full potential and experience the joy of fulfilling its purpose.

The same principles apply related to your purpose as well. Change is a necessary process in the fulfillment of your purpose. Your potential cannot remain in the unhatched state. If that happens, you will never change into who were born to be. Like the bird, if you never transform into who you were born to be, then you will never experience the joy that comes from living a life of purpose. In this regard, change is an essential process in the fulfillment of purpose. Unfortunately, halting the process of change also stops the process of realizing your full potential and discovering your purpose for living.

STOP!!! Be aware of information overload. We are almost finished with this chapter. The objective of this chapter was to give you an overview on understanding key concepts related to purpose. As you can see, there is a lot of information to think about. Perhaps, it would be good for you to take a few moments to reflect on some of these principles. The priority is not for you to rush through the material because I am aware that it is technical and thought provoking. Be patient as you continue to read. Your transformation has started to take place.

## Transformation and Time

Time is another key component in the process of transformation. For many years, I devoted my thoughts to the issues of potential and purpose. I looked for answers at every stage in life. Now, I understand how time plays a major role in the transformational process. The season of transformation happens at the right time and moment in your life. Whenever you pursue the path of purpose, it is important to recognize your season to shine and act upon the moment.

> **Time exists for the fulfillment of purpose.
> Without time, purpose has no meaning.
> Without purpose, there is no true value for time.**

Have you ever heard the saying from Robert Frost that, *"Time and tide wait for no man…?"* This statement is true regarding time, but it is not true for purpose. Purpose waits for you. It beckons you and assists you in discovering the meaning of life. Purpose also creates the passion and reason to maximize time.

Stay with me, we are almost at the end of this chapter. I hope that the next statement does not apply to you. Purpose is embedded in the heart of every man but only a few understand why, when, and how to draw this information out. Those that find purpose also find their career assignment in life. Although the pursuit of it is necessary for sustained peace of mind, it is subject to desires of the heart and information.

*"Imagination is the beginning of creation. You imagine what you desire, you will what you imagine and create what you will,"* according to George Bernard Shaw. In other words, desires of the heart tend to influence your thoughts and actions in goods ways and bad ways. If your desires line up with your purpose and God's will for your life, then it becomes easier to make the right choices at the right time. The conclusion to Shaw's quote is that

transformation into who are destined to become is a natural occurrence in the life of those that maximize their potential on the path of purpose. Is your purpose calling you to transform into the desires of your heart?

## THE NEXT STEP

Well done!!! You have just reviewed the foundational information necessary to understand the concept of purpose. When you add this basic knowledge to the information that you have received about your potential, then hopefully you will start to see a clear picture of your future unfolding before your eyes. Your purpose is a serious issue that requires your undivided time and attention. Therefore, I am happy that you are becoming more knowledgeable about the subject.

As you continue to read, remember that there are many ways that will lead you to discovering your purpose. If you find it and live it, then you will discover the ultimate satisfaction of being all you can be in life. Let's move on together and address the "calling of your heart" in the next chapter. Remember these words from Dr. Myles Munroe, *"The past is the past. Who or what we used to be doesn't matter anymore. What matters is who and what we are now and who and what we can become in the future."*

## Quick reference to understanding purpose principles:

1. There is a season for everything including your purpose.
2. If you recognize the season that you are in, then it will help you understand where you are and what you need to do to fulfill your purpose.
3. Obtaining the proper understanding about your purpose and potential requires that you spend quality time thinking about your passion and natural abilities.
4. The primary objective of the pre-conceptualization season is to direct you towards an awakening of your purpose for living through information overload.
5. The awakening season begins the moment your mind identifies and persuades you to pursue a course in life that coincides with your natural potential.
6. It is important to understand that the awakening season is a planned moment in your life when glimpses of who you are and what you should do in life occurs frequently.
7. When you transform into the person that you were born to be, then the continuous releasing of potential will lead to explaining why you exist.
8. Purpose is fulfilled through the process of change.
9. Time exists for the fulfillment of Purpose. Without time, purpose has no meaning. Without purpose, there is no true value for time.
10. Purpose is innate to every human being, but it must be discovered in the secret depths of your heart.

# Chapter Seven

## Purpose Lives on The Inside of You

*"Being busy does not always mean real work. The object of all work is production or accomplishment and to either of these ends there must be forethought, system, planning, intelligence, and honest purpose, as well as perspiration. Seeming to do is not doing."*
**Thomas Edison**

Hundreds of preoccupied pedestrians walked briskly along the overcrowded sidewalks. As usual, they seemed immune to the loud symphony of blaring horns and speeding cars that filled the congested streets. The normal sounds and busy walkways indicated that the chaotic morning rush hour was in full swing.

For MJ, this day started no differently than others. With a steady and brisk cadence, he blended into his surroundings distracted by the same thoughts. Each day, he struggled with getting motivated to go to a job that he did not like and working with individuals he did not want to be around. Unbeknown to him, the events surrounding this morning would steer him towards a life altering collision course fueled by unfulfilled purpose.

Suddenly, MJ experienced something out of the ordinary. As he walked along the familiar path, he heard a loud voice shout out, "MJ, stop! Help me!

*Purpose Lives on the Inside of You* 163

I need your assistance. Please stop!" Startled by the distressed cry, he came to an abrupt stop, causing a minor disturbance on the bustling walkway.

Immediately, the piercing voice and agonizing plea disrupted his normal train of thought. The voice seemed familiar and vaguely recognizable. MJ stood motionless pondering the location and identity of the person in despair. His heart and mind raced with anxiety. *"Was it a colleague? An old schoolmate? Or, even a former teammate? Is the person in the coffee shop I just passed? Where is he?"* After spending several unsuccessful minutes pondering this mystery, he composed himself and restarted his journey.

MJ could not relax until he found the source of the urgent cry for help. Again, the voice screamed out, but this time with a greater sense of urgency, *"MJ, don't leave me alone, I can't make it without you. You are my only hope for survival. Please, please don't leave me!"*

Visibly perplexed, he made another abrupt stop this time turning completely around. With his head swinging from left to right, eyes stretched wide open, arms swaying up and down, he exhaled in frustration, *"What's happening to me, What's happening to me?"*

MJ's reactions, by this time, were causing him to make a scene. The other pedestrians became noticeably annoyed by his traffic blocking actions. Some stared at him with anger and hostility, while others shouted forcefully, *"Get out of the way or keep moving."* Heeding the external warning signs, he started his familiar journey again. After walking several feet, the unseen person yelled with an elevated cry for attention, *"MJ, MJ stop! Don't leave me alone. Please stop!"*

Nevertheless, he proceeded to work, but MJ couldn't forget about the voice. He sat anxiously at his desk gazing at the empty computer screen, questioning his sanity. The memorable events replayed in his head repeatedly like an unforgettable movie. He thought for a moment, *"Am I dreaming, or did this just happen to me?"* Following several silent minutes of questioning his mental stability, he decided to call 911 to report the disturbing incidents. The operator asked a series of questions, none of which he could answer. Finally, he agreed to assist the response team in locating the injured person by returning to the place where the voice was heard.

Nervously optimistic that the situation was already resolved, he arrived at the site just before the response team. Immediately, the familiar voice shouted, *"Thank you for returning. You can't leave me again. MJ, why won't you help me?"* Fuming from the morning drama, MJ exploded in anger, *"WHO ARE YOU? WHAT DO YOU WANT FROM ME?"*

The voice replied with the same degree of frustration but in a calm fashion, *"You pretend as though you don't know me, and you continue to disregard my pleas for help. I am…"* Rudely interrupting the voice, MJ shouted irately, *"I don't know you and I don't want to know you. Why did you choose to ruin my morning?"*

He continued, *"Don't you realize that I cannot help you if I can't find you? Will you please just LEAVE ME ALONE?"* Also, very annoyed, and sad, the voice replied, *"It's a shame that after all of these years you still don't remember me and now you can't find me, I can't take this anymore."* Exhausted from the years of neglect, the voice confessed, *"I've been overlooked for so many years? MJ, I'M INSIDE OF YOU!"*

> **T**he natural beacon in the form of reoccurring thoughts illuminates the path of purpose.

Do you wonder what your purpose is in life? This chapter will give you information to assist you in discovering it. However, at the end of the day, I can only point you in the direction that will provide helpful insight. Your purpose is individualistic which means that it is inside of you and nobody else. It is hidden in the one place where you are sure to find it.

The heart serves as an internal beacon that shines attention on your purpose. This internal beacon directs your thoughts and sounds an alarm to steer your course in life. If you are pursuing the wrong path, then this beacon sounds out with a symphony of negative mental and emotional effects. Alternatively, when you are traveling along the right path, it rings with a tremendous shout of joy and contentment.

The MJ story is intended to bring attention to the dilemma of pursuing the wrong path in life. It is important to understand that if you pursue the wrong path then you are also pursuing the wrong purpose. To make matters worse, it would also mean that your potential is being used for the wrong reason or not being used at all. Listed below are additional life issues and situations surrounding purpose that are directly or indirectly highlighted in the story:

1. As a matter of routine, many are preoccupied with going in a certain direction in life, but few are traveling along the right path.
2. Life is filled with distractions that are typically accepted as the norm. Often, these distractions play no role in releasing your potential or pursuing your purpose in life.
3. Many people choose the path of comfort that produces the same unfulfilling outcomes, follows the status quo and results in wasted potential.
4. Often, the desire to be accepted, blend in or follow the crowd causes you to settle for a path in life not in line with your true purpose.
5. Although purpose may direct you towards a path or career that is common in society, your uniqueness adds a different perspective and dimension to the assignment.
6. Discontentment is the end-result of continuing to pursue the wrong career path, job, or employment. Your career path is a product of your purpose for living. It is also the designated path that yields the most from your potential.

MJ was traveling along a path that is familiar to many people in life. He chose to follow the expected path based on societal standards and popularity.

He also became accustomed to moving in the same direction just to keep pace with his peers. He became a product of his environment and not his purpose. Although each day produced a sense of unhappiness, he chose to disregard the internal warning signs because the discontentment became an acceptable norm.

## The Calling From Within

Did you know that the vison that you see through the window of your dreams, desires and reoccurring thoughts is your future? Therefore, the best approach to understanding yourself and discovering your purpose is to look within. ***The vision seen through the window of your heart is the path of purpose.*** As previously mentioned, your beacon manifests itself in the form of an inner voice. Often the voice is referred to as a calling. According to Merriam-Webster's online dictionary, a calling is *"a strong inner impulse toward a course of action especially when accompanied by conviction of divine influence."*[29] **The yearning, tugging, and calling from within is the voice of your heart prompting you to give life to your seeds of potential.**

The cry of the heart that MJ heard was his inner voice of direction seeking attention. Do you believe that natural thoughts that guide you along the path of purpose are common, normal, and unprovoked? Within you lies the secret to understanding yourself and the most appropriate path for you in life. Fulfillment of these thoughts lead to addressing psychological needs common to people from every walk of life.

Let's stop at this moment for a time of reflection. Spend time thinking about the cries of your heart. Your heart is conveying a message about your purpose. What is it saying to you? What's on your mind about your future? Can you still hear the voice loudly or is it faint? Your future is calling you, don't ignore it.

## Objectives of Your Calling

Years ago, Helen Keller concluded that there is a misunderstanding about the significance purpose plays in sustaining your happiness in life. She stated, *"Many persons have a wrong idea of what constitutes true happiness. It is not attained through self-gratification but through fidelity to a worthy purpose."* It is important to add to Keller's comments by stating that a worthy purpose must satisfy your psychological needs.

One of the most effective ways to sustain happiness in life is through the pursuit of purpose because purpose provides answers to psychological needs. Therefore, be mindful that the calling of your heart comes to give you the following:

- Sense of Meaning: Purpose gives meaning to your purposeful thoughts, actions, and potential.

- Sense of Direction: Purpose points you in the right direction and ensures that you are following the right path in life.

- Sense of Relevance: Purpose gives relevance to some unprovoked life circumstances, issues and challenges that you face.

- Sense of Significance: Purpose ensures that your life is significant and an important solution to an existing need in society.

- Sense of Value: Purpose guarantees that you are a person of value. When you understand and pursue your purpose in life, the opinions of others are not needed to justify your self-worth.

- Sense of Personal Power: Purpose is the reason why you possess personal power to accomplish things that are impossible for others but possible for you.

Based on what you now know, think for a moment about what life would be like without purpose. ***Without purpose, life would have no meaning, no direction, no relevance, no significance, no value, no order, and no personal power.*** Nevertheless, you do not have to worry because everyone has purpose on the inside and access to the tools to fulfill it. Although you have the innate attributes to fulfill it, you have a responsibility to develop, define and refine it.

## Needs of the Heart

One of the keys to effectively understanding the tremendous significance of purpose is to have the proper appreciation for the phrase "*needs of the heart.*" In this case, the word heart is interchangeable with "mind." Therefore, the phrase can also read as the "*needs of the mind.*" I believe that needs of the mind are issues, questions and concerns about self that develop when purpose is unknown. On the contrary, ***whenever purpose is known then the meaning of self is also known***.

Years ago, I worked briefly as an independent insurance producer for an insurance agency. As a self-employed contractor, I was responsible for generating my own income and paying for my expenses. The company that I was associated with appreciated my success and continuous effort to generate revenue. Fortunately, my talents and abilities were also noticed by others in the insurance industry resulting in an offer to become the General Manager of a small agency.

After several days of negotiations, I agreed to accept the offer. It was a tremendous opportunity that offered a chance to maximize my potential and earn more income. Shortly after accepting the offer, I informed the company I was working with that I would be leaving. The Chairman of the company took the decision of me leaving personally and became very upset. Although his opinion in the matter did not change my decision, something interesting happened after I left his office. A short period after our conversation, I received the thought, *"Someday, you will be required to go back and help them."*

The thought entered my mind, even though I had no desire to return. Years passed, I moved to another country and was working for another insurance agency, but I never forgot the message. In fact, occasionally the thought, *"You will be required to go back and help them,"* would reoccur without my prompting. Over eight years later, my wife and I were approached by the Chairman of the former company asking us to return to help the company chart a new direction.

After the conversation, the thought, *"You will be required to go back and help them,"* intensified into a consistent urging. I realized that the time had finally arrived. Shortly thereafter, we agreed to move back, and I took a senior position in that former company. From that experience, I learned the importance of being aware of the reoccurring thoughts that come to provide direction in life.

Sometimes, the thoughts appear years prior to you being required to decide. Acting upon reoccurring thoughts relative to purpose leads to confidence and a sense of peace of mind. Failure to act upon your purpose leads to an unrelenting cry or yearning from within. The calling from within is the cry of purpose seeking to direct your path, initiate self-manifestation and shed light on why you exist in life.

> **P**urpose is your natural wellspring; it rejuvenates the soul and quenches the thirst for self-manifestation.

Are you okay? Are you understanding the information? Hopefully, your answer is "YES" but if not, don't worry. It will make sense as you meditate on the information in your quiet time. We are moving in the direction of helping you manifest the hidden you. Dr. Myles Munroe concluded, *"Every human heart cries and yearns for the same thing: a chance to fulfill his or her own dreams and desires. Even the poorest man has a dream."* In this regard, the cry of your heart is not a strange occurrence but merely your beacon sent to assist you in navigating your path and exposing self.

## Truths About Self-Manifestation

As a worldwide traveler, diplomatic advisor and international leadership trainer, Dr. Munroe's observations were noteworthy. He concluded that the human hearts cries and yearns for the manifestation of self in the form of released potential. Self-manifestation is a visible expression of your natural internal attributes and capabilities. **Embedded within every heart is the calling to manifest and expose the hidden self to the world through self-manifestation.** The following additional points are worth noting about the concept of self-manifestation:

1. Self-manifestation is the reason why purpose and potential exist.
2. Self-manifestation occurs when you release your TAGs to fulfill a void or need in society.
3. Self-manifestation is the foundation for a successful life.
4. Self-manifestation identifies your sphere of dominion and leadership.
5. Self-manifestation brings notoriety and publicity to yourself.
6. Self-manifestation mobilizes resources that become available at certain checkpoints along the path of purpose.

Hopefully, you understand the importance of giving attention to the cries of your heart because action is required to establish peace of mind. To live and not reveal your true self is a tragedy because self-manifestation is the primary objective of purpose. Included below is a chart that identifies the action steps necessary for you to reach the level of self-manifestation:

## Process of Self-Manifestation Chart

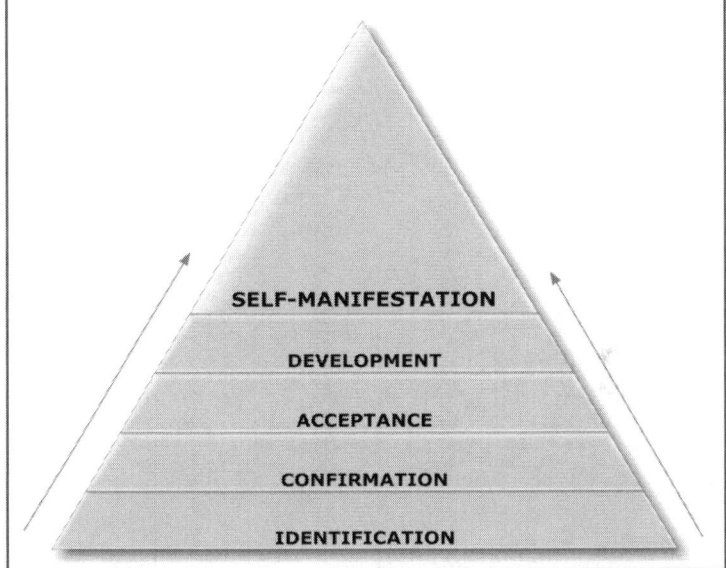

*Pyramid diagram with levels from bottom to top:*
- IDENTIFICATION
- CONFIRMATION
- ACCEPTANCE
- DEVELOPMENT
- SELF-MANIFESTATION

**Identification** – Identification of your purpose in life starts with an awareness of your natural potential in the form of your TAGs. The first stage of identification requires that you display or use your TAGs naturally. In other words, when you discover what comes naturally to you, then you can identify it as a TAG. If it does not come naturally, then it is not associated with your purpose. Therefore, the identification of natural TAGs is key to beginning the process of discovering your purpose for existence.

**Confirmation** – Confirmation of your TAGs and purpose is the next step in the process of living a purpose driven life. Confirming your TAGs through application is a simple process. If you do not possess the natural ability to do something, then there is a strong possibility that it is not associated with your purpose. Linking your potential to the assignment, task or dream that reoccurs in the form of desires or thoughts is essential to confirming your purpose. These thoughts and desires play a vital role in introducing you to yourself and purpose. In other words, you are a product of your thoughts and desires.

Best-selling author and motivational speaker Wayne Dyer believed, *"Your highest self is not just an idea that sounds lofty and spiritual. It is a way of being. It is the very first principle that you must come to understand and embrace as you move toward attracting to you that which you want and need for the parenthesis in eternity that you know as your life."* In simple terms, Dyer's comments suggest that your purpose is a way of being that you must embrace and accept.

**Acceptance** – Moving up the pyramid, acceptance of your purpose is the next step in the process. Your mental stability and well-being are based on your acceptance of purpose. Acceptance of your purpose means that you desire to live an intentional life. Living a purposeful life leads to intentional actions and decisions that are motivated by the knowledge that you possess about yourself and your path of destiny. Let's go back to Wayne Dyer for words of wisdom. Dyer stated that, *"Everything in the universe has a purpose. Indeed, the invisible intelligence that flows through everything in a purposeful fashion is also flowing through you."*

Like Dyer, I believe that everything has a purpose in life and that includes you. Flowing through you are reoccurring thoughts that come to introduce you to the person you are destined to become. Accepting your purpose for living is not an option but a requirement. Once you accept your purpose, then you can begin the process of developing a life suitable for releasing your potential

**Development** – Merriam-Webster defines development as *the act or process of growing or causing something to grow or become larger or more advance.*[30] It is interesting that the responsibility associated with pursuing the path of purpose grows as your potential matures. Developing yourself to grow into your purpose requires knowledge and information. You must have knowledge about your purpose and information about your potential.

What does grow into your purpose mean? It starts by taking active steps towards fulfilling your purpose in life. In order to do this, you must make decisions that present the opportunity to develop and refine your potential. When you become confident in your ability to fulfill your assignment, then you are ready to move to the next stage in the process. The next step up is manifestation of the hidden you.

**Manifestation** – Wayne Dyer also said, *"Within all of us is a divine capacity to manifest and attract all that we need and desire."* Manifestation occurs when there is a physical representation of something that existed in the unseen realm. Self-manifestation is the outward expression of the hidden you exposed for others to see and experience. Another way to view self-manifestation is to say that it is an outward display of your purpose in life and a representation of your released talents, abilities, and gifts.

## Calling of Your Heart

Hopefully, now you understand that the calling of your heart is not a strange phenomenon but a natural beacon. You have access to Holy Spirit. He promised to guide and lead you into all righteous. Now, you also realize that you have another source of information on the inside as well. The next point is very critical to understand.

Contaminated, corrupt, evil, or bad thoughts and desires are detrimental to the process of purpose. God is a good, righteous, and holy God. He is not the source of thoughts that contradict and promote a lifestyle of unrighteous living. Therefore, if you yield to these negative thoughts then understanding your purpose in life becomes a challenge because purpose comes from God. In other words, you cannot fully understand His purpose if you are listening and reacting to the wrong voice.

Meditating on God's word will give perspective on the calling or desires of your heart related to purposeful living. Accordingly, it is necessary that you ensure that your desires are in sync with His word and nothing else. Listen to His voice of instructions:

Blessed is the one who does not walk in step with the wicked or stand in the way that sinners take or sit in the company of mockers, but whose delight is in the law of the Lord, and who meditates on his law day and night. That person is like a tree planted by streams of water, which yields its fruit in season and whose leaf does not wither – whatsoever they do prospers. Ps. 1:1-3 (NIV)

Do not fret because of those who are evil or be envious of those who do wrong; for like the grass they will soon wither, like green plants they will soon die away. Trust in the Lord and do good; dwell in the land and enjoy safe pasture. Take delight in the Lord, and he will give you the desires of your heart. Commit your way to the Lord; trust in him and he will do this: He will make your righteous reward shine like the dawn... Ps. 37:1-6 (NIV)

The introductory short story conveyed the message that some internal thoughts enter your mind and reoccur for good reasons. Your purpose for living is a very good reason to explore your healthy thoughts that point you in the right direction. Would you agree? Are you too comfortable with your present circumstances to explore these thoughts, or are you too afraid of the "unknown" to launch out in faith towards your purpose in life?

## THE NEXT STEP

Wow!!! We discussed some amazing things about the cry of your heart and self-manifestation. I am very excited about what happens next in your life. Good things will happen now that you know the value of self, potential and purpose. You are destined to experience greatness. Can you feel it, taste it and see it? Let's agree with these words of Ralph Emerson Waldo, *"What lies behind you and what lies in front of you, pales in comparison to what lies inside of you."* What's on the inside of you? How valuable is it to you and the world?

The next step is for you to believe that your birth signifies that you qualify to have a fruitful and purpose filled life. The knowledge revealed in this chapter is useless if you either pursue the wrong path in life or decide to forgo the lifelong pursuit of purpose for unsustainable or trivial moments of leisure. Have you really accepted the reality that time never stops moving forward? Therefore, if you fail to accomplish your dream in the time that you are allotted, then eventually it will succumb to lost time. It is possible that a moment of leisure is the reason why you are experiencing unfulfilled purpose related dreams?

Contrary to what some people may believe, the most popular moment of leisure is not found in the Caribbean resting on a pristine beach, overlooking a mesmerizing view of the turquoise waters. The most popular moment of leisure is associated with the comfort zone. The comfort zone is where most people retreat to shut down for an extended period. For this reason, the issue of comfort zones is discussed in the next chapter, as it is the place of rest for purpose and potential. Remember that **the future captured in your dreams will never become a reality if there is no starting point.**

> **Quick reference to purpose lives on the inside principles:**

1. The natural beacon in the form of reoccurring thoughts illuminates the path of purpose.
2. The vision seen through the window of your heart is the path of purpose.
3. The yearning, tugging, and calling from within is the voice of your heart prompting you to give life to your seeds of potential.
4. Without purpose, life would have no meaning, no direction, no relevance, no significance, no value, no order, and no personal power.
5. Needs of the heart point to self-manifestation.
6. Purpose is your natural wellspring; it rejuvenates the soul and quenches the thirst for self-manifestation.
7. Embedded within every heart is the calling to manifest and expose the hidden self to the world through self-manifestation.
8. Self-manifestation is the reason why purpose and potential exist.
9. Self-manifestation occurs when you release your TAGs to fulfill a void or need in society.
10. Self-manifestation is the foundation for a successful life.
11. Self-manifestation identifies your sphere of dominion and leadership.
12. Self-manifestation mobilizes resources that become available at certain checkpoints along the path of purpose.
13. The future captured in your dreams will never become a reality if there is no starting point.

# Chapter Eight

## Comfort Zones Impact Your Potential & Purpose

> *"If you put yourself in a position where you have to stretch outside your comfort zone, then you are forced to expand your consciousness and to strive and achieve."*
> **Les Brown**

Early on a beautiful summer morning, a middle-aged family man took his boat out to sea for a day of fishing and relaxation. The sparkling turquoise water was calm and the outlook for having a good fishing trip was very promising. After reaching his favorite fishing grounds, he dropped anchor and set out a couple of lines. Before long, the fish started biting and his cooler began to fill up. Ignoring the visible signs of inclement weather approaching, he continued to reel in fish after fish.

After seeing his nice catch for the day, he thought, *"Life is good. This is my best day of fishing ever."* Gradually, the environmental conditions started to deteriorate from the fast-approaching weather system. A dangerous thunderstorm moved quickly across the warm water and developed into a life-threatening situation. Soon after, the man found himself battling strong winds and ferocious waves. The experienced and confident seaman was accustomed to fighting bad weather, but this occasion was different.

On this day, he was losing the battle to keep his vessel from tipping over. Each time the powerful waves crashed into his small boat, his heart raced faster, as the fear of dying increased. For several terrifying minutes, the boat was tossed uncontrollably.

Afraid of succumbing to the situation, his heart screamed for mercy and calm seas. Nevertheless, the onslaught from harrowing winds, piercing thunder and violent seas continued to drain his confidence. With each nervous breath, his adrenaline and desperation intensified. Looking at his bleak surroundings through terrified eyes, two thoughts penetrated his mind. His first thought was *"Surely, today I will meet my Maker."* However, as he reflected on life and things yet to be accomplished, he had a second thought. He found reassurance from a confident voice from within that said, *"You can make it. Just believe and remain engaged."*

Those positive words of encouragement were what he needed to hear during his hour of desperation. Energized by the internal voice of comfort, he worked feverishly to keep the huge waves from capsizing his vessel. Determined to overcome his sudden adversity, he shouted with a loud confident voice to the forces of nature, *"I will not die today but live to see land again."*

As midday approached, the intense storm moved away, and the clear blue sea returned to a serene state. Fortunately, the man did not perish in the ferocious storm. With land in his sight at the horizon, he made another declaration, with a sigh of relief, he shouted, *"It's over. Now I can finally relax!"* After plotting his course and turning towards home, the same message repeated in his mind, *"It's over. Now I can finally relax!"* Reclining into a comfortable position in the captain's seat, he thought about the overwhelming troubles of the day while privately celebrating his victorious outcome.

He raced towards the comfort of land unaware of the hidden damage to his engine caused by the turbulence. As land drew closer, his heart filled with relief and great anticipation. He cracked a smile and said, *"I made it, I can't believe I did it."*

Suddenly, there was a loud "**BOOM**" as chaos struck again. His inboard engine erupted into a thunderous explosion. The explosion and resulting fire damaged the hull and caused the boat to take on water rapidly. Although his physical injuries were not life threatening, the same was not true regarding his mental state of mind. Unfortunately, after reaching a hundred yards from shore, a fatal dose of fear took complete control over the seasoned captain. Thus, immobilizing his body and ability to react as quickly as before.

After a few seconds, it was over. Completely overwhelmed by unbearable fear, he vanished in the depths of the dark ocean. His last thought was, *"Why is this happening to me?"*

## Understanding Comfort Zones

According to Roy T. Bennett, a former Zimbabwean politician, *"The comfort zone is a psychological state in which one feels familiar, safe, at ease, and secure…"* In addition to Bennett's definition, I believe that a comfort zone is also *a state of mind that promotes a lifestyle of mediocrity under the premise of relaxed living.* Perhaps, you have your own definition for comfort zone. Nevertheless, I am curious to know your opinion on comfort zones. Do you believe that they are harmless?

One more question, did you know that comfort zones are the most subtle and effective opposition to purpose and released potential? Why is this statement true? It is true because comfort zones neutralize the power contained within your potential to grow and produce fruit. *"If we are growing, we're always going to be out of our comfort zones,"* according to John Maxwell.

It is an unchangeable condition that every living thing must undergo the process of growth to reach its original intended state. In other words, a seed must release its potential to grow into a fruit bearing tree. The fruit bearing tree is the intended result of the seed, but it would not exist without the released potential of the seed. Likewise, it is important to understand that desires related to expressing your potential and fulfilling your purpose in life must grow into unyielding passions. Comfort zones convince you to halt or forgo the growth and development process necessary to achieve self-actualization, which is the highest level of personal attainment.

Comfort zones also promote the thought that potential and the fulfillment of purpose are not time sensitive. Unfortunately, life and time are the regulators determining what you can achieve at each stage. As you get older, the physical clock begins to limit the terms for releasing your potential. Comfort zones are in direct opposition to releasing your full potential because they create the mindset that extended pursuits of unproductive tasks or idleness is harmless. Although this is true, don't be persuaded to fall into that trap.

One of the biggest obstacles to your motivation to push forward is the perceived comfort from resorting to a phase in life that is void of persistence and upward mobility. Potential requires that you reject the desire to settle for less than the image portrayed through the window of your heart. You owe yourself the courtesy of being honest concerning the void created by unfulfilled purpose and unreleased potential. *"We have to be honest about what we want and take risks rather than lie to ourselves and make excuses to stay in our comfort zones."* Why was this advice Roy Bennett true? It's important because there are effects of comfort zones that have a negative impact on your potential, purpose, and destiny in life.

## Effects of Comfort Zones

The psychological responses to life's issues initiated by comfort zones cross boundaries such as culture, race, religion, age, and gender. I am sure you will agree that making decisions is a part of everyday living. Each day, you make decisions related to all aspects of your life. Since thoughts precede your decision and the corresponding action you take, it is not possible to separate the effects of comfort zones from your mind. This means that the precursor to every comfort zone is a thought that directs your actions and responses to situations. For this reason, comfort zones present the greatest hindrance to releasing your full potential and pursuing your purpose for living. Listed below are 12 reasons why this statement is true:

1. Comfort zones place boundaries on personal and corporate advancement.
2. Comfort zones cause you to choose the wrong career path and prevent you from moving beyond the bad decision to a place of true contentment.
3. Comfort zones alter purpose and block potential.
4. Comfort zones hold dreams and desires of the heart in captivity.
5. Comfort zones breed excuses for why you can't, shouldn't and won't make the decision to pursue the correct path in life.
6. Comfort zones lead you down a path of discontentment, unfulfillment and uncertainty.
7. Comfort zones alter your sense of self-worth and minimizes the importance of the things you desire to accomplish in life.
8. Comfort zones convince you to believe that time is endless.
9. Comfort zones alter life's priorities and create a false sense of security.
10. Comfort zones promote internal voids and inaction.
11. Comfort zones impact your ability to make the right decision at the right time.
12. Comfort zones produce temporary results, solutions, and a false sense of satisfaction.

Irrespective of the above truths, many people believe that it is always best to make decisions that promote comfortable living and prevent emotional, mental, or physical strain. Nevertheless, purpose challenges you to transform into the person you are destined to become. To accomplish this objective, you may be required to overcome and to adjust by stepping out of your area of comfort. Why would you or anyone else support a position in life that robs you of peace of mind?

Do you fall into the same category as others believing that they are harmless? If so, can you identify accomplishments related to your purpose that you were able to achieve because of comfort zones? Did a comfort zone help you discover or release your potential? Or, did a comfort zone help you fulfill some aspects of your purpose in life?

Let's go back to Bennett for additional words of wisdom, he also said that *"You never change your life until you step out of your comfort zone; change begins at the end of your comfort zone."* What does this mean? It means that the pursuit of your purpose for living stops at the beginning of the comfort zone and starts again at the end of the comfort zone. Another way to state this point is to say that comfort zones halt progression towards fulfilling your purpose for living. Unfortunately, when you linger in a mental state of complacency, then you unknowingly expose yourself to several negative effects that are hard to overcome.

> **Comfort zones create a false sense of security and minimizes the importance of maximizing your potential.**

Although the introductory chapter story is fiction, it captures the subtleness and the inherent dangers hidden in comfort zones. It is written to convey a message that comfort zones impact your life in a negative way. The fisherman did a commendable job handling overwhelming obstacles. His response to the difficult circumstances proved that he possessed exceptional seamanship abilities. What happened to cause this skilled captain to perish just a hundred yards from shore? Let's review some of the details in the story:

- He was busy pursuing his desire of the heart. - ***Fishing***
- An unanticipated situation occurred that caused him to fear for his life. - ***Bad weather***
- Motivated by a positive thought, he remained engaged and fought to keep the boat from capsizing. - ***Physical and mental struggle***

- Consequently, his difficult circumstances changed, and life returned to a good state. - *Life changes*
- He relaxed mentally and headed back to shore. - *Comfort zone*
- Close to accomplishing his objective of safely reaching land another unexpected situation occurred. - *Catastrophic boat damage*
- Overwhelmed by fear, he failed to regain his confidence and make the best decision. - *Fear*
- The emotional and mental stress was unbearable. He succumbed to the pressure and died in despair. - *Pit of despair*

Do you realize that there are three options when you are faced with having to make decisions? *"In every moment of decision, the best thing you can do is the right thing, the next best thing is the wrong thing, and the worst thing you can do is nothing,"* according to President Theodore Roosevelt. His comments were true. You can decide to make the right decision, wrong decision, or no decision at all. It is important to understand that comfort zones tend to influence two of the choices. Comfort zones may cause you to make the wrong decision or no decision but never the right decision.

> **Comfort zones create false perceptions that attract negative symptoms.**

Comforts zones are dangerous because of the emotional and mental affects attributable to voluntary complacency. Attached to every comfort zone is a host of characteristics that influence your decision-making ability. What goes through your mind whenever you are required to make a major life or career decision? One of the most effective ways to determine if you are experiencing the effects of comfort zones is to examine whether your decisions are impacted by the symptoms listed on the following chart:

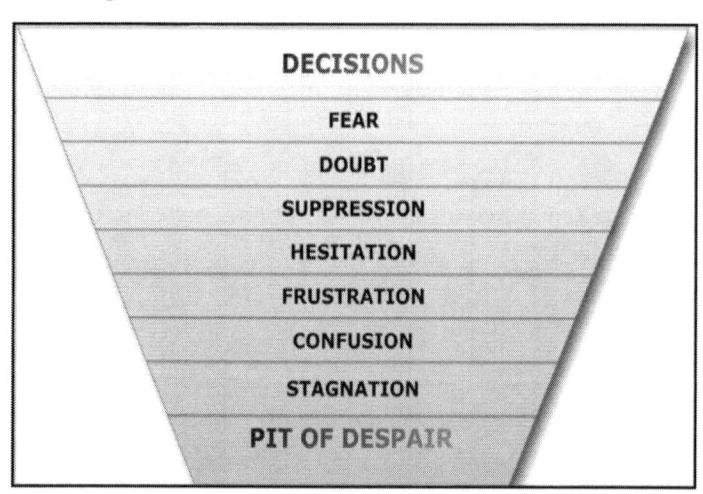

## Negative Effects of Comfort Zones Chart

| DECISIONS |
|---|
| FEAR |
| DOUBT |
| SUPPRESSION |
| HESITATION |
| FRUSTRATION |
| CONFUSION |
| STAGNATION |
| PIT OF DESPAIR |

The above chart highlights seven major symptoms of comfort zones. Deciding or failing to decide opens the gateway that may lead to a mental or emotional fall into a pit of despair. Any one of the symptoms can cause you to slip into despair. Understanding the motivation behind your actions is necessary when looking to address the mental ramifications. Therefore, it is important to evaluate and analyze why you make certain decisions and why you fail to make other decisions. In the context of potential and purpose, what is the true reason why you are experiencing uncertainty, discontentment, or a lack of fulfillment?

The fisherman settled into a comfort zone when he decided to relax before reaching home safely. Although it is understandable why he did it, his comfort zone produced unfavorable results. Fear is one of the powerful effects that typically surfaces before and during comfort zone retreats. This onset is initiated by uncertainty about the outcome of a situation or a negative reaction to frightening life events. Unfortunately, once fear enters the mind, it inhibits your ability to make the right decision at the right time.

## Fear

In a Forbes article entitled, *7 Things Successful People Overcome,* fear is listed as a negative emotion that successful people confront and overcome.[31] The voice of fear is the main perpetrator behind the false or fictitious belief that it is always safer to remain in the "shelter" of your comfort zone. Ask yourself this simple question: *"What's preventing me from experiencing true contentment regarding the path that I have chosen?"* Perhaps, you are afraid to upset your "perfect world?" Or, are you afraid to acknowledge your hidden uncertainty?

> **C**omfort zones magnify challenges with a heavy dose of fear.

Are you starting to sense that fear is a good friend of comfort zones? If you truly want to choose the correct path in life, then fear must be defeated. You must not become comfortable with entertaining or embracing it, because it will hinder your ability to fulfill your goals and maximize your potential. Do you recall reading these words of Dale Carnegie, *"Inaction breeds doubt and fear. Action breeds confidence and courage. If you want to conquer fear, do no sit home and think about it. Go out and get busy?"*

My words to you are to fear not, *"For God has not given us a spirit of fear and timidity, but of power, love, and self-discipline."* Think for a moment about this statement. God does not intend for you to be afraid of moving towards your future with confidence. However, to achieve your purposeful objectives, you will need to counteract the urge to fear with action, confidence, courage, and self-discipline. Remember you must resist the impulse to stop moving and relax for extended moments. Your potential and purpose are too important. Furthermore, the longer it takes to activate your potential, the greater the chances that doubt will slip into your mind. If your potential and purpose are being negatively impacted by fear, meditate on this assurance from God, *"Don't be afraid, for I am with you. Don't be discouraged, for I am your God. I will strengthen you and help you. I will hold you up with my victorious right hand."*

**Doubt**

If you suffer from the effects of fear during the decision-making process, then you will also suffer from doubt. Initially, you may have an indication regarding what decision to make. Nevertheless, the longer you wait before choosing the right option, the more difficult the decision becomes because of increasing doubt. At the end of the day, doubt causes you to question your abilities, options, and chances of accomplishing your objective. God can and will help you find peace of mind. If you ask Him. *"But when you ask him, be sure that your faith is in God alone. Do not waver, for a person with divided loyalty is as unsettled as a wave of the sea that is blown and tossed by the wind."*

Faith is the opposite of doubt. Think for a moment, what good thing results from doubt? Benjamin Franklin once said, *"When in doubt, don't."* When the urge comes to doubt the greatness of your future, a simple response is, *"don't do it."* If you apply faith, there is hope. There is no hope in doubt. Instead, you are plagued with uncertainty and frustration. Now I ask you, *"Is it better to have hope, faith and belief or doubt, fear and frustration?"* I believe that you will succeed in defeating the negative mental reactions preventing you from self-actualizing, but you must overcome the urge to doubt. As you continue to read, remember that suppressing the truth about comfort zones and the value of potential is not beneficial.

**Suppression**

We have covered fear and doubt thus far. However, suppression is the most deceptive symptom of comfort zones. It is deceptive because it seeks to muzzle the voice of your heart and disregard the consequences of doing so. As previously mentioned, the voice of your heart is the warning beacon and guiding light directing you along the path of purpose. Comfort zones seek to suppress the true value of potential and purpose by redirecting your thoughts to other areas. Nevertheless, redirecting your thoughts to focus on fleeting comfort cannot silence the yearning of your heart indefinitely. This action causes mental confusion and dissatisfaction because the needs of your heart will always prompt you to give attention to your purpose.

I encourage you to not hesitate or suppress the voice of your heart by allowing comfort zones to consume your life. Instead, plan to move forward towards peace of mind. The voice of your heart is speaking the truth about your potential and the future that God has reserved for you. Hold fast to God's words and principles, *"Then you will know the truth, and the truth will set you free."* You have the power to defeat the effects of comfort zones and live victoriously. Don't hesitate, continue to move in the direction of fulfilling your purpose.

**Hesitation**

Next on the list of negative consequences of comfort zones is hesitation. Hesitation occurs after receiving information about your purpose that requires some degree of change to take place in your life. Be mindful that the strongholds of fear, doubt, and suppression seek to prevent you from moving forward. The act of not moving forward creates a comfort zone.

Are you aware that comfort zones cause extended periods of hesitation that could last a lifetime? Think for a moment, after addressing the questions or concerns about your potential and purpose, what's a key element stopping you from moving in the right direction? Perhaps, hesitation is the culprit blocking your path. Since there is a time and season for every purpose, it is important to acknowledge the impact hesitation has on your life.

Patrick Swayze's commented that, *"Fear causes hesitation and hesitation will cause your worst fears to come true."* The introductory story conveyed this message. Fear caused the man to hesitate at the most inopportune time. What he feared the most, became his reality. Are you starting to sense that comfort zones sustain fear, not defeat it? If you are frustrated by your hesitation to shake off the fear preventing you from pursuing your purpose in life, then make a firm decision to move in the right direction. God created you and blessed you to be an overcomer.

Repeat after me, *"I am an overcomer, and I will not be defeated by fear."* Can you fulfill your purpose during your lifetime? I will answer that question for you. Yes, you can fulfill it!!! Speak these words as you move forward, *"I have not achieved it, but I focus on this one thing: Forgetting the past and looking forward to what lies ahead, I press on to reach the end of the race and receive the heavenly prize..."*

## Frustration

*"Unless a man believes in himself and makes a total commitment to his career and puts everything he has into it - his mind, his body, his heart - what's life worth to him?"* Those were the words of Vince Lombardi. The statement addresses the pitfall of not being able to devote maximum effort into your planned course in life. Frustration results from not being able to reach the pinnacle expressed through the window of your heart and reoccurring purpose related thoughts.

For decades, statistics have confirmed that many Americans are not happy with their careers and jobs. Lack of job satisfaction is a major cause of frustration in life. Even though this is true, **how many people do you know will contribute their lack of job satisfaction to a personal comfort zone?** The probable answer to this question is "not many." Reason being, frustration resulting from comfort zones lead to excuses and the tendency to blame everyone or everything but yourself.

If you are frustrated by the inability to find peace of mind in your pursuit of purpose, it is important to remember the words of Thomas Edison. He said, *"Many of life's failures are men who did not realize how close they were to success when they give up."* Reading this book is a step in the right direction. This means that you are on the path to achieving success in your pursuit of purpose. Along the way, do not become confused about the dangers of comfort zones. *"For at the proper time you will reap a harvest if you do not gave up."*

**Confusion**

We are almost finish exposing the myths surrounding comfort zones. Remember that the true needs of the heart always point in the direction of fulfilling your purpose and releasing your potential. Contrarily, comfort zones always promote what is convenient, easy, popular, or is politically correct. Prevalent societal views tend to also add to the misunderstanding surrounding the effects and dangers of comfort zones. Society promotes making decisions that will either make you "feel good," or result in more money. There is nothing wrong with legitimately obtaining the finer things in life. However, you don't have to sacrifice your purpose to get them.

Have you ever read an article or seen a television report on a famous person who became an alcoholic or a drug addict, or who committed suicide? What prompts a person to waste their life even though they seemingly have the best things that life offers? Perhaps, the answer can be traced back to the persistent needs of the heart that are unfulfilled. Ultimately, I believe that confusion smothers the joy of having material wealth without a sense of purpose.

Confusion occurs when people, places or things cannot replace the void created by pursuing the wrong path in life. Additionally, confusion sets in when the heart wants something more than what has already been achieved. Unfortunately, the end-result of this problem is a stagnant mind and life. Your future is too great to let confusion stagnate your life and dreams. *"For God is not the author of confusion, but of peace..."* Is it better to have peace of mind or confusion?

**Stagnation**

Stagnation is the last negative effect of comfort zones. Remember that it only takes one symptom to cause your life to become stagnant. Don't let your guard down. Stagnation is subtle but powerful. It will eventually lead to a mental pit of despair. Leonardo da Vinci once said, *"Iron rusts from disuse; water loses it purity from stagnation...even so does inaction sap the vigor of the mind."*

> **Comfort zones freeze potential. Potential is maximized when your comfort zone thaws.**

Leonardo achieved tremendous success during and after his lifetime. Based on his words, inaction was not an option related to his career pursuit. Perhaps, the reason he made the comment was because stagnation contradicts the principles surrounding potential, purpose, time, and seasons. Time and seasons produce change which is necessary for continual growth and development.

Inevitably, if you are experiencing periods of stagnation, then moments of despair are not far away. I encourage you to *"work hard so you can present yourself to God and receive his approval. Be a good worker, one who does not need to be ashamed..."* Remember that your work or assignment is your purpose in life. At some point, if you let comfort zones stop you from releasing your full potential, then the pit of despair is a realistic landing spot.

## Pit of Despair

Although we have discussed each negative symptom of comfort zones, we are not in the clear. Why? If allowed, each symptom can independently or collectively cause you to spiral down into a pit of despair. Based on the knowledge that you have acquired from reading this book; how would you define a pit of despair regarding your purpose and potential? Take a few moments to think about your answer.

Unfortunately, the pit of despair is the unintended landing spot for those suffering from the negative effects of comfort zones. Comfort zones and the negative symptoms that follow cause you to see life from the wrong perspective. At this stage, I hope you accept the fact that comfort zones are not mentally, emotionally, or physically healthy, if your stay is protracted. Eventually, they will cause the mind to see challenges as huge obstacles that are invincible or impossible to overcome.

When mountains in your life seem too high to overcome, the onslaught of hopeless thoughts and an attitude of defeat are not far behind. Entertaining these negative thoughts will lead to inaction in your life because the pessimistic attitude robs you of faith. For this reason, I believe that Lord Alfred Tennyson stated, *"I must lose myself in action, lest I wither in despair."*

## How to Defeat the Feeling of Despair

Previously, I shared quotes from Roy T. Bennett. Bennett rose to political influence in Zimbabwe after experiencing tremendous obstacles and disappointments. In his latter years, he faced harassment, economic hardship, and prison. Nevertheless, he loved sharing positive and motivational messages to inspire individuals to rise above their circumstances. He also possessed a keen awareness of the power of potential and the pitfalls associated with comfort zones. Listen to this advice once spoken by Bennett, *"Step out of your comfort zone. Comfort zones, where your unrealized dreams are buried, are the enemies of achievement. Leadership begins when you step outside your comfort zone."*

It is encouraging to know that he did not fall into a pit of despair when his farm was seized by the government without proper compensation. That unjustifiable event caused his life to change drastically overnight. Instantly, his economic status and comfort level went from stable to unstable. How did he survive the harsh reality of losing his source of income through unprovoked and unfair means? Perhaps, Bennett answered the question when he stated, *"You need to have faith in yourself. Be brave and take risks. You don't have to have it all figured out to move forward."*

His experience is an example of the importance of believing that *"...God causes everything to work together for the good of those who love God and are called according to his purpose for them."* God called you to do a great and important work during your lifetime. Therefore, you have the assurance of knowing that everything will work out in the end. I realize that you may not be able to see the end at this point, but trust God. *"Every word of God proves true. He is a shield to all who come to him for protection."* Bennet's success in overcoming tremendous obstacles is a testament to the power of faith.

If you have fallen into a pit of despair or suffer from the effects of comfort zones, then I encourage you to believe that a brighter future is possible. Your released potential can pull you out of your moment of despair and cure the symptoms of comfort zones at the same time. The healing process begins when you point your faith in the direction towards fulfilling your purpose in life. Along with the application of faith, you will need to take the appropriate action.

Do you remember the truthful advice spoken by Thomas Jefferson, *"Do you want to know who you are? Don't ask. Act! Action will delineate and define you?"* Taking action also means that you are persistent. According to Napoleon Hill, *"The majority of men meet with failure because of their lack of persistence in creating new plans to take the place of those which fail."*

## Tools to Defeat Comfort Zones

*"Therefore, prepare your mind for action; and exercise self-control."* Jefferson's comment that action will define you is understandable, because your potential and purpose are already on the inside. When you release your

potential, you are introducing the world to who you are. Taking the right action also leads to healing your internal voids and overcoming moments of despair.

Faith is an effective tool in defeating the effects of comfort zones. One of the other tools that you will need is perseverance. When you persevere, it signifies your maturity and passion to live a purpose driven life. Perseverance is also a sign that you have positive and healthy thoughts regarding the possibility of achieving a successful outcome.

In addition to action, faith, perseverance and positive thinking, there is another essential comfort zone fighting tool. The final tool that you should use to offset the effects of despair is positive speaking. The ability to speak positively during challenging circumstances is hard, but therapeutic if you believe what you say. Positive speaking reinforces an optimistic attitude which is needed to climb out of despair. Let's go back to the words of Roy T. Bennett for wisdom. Bennett once stated, *"Don't be pushed around by the fears in your mind. Be led by the dreams in your heart."*

His comments suggest that it is counterproductive to let fear and the feeling of despair ruin your life. Your dreams are glimpses of your predestined future. That is why suffocating the cry of your heart because of fear is counterproductive. When you walk by faith and not sight, persevere, think positive and actively engage in pursuing your purpose, then positive speaking becomes second nature. This is true because what comes out of your mouth is what you already see through the window of your heart. I encourage you to make a mental picture of the chart shown below:

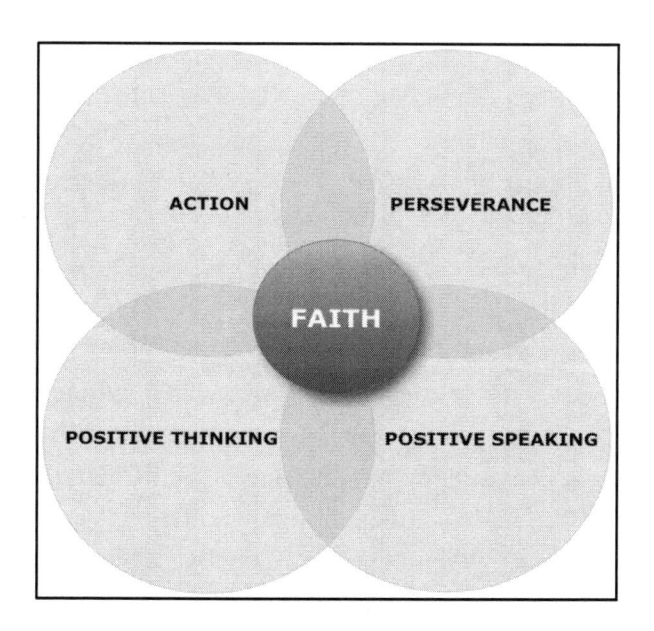

## Tools for Defeating Despair Chart

*[Diagram: Four overlapping circles labeled ACTION, PERSEVERANCE, POSITIVE THINKING, POSITIVE SPEAKING, with FAITH at the center]*

In my opinion, one of the greatest examples of defeating comfort zones in found in the Bible. Jesus Christ's experience in the Garden of Gethsemane epitomized the correct approach to defeating comfort zones. Being fully aware of what was to come, he desired to avoid the pain, humiliation, suffering and death. His agonizing plea was, *"My soul is overwhelmed with sorrow to the point of death."*

He spoke those words to his disciples, went away, fell on the ground and prayed, *"My Father, if it is possible, may this cup be taken away from me Yet, not as I will but as you will."* Afterwards, he went back to check on his disciples before returning a second time to pray. On the second occasion, he prayed *"My Father, if it is not possible for this cup to be taken away unless I drink it, may your will be done."*

It is very important to note that Jesus had a choice regarding his future. His choice was either die for the sins of the world or turn his back and walk away. Thankfully, he chose to act upon his purpose. In doing so, he had to persevere through the agony, think positively when confronted with despair and speak positively about the will of God. Jesus chose the right option according to his divine purpose, even though it took him down a painful and difficult path. However, the end result of his pursuit of purpose was the reconciliation of mankind back to God. Have you ever thought about the end result of your pursuit of purpose?

Overall, it is better to avoid comfort zones rather than attempt to recover from despair. When applied collectively, the tools in the chart can cure the effects of comfort zones. As noted, faith is the primary foundational tool; however, your faith needs ACTION. Being proactive about releasing your potential and pursuing your purpose is imperative. How can you change your circumstances without some sort of action, whether mental, physical, or spiritual? The conclusion is that you must respond and act in the way that supports your purpose.

Approaching decisions from the right perspective will ensure that you are not motivated to pursue the path of comfort zones. Again, I would encourage you to not believe the hype surrounding comfort zones. Traveling down the wrong path can cause more harm than you initially realize. Since comfort zones stop or prevent you from maximizing your full potential, then they are also stumbling blocks that prevent self-actualization.

## The Path to Self-Actualization

Unfortunately, it is possible for you to live a long life, but never find a way to discover or expose the real you. *How is it possible to live the wrong life?* It happens when your actions are dictated by comfort zones instead of being governed by your purpose for living. Since change is an expected process of purpose, making decisions that challenge the status quo is required. Comfort zones cause you to settle for the status quo instead of challenging it. Therefore, comfort zones are serious threats to self-actualization because they prevent the hidden person from being fully revealed. Action is the opposite of comfort zones. It is needed to move you towards manifesting self. Your decisions hold the key to making this happen.

It is also important to realize that developing a life strategy that centers on exposing self is advantageous when faced with making life decisions. A life strategy also helps you live a focused, intentional, and fruitful life. Did you know that focused and intentional decisions are the foundation for a purposeful life strategy? When you choose the focused and intentional path, then it is possible to evade comfort zones while moving in the direction of self-actualization. <u>Self-actualization is not an accident, but the result of an effective and methodical approach to life that results in the maximization of your potential.</u> The chart below identifies this approach:

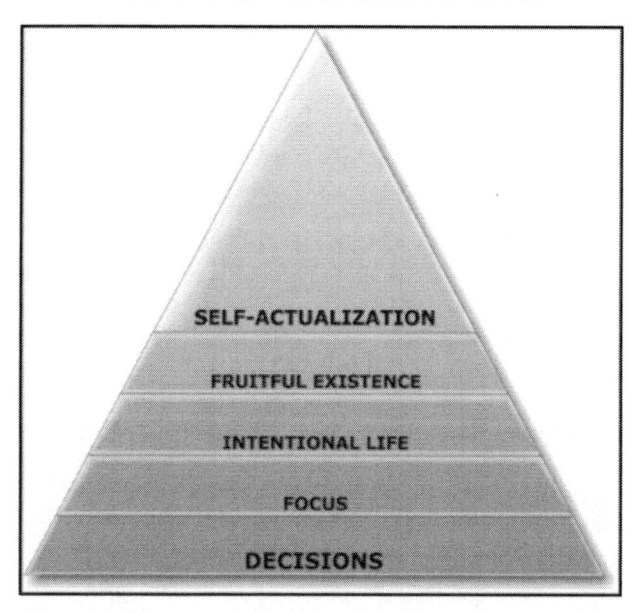

## Path to Self-Actualization Chart

*(Pyramid chart with levels from bottom to top: DECISIONS, FOCUS, INTENTIONAL LIFE, FRUITFUL EXISTENCE, SELF-ACTUALIZATION)*

## Decisions

*"The greatest danger for most of us lies not in setting our aim too high and falling short, but in setting our aim too low, and achieving our mark,"*

according to Michelangelo. Re-read that quote and think about your goals and accomplishments. Be mindful that comfort zones appear as viable options when you set your aim too low. Your decisions can lead you in the direction of either self-actualization or comfort zones and the pit of despair. At this point, you now realize that decisions hold the key to discovering self, releasing your potential, and fulfilling your purpose in life.

Therefore, making the right decisions is critical to living a successful life. Again, going back to the insightful words spoken by Roy Bennett, *"You are not the victim of the world, but rather the master of your own destiny. It is your choices and decisions that determine your destiny."* I agree with his conclusion because decisions precede every action that you take or neglect to take. I also agree with these words spoken by Amelia Earhart, *"The most difficult thing is the decision to act, the rest is merely tenacity. The fears are paper tigers. You can do anything you decide to do. You can act to change and control your life; and the procedure, the process is its own reward."* The key is to remain focused with your heart fixed on releasing your potential while fulfilling your purpose.

**Focus**

*"The secret of change is to focus all your energy, not on fighting the old, but building the new."* That observation from Socrates is still true. If you spend your energy dwelling on the past decisions that led you down the wrong path, then it leads to pessimism, depression, and doubt. On the contrary, if you focus your energy on moving in the right direction, then the decision will lead to self-actualization and contentment.

What is the starting point for self-actualization? Wait, don't answer the question, pause for a moment and think about your response. Based on previous experience, I believe that the path to self-actualization starts with the decision to live a focused life. Did you come to the same conclusion? This is important because the path to self-actualization requires that your focus is narrow, clear and set on a mark. Following a narrow path in life means that you understand the importance of making key decisions based on your potential and purpose for living. Having clarity of thought and a vision adds to your ability to stay focused. When this happens, you can see the mark, which is your destination or destiny clearly.

*"People think focus means saying yes to the things you've got to focus on. But that's not what it means at all. It is saying no to the hundred other good ideas that there are. You have to pick carefully."* That analysis from Steve Jobs is enlightening. Perhaps, he made that statement because you must be certain about your purpose and not be inclined to deviate from the designated path. When you agree to pursue your purpose, you are on a mission. Your destination in life must be clear if you want to stay on the narrow path that leads to fulfillment. Additionally, if you want to hit the right mark, then you must be deliberate and intentional during the decision-making process.

**Intentional Life**

Living an intentional life is a good principle to live by. There are many distractions that come to get you off track. It is good to know that when you combine the willingness to remain focused with clarity of purpose, then it means that you are committed to living an intentional life. Living an intentional life suggests that you base key life choices on whether the decision will allow you to release your potential and fulfill your purpose. John Maxwell articulated this point in his statement, *"An unintentional life accepts everything and does nothing. An intentional life embraces only the things that will add to the mission of significance."*

Maxwell's statement is brief but correct. Living an intentional life means that you are focused on embracing the things that add to your purpose and self-worth. Deciding that you will be a person of value and worth starts with choosing to believe that it will happen. Your potential ensures that you have the capacity to live a fruitful and productive life, but the choice is yours.

## Fruitful Existence

You have arrived at a critical juncture in understanding vital aspects about self-actualization. I commend you for continuing to read. Self-actualization and comfort zones are mutually exclusive, as you can only have one or the other. Therefore, you cannot reach the self-actualization pinnacle if you entertain comfort zones.

At this point, have I persuaded you to believe that comfort zones impede your decision to pursue purpose and hinder the release of your full potential? Now, it is important to realize that your decisions must position you to have a fruitful existence on a continual basis. A fruitful existence means that you are allowing your potential to flourish and produce significant results. The nature of comfort zones suggests that it is more reasonable and comfortable to place limits on yourself. Maximizing your potential on the path of purpose is the alternative to placing limitations on your accomplishments.

The objective is for you to stay at the top of the self-actualization pinnacle. For this to happen, you will need additional information on getting to the summit point of self-actualization and remaining in that position. Making the right decisions regarding your potential and purpose is essential to successful living. Self-actualization does not happen overnight. You achieve this level by having knowledge about yourself and the wisdom to process information correctly. Stay with me, please continue reading, good job thus far. You are on the verge of becoming a self-actualizer. Are you excited?

## THE NEXT STEP

This chapter emphasized the dangers of comfort zones. As you learned, comfort zones are not comfortable when the heart cries to release its hidden potential and your destiny yearns for the call of purpose. Hopefully, this information will help you avoid the pit of despair and the onslaught of negative effects. Nevertheless. if you have fallen in the pit or if you are suffering from the effects of comfort zones, then remember the earlier quote from Roy T. Bennett. As you know, he said, *"Don't be pushed around by the fears in your mind. Be led by the dreams in your heart."*

When you are led by your TAGs, dreams, and needs of the heart, then finding your path of purpose is made easier. In the next chapter you will receive additional information about making the right purposeful decisions and using wisdom to assist you in choosing the right path in life. Your future is calling you towards a path that leads to your greatness and personal satisfaction. Do you believe that the world awaits the wonder of your TAGs? If so, join me as we discuss how to use wisdom to chart your course of destiny. Along the way, remember these words spoken by George Bernard Shaw, *"We are made wise not by the recollection of our past, but by the responsibility for our future."*

> **Quick reference to comfort zones impact your potential & purpose principles:**

1. The precursor to every comfort zone is a thought that directs your actions and responses to situations.
2. Comfort zones place boundaries on personal and corporate advancement.
3. Comfort zones cause you to choose the wrong career path and prevent you from moving to a place of contentment.
4. Comfort zones alter purpose and block potential.
5. Comfort zones hold dreams and desires of the heart in captivity.
6. Comfort zones breed excuses for why you can't, shouldn't and won't make the decision to pursue the correct path in life.
7. Comfort zones lead you down a path of discontentment, unfulfillment and uncertainty.
8. Comfort zones alter your sense of self-worth and minimizes the importance of the things you desire to accomplish in life.
9. Comfort zones convince you to believe that time is endless.
10. Comfort zones alter life's priorities and create a false sense of security.
11. Comfort zones promote internal voids and inaction.
12. Comfort zones impact your ability to make the right decision at the right time.
13. Comfort zones produce temporary results, solutions, and a false sense of satisfaction.
14. Comfort zones create a false sense of security and minimizes the importance of maximizing your potential.
15. Comfort zones may cause you to make the wrong decision or no decision but never the right decision.
16. Comfort zones create false perceptions that attract negative symptoms.

17. The pit of despair is the unintended landing spot for those suffering from the effects of comfort zones.
18. Comfort zones freeze potential. Potential is maximized when your comfort zone thaws.
19. Comfort zones are not comfortable when the heart cries to release its hidden potential and your destiny yearns for the call of purpose.

# Chapter Nine

## Wisdom And The Mind

> *"Blessed are those who listen to me,*
> *watching daily at my doors,*
> *waiting at my doorway."*
> **King Solomon**

As usual, Richard's countenance glowed with an air of leadership and discipline. Confidence and quick decision-making came natural to this former decorated veteran of the US Marine Corps. Prior to his vacation, he informed his childhood friend and neighbor that he would be in his city for a few days. Excited about the opportunity to spend time together and reminisce about the early years, the men committed to meeting each other.

When Richard arrived at the meeting, he met Dan who was eagerly waiting to receive updates on his life and family. After several minutes of jovial conversation, it became apparent to Dan that this meeting was a planned encounter to discuss a serious issue related to purpose, potential and self-manifestation. For several weeks, Richard was wrestling with making a major life decision that would require significant short-term adjustments to his current lifestyle.

In Richard's current position as a successful corporate executive, things were going extremely well. On a consistent basis, he exceeded his revenue projections and provided exceptional service to his valued customer base. His first words about his current job were, *"Man, things are working out really well on the job. I like what am doing."* He went on to say, *"But I have an opportunity to pursue my passion. I need to make a firm commitment in 30 days whether to pursue it or not."*

Several weeks prior, Richard decided to start the process of completing the final educational requirements to obtain his certification in a completely different field of interest. The new career path seemed to match his natural potential and purpose for living, more so than his current job. Additionally, it would allow him to do something that he loves on a full-time basis.

As Richard carefully articulated the situation to Dan, he vacillated about leaving his current job. Therein was his dilemma, the stress of which option to select was creating a significant level of anxiety and uncertainty. The weight of the situation was starting to impact him and his family. He questioned, *"Should I choose the corporate option with great pay and benefits or choose my passion which comes with no guaranteed income or benefits?"* He went on to say, *"Mind you, I enjoy my job, working with my clients and employees. I love serving others."*

Based on previous knowledge, he realized that Dan's wisdom and input could help in confirming which direction to take. Dan listened attentively with vivid recollections of the former years admiring Richard's military bearing, commanding presence, and strong character. Serving his country and people was a cherished privilege that he still reflects on.

Honored that he would choose to share his secret struggle for clear direction, Dan looked into Richard's eyes and drilled him in rapid succession. *"Have you defined your self-identity? Where is your passion taking you? Why are you seeking to pursue this direction in life? What are you seeking to accomplish by selecting this option?"*

Richard replied, *"I can't answer those questions right now. I don't know, but it is something that I feel strongly about. Honestly speaking, I don't know where it will lead me."* Making the decision even harder, he disclosed with a sense of uncertainty that, *"I was asked to take on a new and rewarding assignment with my company, but I am stalling because I feel as though I should be pursuing this other direction."*

*Wisdom and the Mind*

For Richard, the new career path represented much more than a basic job. With excitement, he revealed that, *"It is a part of my legacy, as my grandfather and father pursued similar paths."* He felt a sense of obligation to pursue the change in career direction and guilty for earning a good income doing something else. The situation made him feel as though he was sacrificing his true purpose in life for financial reasons. His heart was crying for relief.

Dan understood his dilemma and desire to select the right option. He proceeded to offer words of wisdom. After receiving the advice, Richard exclaimed, *"I feel like the weight of the world has been lifted off of my shoulder."* What advice do you think Dan gave him? Did he recommend Option #1, the great corporate job that Richard enjoyed or Option #2, pursing the passion of his heart and extending the family legacy? We will re-address the outcome of Richard's decision at a later point in this chapter.

> **W**isdom reveals the right path to take according to your purpose in life.

## Understanding Wisdom

Merriam-Webster's online dictionary provides a comprehensive definition of wisdom. It defines wisdom as *"knowledge, and the capacity to make due use of it; knowledge of the best ends and the best means; discernment and judgment; discretion; sagacity; skill; dexterity."*[32] In other words, wisdom is the application of knowledge that produces the right result. It is important to recognize that knowledge about something does not make you wise. You can have several college degrees, but you still lack wisdom in making personal, professional and career decisions.

Another simplistic meaning of wisdom is possessing the right understanding and knowledge that leads to the recipient making the right judgment or decision. This knowledge also gives some the uncommon ability and skill to produce outcomes previously unseen, undone, or unknown. When you focus on Webster's dictionary use of the phrases *"best ends and the best means,"* then you can distinguish the difference between having wisdom and basic knowledge. The best ends and the best means concept relate to using wisdom to select the best option based on the best resources at your disposal.

While living in the Bahamas, I enjoyed spending time snorkeling and seeing the many beautiful tropical fishes. One day, the thought entered my mind to acquire a 50-gallon fish tank and a small net to catch fish for the tank. Additionally, I spent several hundred dollars buying the accessories for the tank such as filters, pumps, buckets, and lights. Realizing that I would also need a sturdy cabinet for the heavy tank, I decided to build a special cabinet from scratch. In total, the entire project was expensive and very time consuming.

The saltwater fish tank project took a lot more effort than I had anticipated. Nevertheless, I did not mind because I had visions of having a beautiful aquarium filled with a stunning array of hand caught tropical fishes and other sea life. After spending several weeks constructing the cabinet and setting up the tank, the day finally arrived to start filling the tank with water. I made three visits to the beach with 5-gallon buckets. I filled the tank with fresh saltwater. Over the next two weekends, the kids and I collected rocks, sand, caught a variety of small reef fishes, two lobsters, a sea anemone, and starfishes.

The beauty of the finished tank was beyond my expectation. It was an amazing exhibit of reef life that transformed the ambiance of our home. Everything was convenient. When I needed to add more water to the tank, I traveled to the beach, which was a minute away from the house. When we wanted to add more sea life, we went snorkeling and caught it. After two months, my beautiful and diverse array of species started to die off. One by one, everything in the tank died. We replenished the tank, but everything continued to die shortly thereafter.

I had a good idea, basic knowledge, understanding and plenty of motivation, but I lacked wisdom. Instead of changing all the water at a time, I was refilling the tank to top it off as the water evaporated. This process created a toxic chemical imbalance that prevented my tank from sustaining life. When I discovered my error, I fixed the problem, but it was too late. I could not recreate the same array of sea life that made it special.

> **Having basic knowledge about something does not mean that you possess wisdom.**

Based on my life experiences, I realize that having knowledge or information does not make you wise. How you use that information or knowledge makes you wise. A wise person possesses the right knowledge that creates the best outcome. A wise person also uses the best means to produce the right outcomes. For these reasons and others, wisdom is a tremendous asset to have in life, as it gives you the ability to make the right decisions.

## Wisdom is Valuable

Richard's dilemma is an example of the importance of allowing wisdom to direct your decisions in life. He revealed that his passion in life is serving others. After his military tenure, he enrolled into a prestigious university and graduated with several degrees. Eventually, he became a pastor and leader of a local church. The decision to become a full-time local pastor was a good decision, but it was not the right long-term fit for him. After several years of mentoring and training a great team of ministers, he resigned and took a position in corporate America and continued ministry on a part-time basis.

Both, his grandfather, and father served in the ministry as pastors. Having already served as a pastor, he now feels a strong urge in his heart to pursue the path of counseling. Recently, he was accepted into a residency program to finalize his counseling credentials. Choosing this option would require complete dedication, which means that he would have to leave his current job.

After hearing these details, Dan became aware of the core issues preventing Richard from seeing the correct path to take. The issues preventing him from seeing the correct path to take included pressure to follow the path of his role models, a lack of understanding about his purpose and a lack of clarity about his destination. As you recall, Richard could not definitively answer the questions related to clearly defining his future path or desired destination. In other words, he did not have a clear vision for his life, only recognition of his TAGs.

Hopefully, information contained in this chapter will help you make the right decision regarding your pursuit of purpose. Albeit, it is important to note what Christian theologian, J.I. Packer said, *"Wisdom is the power to see and the inclination to choose the best and highest goal, together with the surest means of obtaining it."* Knowing what you would like to accomplish but not knowing how, is part of the struggle with defining self and pursuing purpose. Be mindful that wisdom gives you the ability to choose the correct path to take and the best means to accomplish the objective.

> **W**isdom is a powerful source that helps you choose your goal and obtain it.

Jan Ernst Matzeliger was an immigrant that migrated to America seeking a better life. Originally, from Suriname, he was of Dutch and Surinamese decent. In 1873, life for a young brown-skinned immigrant that spoke very little English was extremely difficult. With the help of others from the African American community, he was able to find work as a cobbler, which is a person that repairs, or mends shoes. Eventually, he moved on to working as an apprentice in a shoe factory. From the beginning, he enjoyed his new job and spent considerable time independently learning the entire process of making shoes.

Naturally mechanically inclined, Matzeliger began a quest to create a mechanical solution to the manual process of attaching the sole to the upper shoe part. At that time, sewing machines were used to create the upper part that was attached to the sole by individuals known as "hand lasters." The most skilled hand lasters could attach up to 50 soles during an average workday. As a visionary leader, Matzeliger believed that a mechanized process would greatly improve the production of shoes.

In addition to industry experience, Matzeliger studied books on physics and mechanical science to gain knowledge. Against all odds, he used his skills, knowledge, and experience to create a model of the first machine to connect the upper shoe to the sole. After successfully securing a patent from the United States Patent Office, he continued his project and later developed a working machine. Matzeliger refined his machine until it was able to produce up to 700 pairs of shoes per day.[33]

His invention increased production and lowered the price of shoes. A young man from humble beginnings changed the lives of millions worldwide. He did something that no one else could do and created something no one else could create. Matzeliger's successful story embodies the definition and application of wisdom. His wisdom added unbelievable value to his potential and purpose in life. Do you recall the definition of wisdom which states that it is *"knowledge, and the capacity to make due use of it?"*

Why is wisdom valuable? It is valuable because it provides information, answers, solutions, and the best course of action for your complex life issues? Additionally, is wisdom valuable because it gives you the ability to think creatively, find undiscovered options and see the "impossible or unknown?" As you may have realized, your natural potential is obvious and easily recognizable, but matching your potential with your purpose may prove to be challenging. Having knowledge about your potential and purpose in life does not guarantee that you will be able to make the right decisions at the right time and for the right reasons. Wisdom is the key to this dilemma.

> **W**isdom suggests the best course of action during the decision-making process.

Now that you have additional information about the decision-making capabilities of wisdom, let's return to the introduction story. Richard realized that wisdom was the solution to his dilemma. He wanted to make the right decision at the right time in his life. For that reason, he was eager to receive input from Dan.

Previously, the question was asked whether you believe that Dan recommended pursuing Option #1, the great corporate job or Option #2, the family legacy. While both seemed to be good options, Dan encouraged Richard to focus on clarifying his purpose in life. Richard did not have a clear vision; he was unable to answer why it was necessary to pursue the educational opportunity and he did not know if the new career path would ensure his peace of mind.

In consideration of these points, Dan said, *"I would encourage you to spend quality time thinking about your purpose in life before making a significant life change."* He continued, *"Richard, you were a pastor of a church and left because it didn't seem like the right assignment. Let's make sure that the new path is right for you before you follow it."* Richard's response was, "I have some work to do, man I feel like the weight of the world has been lifted off of my shoulders."

This situation is a dilemma that many people encounter during their lifetime. The question is whether to choose to do what is good or choose to do what is right. Could it be that "good" choices are significate hinderances to identifying and selecting the "right" choices? Finding the right path tends to present the greatest challenges and obstacles which leads many to choosing the good path.

Richard was leaning towards selecting the option to pursue a new career path which appeared to be the good path. However, after discussing this matter with Dan, he concluded that the right decision was to stay on his current career path. It is still possible that he may choose, at some point, to pursue the new career direction. However, the timing or season was not right at that moment. Therefore, the issue was causing him major anxiety and uncertainty. Richard's encounter is an example of how valuable wisdom is in the decision-making process regarding your purpose.

We have reviewed two examples related to the application of wisdom. Richard used the wisdom of Dan to help him identify the right path. Matzeliger used wisdom to invent a machine to solve a problem. In both cases, the underlining factors that each had to understand were the necessity of making right decisions, releasing potential, the season of purpose, and the importance of a clear vision in life. Wisdom was the link that merged everything together for them.

The knowledge and understanding that you receive from wisdom adds tremendous value to your life. It also gives you exciting information about your vision, potential and purpose. The information comes to assist you in making the right decisions at the right time. The following chart highlights the main areas to target when applying wisdom for the purpose of self-discovery and self-actualization:

## Wisdom Chart

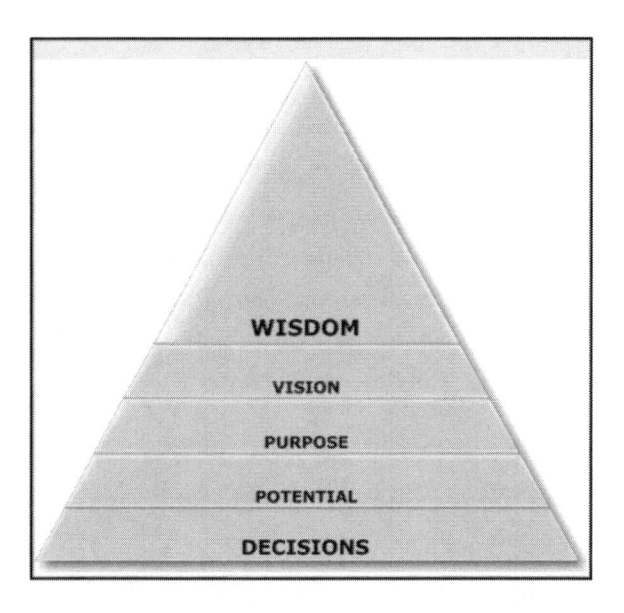

*Pyramid chart with levels from top to bottom: WISDOM, VISION, PURPOSE, POTENTIAL, DECISIONS*

## Interpreting the Wisdom Chart

The chart suggests that wisdom is key to discovering and applying vital information necessary to reach the pinnacle level of self-actualization. This is true because wisdom penetrates your thoughts and assist you in the following ways:

- Wisdom provides information and shows you how to develop a vision for your life.
- Wisdom provides information about the right path of purpose for your life. It assists you in developing the right course of action to fulfill your purpose for living.
- Wisdom assists you in creating the right environment and opportunities for you to maximize your potential.
- Wisdom assists in the decision-making process by providing you with information about the right option to take based on the situation.

In consideration of these points, it is clear to see that wisdom is the most comprehensive source of direction at your disposal to assist you in living a successful and fruitful life. Navigating through the maze of options to find the path of purpose requires information, knowledge, and direction. When a word of wisdom enters your thoughts, it provides the right answers in life.

*"Wisdom is the principal thing; Therefore get wisdom. And in all your getting, get understanding."* Wisdom is the most important component in the decision-making process, but understanding is necessary as well. Are you beginning to recognize how important your life is and the tremendous value of your potential? Wisdom helps you discover and appreciate your area of personal leadership. In other words, when you get wisdom, you acquire the right information, understanding and the best application of your personal leadership ability.

## How to Obtain Wisdom

Let's revisit on the philosophy of Aristotle as we initiate our response to the question of how to obtain wisdom. Starting with this important point, remember that he said, *"Knowing yourself is the beginning of all wisdom."* As you are fully aware, we have discussed potential, purpose, and self-actualization in detail. Is it safe to say that at this stage, you have a much better understanding and more knowledge about yourself? If you agree, then the process of obtaining wisdom has already begun for you.

Moving on, Socrates said, *"Wisdom begins in wonder."* Curiosity is a definition for wonder and an important element in the process of receiving wisdom. Are you curious to know if your future is as valuable as alluded to in this book? Are you eager to explore the realms of maximized potential and a purpose filled life? If so, then additional wisdom regarding living a successful life is knocking at your doorstep.

Now let's look at the question of obtaining wisdom from a contemporary and a traditional perspective. It is common knowledge that you can obtain wisdom from receiving knowledge from others. Likewise, you can obtain wisdom from personal experiences. You can also obtain wisdom through spiritual revelation. Irrespective of the method used, remember that wisdom is accessible to young, old, rich, and poor, as nobody is disqualified from receiving it.

## Wisdom Acquired From The Creator

Although wisdom is not common, it is available to everyone. God holds the secret to your purpose and the wisdom you need to manifest it. *"If any of you lacks wisdom, you should ask God who gives generously to all without finding fault, and it will be given you."* When you receive wisdom from God, you gain access to information, ideas, solutions, and answers that were previously unknown.

Additionally, there are five important facts you should know about the wisdom you receive from God, as His wisdom differs from wisdom acquired through natural experiences. Firstly, God's wisdom gives you uncommon information or knowledge that allows you to perceive a solution that previously seemed impossible. Secondly, God's wisdom gives you knowledge that was previously unknown by you and others. Thirdly, God's wisdom reveals the original intent, correct usages, or best solutions to remedy any problem. Fourthly, God's wisdom provides answers to the most difficult questions about your self-identity, purpose, and destiny in life. Lastly, God's wisdom is the most valuable free and non-tangible resource available to everyone. Furthermore, the information that you receive from Him is always right.

> **W**isdom is the most valuable free and non-tangible personal resource.

God is a primary source for obtaining wisdom. *"For the LORD grants wisdom! From his mouth come knowledge and understanding."* When you acquire wisdom, *"you position yourself for long life, riches and honor."*

Additionally, wisdom is the key to finding the right path which is pleasing God. *"For whoever finds me finds life and receives favor from the LORD."* The statement *"whoever finds me"* is referring to wisdom. Wisdom from God helps you discover the life that He intends for you to live. Guess What? When you find His will for your life, He also promises to bestow favor on your plans, dreams, and desires of the heart.

> **W**isdom from God helps in the interpretation of dreams.

As a young teenager, Joseph's brother sold him into slavery because of jealousy. His unwarranted journey ended in Egypt as a domestic slave. Over time, another unfortunate event occurred, and he was unfairly sent to prison for a crime that he did not commit. One day, he overheard two of Pharaoh's officials discussing their individual dreams. Both men, the cupbearer and baker, were serving time in prison for upsetting Pharaoh, the king of Egypt.

Joseph possessed wisdom from God and was able to provide an accurate interpretation of both dreams. Eventually, the cupbearer was released and returned to serve in Pharaoh's court. Over time, Pharaoh had a disturbing dream that none of his officials could interpret. At that point, the cupbearer remembered Joseph and mentioned him to the Pharaoh.

Pharaoh sent word to the dungeon to have Joseph appear before him. He said to Joseph, *"I had a dream, and no one can interpret it. But I have heard it said of you that when you hear a dream you can interpret it."* Sure enough, with God's wisdom, Joseph interpretation of the dream pleased Pharaoh to the extent that he elevated him to second in command over Egypt. Wisdom promoted Joseph from the dark dungeon and elevated him to the highest leadership position under the king. Do you have a hunger for wisdom?

## Crave Wisdom

Socrates also stated, *"When you want wisdom and insight as badly as you want to breathe, it is then you shall have it."* Accordingly, if you truly wonder about your purpose in life, then wisdom will open the door to understanding. If you wonder about what career choice to pursue, then wisdom will enlighten your path. If you want to understand who you are and what you can accomplish in life, then wisdom will point you in the right direction.

Be encouraged by these words also spoken by Dr. Ben Carson, *"I actually don't think that I'm that much smarter than anybody else. It's just that I frequently just seem to know what to do, and I think that's wisdom."* Your mind holds the key to either opening the wisdom door or closing it. In this regard, having the right mindset is necessary to ensure that wisdom makes a positive difference in your life.

## The Mind

Contrary to popular belief, the prosperous diamond mines and significant oil reserves found around the world are not the greatest natural resources or wealthiest places on earth. The greatest natural resource and wealth is living inside of you. What is the resource and wealth? The resource is your mind. The wealth is the path of purpose and potential stored in your mind. Unfortunately, **whoever or whatever controls your mind also controls the natural resource and wealth contained in your purpose and potential.**

Alcmaeon of Croton was an Ancient Greek medical scholar that lived around 6th century B.C. Against popular belief, he was the first to theorize that the brain is the most complex human organ, home of intellect and the mind, also known as the "heart." According to Merriam-Webster online dictionary, the mind is *"the element or complex of elements in an individual that feels, perceives, thinks, wills, and especially reasons."*[34] When you consider this definition, it is possible to conclude that Alcmaeon was the first to make the connection that the mind possesses a key to discovering the meaning of self and self-actualization.

Scientific and medical communities both agree that the mind is the internal faculty that formulates thoughts and processes information. Therefore, it is reasonable to also conclude that the mind is the home of your purpose and potential. Another way to look at this issue is to say that the mind holds the answers to who you are, why you are here, what you can do and where you are going in life. This means that what you become and what you do in life is initiated by what you perceive in your mind first.

*"You are who you are and what you are because of what has gone into your mind. You can change who you are and what you are by changing what goes into your mind."* I concur with this conclusion made by Zig Ziglar. Where is the information coming from that's going into your mind about your purpose and potential? Granted, it is true that certain thoughts are influenced by your culture, heritage, social environment or will. However, the mind possesses the power of choice and a conscience.

*"In the long run, we shape our lives, and we shape ourselves. The process never ends until we die. And the choices we make are ultimately our own responsibility."* Therefore, at the end of the day, you are responsible for your own actions, as Eleanor Roosevelt suggested when she made that statement. Since the mind controls how you handle your past, present and future, developing a process to ensure that it produces the right decisions is necessary.

*"A man's mind may be likened to a garden, which may be intelligently cultivated or allowed to run wild; but whether cultivated or neglected, it must, and will, bring forth. If no useful seeds are put into it, then an abundance of useless weed seeds will fall therein and will continue to produce their kind,"* according to James Allen. Often, the mind is inundated with thoughts, desires, memories, and emotions that impact your ability to identify the right direction in life. In addition, environmental and cultural influences tend to create

standards in life that become societal norms. Be mindful not to allow contrary thoughts to run wild and create weeds that block your path and progression.

Have you noticed that each day that you live, there is a battle waged for control over your mind? Since your thoughts control your emotions, attitude, actions, and decisions, it is essential that you control your thoughts by guarding what enters your mind. Are you able to distinguish between what is reality versus a temporary setback? Do you have weed seeds that have taken root and continue to sprout unwanted or unnecessary results in your life? If so, the LORD says, *"I will guide you along the best pathway for your life. I will advise you and watch over you."*

## Reality Thinking

A positive mind helps you maintain the right outlook on life and maximize your potential. One of the problems that tend to prevent individuals from having a positive mind is their outlook on the circumstances surrounding their life. In other words, some are confronted with reality, but they choose to live in denial or a fantasy. As a result, their thoughts about future endeavors are not reality based.

Reality thinking is the most productive approach to maximizing your full potential and living a purposeful life. In simple terms, reality thinking is the process of acknowledging the fact that you are loaded with tremendous value and success is your destiny in life. It also means that you do not seek to ignore key elements in your path that are evident. If you have major obstacles impeding your progression, then should you deny the challenge exists? Remember these words from Dr. Archibald Hart, *"Perhaps the greatest benefit of reality thinking as a habit is that it maximizes the likelihood that you will keep God in control."* In other words, there is no mountain, obstacle or stumbling block too great for God. With His help, you can do all things.

When you accept the reality of your situation, then you are ready to begin the process of overcoming the mental hindrances and opposition preventing you from achieving your goals. Accepting the reality of your situation does not mean that you do not have faith, it means that you see the mountain for what it is. In other words, if the hindrance is lack of confidence, then acknowledge it and develop a plan to defeat it. Remember that you are an overcomer with God's help. Stay prayerful and believe that He will see you through the challenge. As Roy Bennett said, *"The biggest wall you have to climb is the one you build in your mind: Never let your mind talk you out of your dreams, trick you into giving up. Never let your mind become the greatest obstacle to success. To get your mind on the right track, the rest will follow."*

> **W**isdom is the key to defeating the mental stumbling blocks preventing you from maximizing your potential and discovering your purpose.

Why is it necessary to have the right mindset and how do you get your mind on the right track? Let's go back to Socrates for a moment to answer the first question. He said, *"May the inward and outward man be as one."* A contradictory life ensues when your actions differ from the desires of the heart. Socrates' point suggests that living your best life occurs when your actions are a true reflection of the inner man. When your actions line up with your natural TAGs along your path of purpose, then you are destined for success.

Are you starting to connect the dots that a wise person must first take control over their mind? If you want to possess a healthy mind and get it on the right track, then you must be prepared to cleanse it from unhealthy thoughts and desires that contradict your purpose in life. It is also necessary that you renew your mind daily with the right information about yourself, as opposed to unproductive thoughts about yourself and the negative opinion of others. After you do this, then you are ready to fill your mind with the right knowledge and wisdom. Staying focused throughout the entire process will ensure your success. The chart below highlights the process that your mind must undertake to ensure that your thoughts line up with your purpose for living:

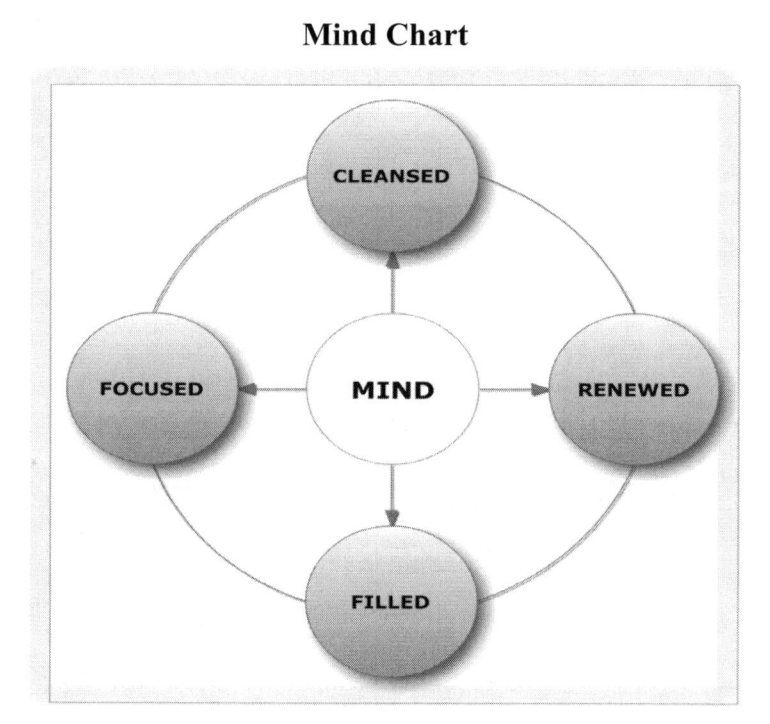

## Mind Chart

**Cleansed**

Let's look at this point from a reality perspective. Cleansing your mind does not mean that you will not have memories, it means that you have decided to purge your mind and block unwanted thoughts from taking root and becoming strongholds. Whenever a bad or negative thought enters your mind, you must convince yourself of the importance of stopping it immediately. Robert Schuller made an excellent point in this statement, *"It takes but one positive thought when given a chance to survive and thrive to overpower an enemy of negative thoughts."* When you overpower negative thoughts, you heal the mind and start a renewal process.

In fact, I encourage you to think about *"whatever is true, whatever is noble, whatever is right, whatever is pure, whatever is lovely, whatever is admirable-if anything is excellent or praiseworthy-think about such things."* Now, when you put this scripture in the context of thinking about your potential, purpose, and destiny in life, then you can clearly see that inundating your mind with these thoughts is healthy and very productive. Training your mind to think this way is a sign of wisdom and an awareness of the truth about who you are.

**Renewed**

Have you ever considered the necessity of renewing your mind? Renewal of the mind is the primary objective of replacing negative thoughts with positive thoughts. To receive the full impact of this point, you must fully understand the word "renew." The prefix at the beginning is "re" and it means to return.

Therefore, to renew your mind means *to return to its original state of being*. It is the same as returning to the basics before your life became complicated and your mind convinced you that accomplishing your dreams is impossible. Therefore, *"We need quiet time to examine our lives openly and honestly – spending quiet time alone gives your mind an opportunity to renew itself and create order,"* as Susan L. Taylor concluded. The process of order requires that you fill your mind with the right information.

*"Do not conform to the pattern of this world, but be transformed by the renewing of your mind. Then you will be able to test and approve what God's will is-his good, pleasing and perfect will."* Renewing your mind is a prerequisite for understanding God's will for your life. Are you able to change your thoughts about your future? Are you willing to fill your mind with the knowledge that God created you to fulfill a plan and achieve an assignment?

**Filled**

Filling your mind with knowledge will give you information, which is good to have. However, be aware that, as the Ancient Egyptians concluded, *"Knowledge is not necessarily wisdom."* Using a parable to elaborate this point, think about this concept. Knowledge says to wisdom, *"We are one."* Wisdom replies to knowledge, *"You are incorrect."* Knowledge asks, why? Wisdom responds, *"To be like me you must have understanding, information and use both to produce the right outcome."* Therefore, *"Getting wisdom is the wisest thing you can do! And whatever else you do, develop good judgment."*

For these reasons, it is essential to follow this approach stated by King Solomon, *"I turned my heart to know and to search out and to seek wisdom and the scheme of things..."* Being determined to find the right answers regarding your purpose and potential in the scheme of things must take priority in your mind. Seeking wisdom to answer purpose related questions is the correct approach to take. Remember, *"Wisdom is a tree of life to those who embrace her..."*

Once filled with the right knowledge, *"prepare your mind for action; be self-controlled."* Staying focus on the path of purpose is an excellent start to finding answers and solutions. The ability to stay focus begins with being proactive and having self-control. Believe it or not, your future is impacted by your ability to stay focused until the objective is achieved.

**Focused**

Think for a moment, what are you focused on achieving in life? Can you honestly say that you are interested in maximizing your potential and fulfilling your purpose? At this stage in your reading, I hope that you are able to answer the question by saying "YES!" Being focused is necessary for you to live the life you were designed to live. It will also help you overcome opposition and achieve those things that seem impossible to accomplish. The words of Steve Jobs are memorable. He commented, *"That's been one of my mantras – focus and simplicity. Simple can be harder than complex: You have to work hard to get your thinking clean to make it simple. But it's worth it in the end because once you get there, you can move mountains."*

The mind is a tremendous asset and potentially your greatest personal liability. As President Ronald Reagan once said, it's an asset because, *"There are no constraints on the human mind, no walls around the human spirit, no barriers to our progress except those we ourselves erect."* Your mind becomes a liability if your thoughts prevent you from making the right decisions, thinking the right things, and pursuing the right path in life. Removing the barriers from your mind will open the window for possibilities, optimism, and calmness.

*"So be careful to do what the LORD your God has command you to do; do not turn aside to the or to the left. Walk in obedience to all that the LORD your God has commanded you, so that you may live and prosper and prolong your days in the land that you will possess."* Those are the words that Moses spoke to the Hebrews after receiving the commandments from the Lord. Are those words applicable to you and me? ABSOLUTELY!!! God expects us to stay focus and calm under the pressures of life.

## Calmness of Mind

*"The more tranquil a man becomes, the greater is his success, his influence, his power for good. Calmness of mind is one of the beautiful jewels of wisdom,"* as spoken by James Allen. Therefore, *"Do not be anxious about anything, but in every situation, by prayer and petition, with thanksgiving, present your requests to God. And the peace of God, which transcends all understanding, will guard your hearts and your minds in Christ Jesus."*

Do you agree with Allen's assessment that calmness of the mind is one of the beautiful jewels of wisdom? A calm mind is an important start to allowing wisdom to filter through your thoughts. Calmness of the mind is the same as peace of mind. Look around you and identify those individuals that seem to possess a calm mind or peace of mind. Would you agree that they seem to remain focused and are a good source for wisdom?

## Sources of Confidence

Based on my experience, a calm mind is normally associated with a confident, prepared, and focused person. However, there are, at least, 9 other reasons that lead to having a calm disposition and confidence. This means that confidence is also associated with having knowledge in certain key areas. I retrieved the list shown below from my personal notes taken during one of Dr. Myles Munroe's training sessions. According to his wisdom, confidence derives from…:

- Knowledge of one's **uniqueness**
- Knowledge of one's **purpose**
- Knowledge of one's **resources**
- Knowledge of one's **source**
- Knowledge of one's **value**
- Knowledge of one's **ability**
- Knowledge of one's **predestination**
- Knowledge of one's **protection**
- Knowledge of one's **creator**

It goes without saying that if you do not have knowledge related to the above points, then calmness of the mind will likely evade you. If you lack this information, do not be dismayed because wisdom from God will give you answers to each of the above points about the source of confidence. Hopefully, you have come to believe that one of the most important things in life on earth is to make it to your future. The words of wisdom conveyed by Dr. Munroe are sound advice. When you possess knowledge as noted above, you become confident and calm when confronted with obstacles, challenges, and disappointments. Did you know that relying on your conscience can result in negative mental consequences that are opposite of calmness of the mind?

## The Conscience

I have an important question for you, *"Did Adam and Eve possess a conscience before they ate the fruit, or did they acquire it after eating?"* Before eating the fruit, it is very clear that Adam had wisdom, as he was able to give names to all of the livestock, birds, and wild animals without any problems. Therefore, wisdom was the only knowledge that Adam was created and expected to live by. He was not designed to entertain good options, bad options, or his opinion on what's considered right or wrong.

Something significant happened to his thoughts, and actions the instant he ate the fruit. *"Then the man and his wife heard the sound of the LORD God as he was walking in the garden in the cool of the day, and they hid from the LORD God among the trees of the garden."* Hiding from an omnipresent and omniscient God is an indication that something went wrong the moment the fruit was eaten. What happened?

Well, after eating the fruit, Adam's eyes were open in the form of knowledge of good and evil. Immediately, he realized that he was naked physically and spiritually. At that point, Adam's reactions were motivated by his conscience and fear. Listen to his response when God asked him if he had eaten fruit from the forbidden tree. *"The woman you put here with me-she gave me some fruit from the tree, and I ate it."*

> **Y**our conscience directs you to choose the good option, but wisdom directs you towards the right option.

Adam knew the fruit that he received from Eve was from the forbidden tree before he ate it. He had the option to throw it away or just refuse to eat it.

The decision to eat it was an unwise act. Let's examine some other issues related to this account:

- When Adam was created, he possessed wisdom, a mind and knowledge, but he did not have a conscience. He was created to respond to life in a wise, righteous, and holy manner.
- Adam chose to disregard wisdom. He allowed his mind to be negatively influenced. That decision led to an act of disobedience and sin.
- After eating the fruit, he acquired something that he was not created to have and was not supposed to live by. He was supposed to live by every word that proceeded from the mouth of God not his opinion on what was good or bad.
- The conscience that he acquired changed his actions, decision-marking, thought process, life, and destiny by exposing him to options that were not supposed to exist.

*"And the LORD God said, the man has now become like one of us, knowing good and evil. He must not be allowed to reach out his hand and take also from the tree of life and eat, and live forever."* This verse provides clear and irrefutable evidence that God has a firm position regarding our knowledge of good and evil. He did not create Adam to have this knowledge which means that Adam was not created to decide what constitutes good and evil. In other words, what seems good to you may not be good to God or what is evil according to God may seem to be good to you.

Merriam-Webster's online dictionary defines conscience as *"the sense of consciousness of the moral goodness or blameworthiness of one's own conduct, intentions, or character together with a feeling of obligation to do right or be good."*[35] In other words, the conscience is defined as having knowledge about what is right and wrong. From a spiritual perspective, <u>it also means having knowledge of good and evil</u>.

It is necessary to understand that the conscience adjudicates information and places it into a specific category. As information filters through your conscience, the mind categorizes it as being good or bad, right, or wrong. The conscience also processes wisdom and classifies the information as either good or bad, right, or wrong. The problem that we all face is that our conscience may know what is right but the action that we take is wrong.

Have you ever experienced a situation whereby you had a choice to do the right thing but after weighing the consequence of doing what was right, you decided that the price was too great? As a result, you chose to do what was wrong even though you knew that it was wrong. Sometimes, a war wages internally as it relates to maximizing potential and pursuing the path of purpose. If the option exists to choose a good option over the right option, what will you do?

## Choose the Right Option

As you are aware, your conscience possesses knowledge about what is good, but this knowledge does not always translate into you doing what is right. Confusion occurs in your mind when the good option to take is not the right option based on the situation or circumstances. Can you recall when you faced a situation that required you to do what was right, instead of what was good or convenient for that moment? Years ago, I recall during my last interview with a major insurance company for a claim's adjuster position, I was asked an interesting question. The divisional manager asked me, *"Is it better to be a good person or a right person?"*

I responded by saying that *"it is better to be a right person."* Why did I choose right over good? The answer reverts to the point that pursuing the right path or approach is better than pursuing what is good or convenient. Selecting the good approach may or may not produce positive and lasting results. For these reasons, it is necessary to possess wisdom, as it will always direct you to respond to situations with the right response that renders the best outcomes.

*"Real integrity is doing the right thing, knowing that nobody's going to know whether you did it or not,"* according to Oprah Winfrey. Are you being

true to yourself, your values and desire of the heart related to releasing your full potential and pursuing your purpose for living? Now that you understand the importance of wisdom, the mind and using your conscience to select the right option, are you prepared to move in the direction of peace of mind? Hopefully, at this stage, the answer to both questions is YES!!!

## THE NEXT STEP

*"The doors of wisdom are never shut."* The most obvious interpretation of that Benjamin Franklin quotation is that wisdom is always available to you when you need it. It is available to guide you through every aspect of your life. Nevertheless, there is a subtle interpretation that you can glean from Franklin's use of the word *"doors."*

His quote suggests that you can find wisdom from various sources at any given point. The process undertaken to acquire wisdom may differ from individual to individual. Some acquire it from personal experiences or from the advice of others. Whereas, others may use different means to become wise in their decisions and interactions. Ultimately, the method that you use to acquire wisdom is a means to a necessary end. The necessary end is for you to have wisdom and learn how to use it to make the right decisions, maximize your potential and fulfill your purpose for living.

Defeating the internal and external opposition that you encounter in life is essential. Think for a moment, *"What are the stumbling blocks hindering you from fulfilling your dreams?"* As you think about the internal and external opposition, always remember that you were born to succeed, achieve and fulfill your destiny. I encourage you to continue reading and continue believing as we navigate this journey of potential and purpose together.

## Quick reference to wisdom and the mind principles:

1. Wisdom reveals the right path to take according to your purpose in life.
2. Wisdom is possessing the right understanding and knowledge that leads to the recipient making the right judgment or decision.
3. Wisdom is key to making the best decision while using the best resources to accomplish your objective.
4. Having basic knowledge about something does not mean that you possess wisdom.
5. Wisdom is a powerful source that helps you choose your goal and obtain it.
6. Wisdom is valuable because it provides information, answers, solutions, and the best decision for your complex life issues.
7. Wisdom suggests the best course of action during the decision-making process.
8. Wisdom is of vital importance whenever you seek to develop a vision for your life, understand your purpose, and maximize your potential.
9. Wisdom provides information about the right path of purpose for your life. It assists you in developing the right course of action to fulfill your purpose for living.
10. Wisdom assists you in creating the right paths and opportunities for you to maximize your potential.
11. Wisdom assists in the decision-making process by providing you with information about the right option to take based on the situation.
12. Navigating through the maze of options to find the path of purpose requires information, knowledge, and direction.
13. When a word of wisdom enters your thoughts, it provides the right answers in life.

14. Wisdom positions you for leadership because it generates self-confidence, solutions and answers that others do not have.
15. Wisdom is the most valuable free and non-tangible personal resource.
16. Wisdom from God helps in the interpretation of dreams.
17. Wisdom is the key to defeating the mental stumbling blocks preventing you from maximizing your potential and discovering your purpose.
18. Your conscience directs you to choose the good option, but wisdom directs you towards the right option.

# Chapter Ten

## What's Blocking You From Maximizing Your Potential

> *"Stand up to your obstacles and do something about them. You will find that they haven't half the strength you think they have."*
> **Norman Vincent Peale**

For hours, Benjamin laid face down and motionless at the waters' edge of a sandy beach inlet that was carved out of the rocky terrain. The cadence of waves smashing against the rocks produced a peaceful and steady rhythm. Back and forth, back and forth, the powerful waves rolled in and pounded the isolated shore.

Around mid-afternoon, he awoke, jumped up soaked, confused, and disoriented. His head swung from side to side. His heart beating rapidly. Frightened and alone, he gasped with enough breath to say, *"How can this be that I am on the opposite side of the mountain."* Somehow, he ended up on the remote uninhabited backside. You see, Benjamin's island home was surrounded on three sides by a dangerous and steep mountain range. Furthermore, the island was also known for its huge waves and strong rip tides, which made escaping his captivity by sea impossible.

The days stranded turned into lonely weeks. For comfort, he would stare into the star filled night sky, and reflect on the humorous experience of visiting his grandfather. Papa, as he called him, often behaved in an unusual manner. Several times during the day, he would say, *"Move Mountain, Move,"* jump up slightly, twist the hips and shuffle his feet as if dancing to the rhythm of a lively Caribbean beat. The dance would only last for a few seconds, then he would continue his chores. The more Benjamin observed this odd ritual, the more he laughed and shook his head. He was convinced that Papa was a little crazy.

Nevertheless, reminiscing about the past soothed his troubled mind. Before his untimely change of events, Benjamin was focused and full of confidence. His future seemed bright. He had a passion for pursuing his purpose in life and possessed the potential to do great things for his small island community. Now, he was left with fond memories, as he faced his greatest obstacle, the mountain.

One day, Benjamin was determined to experience a positive change of circumstances. Strong in spirit, he fixed his gaze on the huge stumbling block and roared sternly from the depths of his weak frame, *"Move Mountain, Move,"* but nothing happened. Again, he shouted, this time a little louder *"Move Mountain, Move,"* but again nothing happened. Throughout the day, he repeated the declaration until late at night.

Emotionally drained, he eventually fell asleep. After several restless hours, he was awakened by thunderous rumbling sounds and the ground shaking violently. The region was prone to experiencing major earthquakes. During the night, a powerful earthquake enlarged a narrow pathway through the mountain that was previously too tight for Benjamin to enter.

At daybreak, he discovered that the crack was a clear pathway to freedom. Although it took many hours to climb and squeeze through the tight crevice, he finally reached the familiar side of the mountain just before sunset. Scratched up, frail, mentally battered and exhausted, he hobbled slowly towards Papa's farm. On arrival, he met Papa waiting on his small wooden porch rejoicing and shouting, *"Move Mountain, Move,"* followed by his unique dance.

You see, Papa wasn't crazy after all. He had a dream that his grandson would find himself trapped on the uninhabited side of the mountain. Papa's dance was a symbolic gesture representing a victorious future outcome. His statement, *"Move Mountain, Move,"* was a seed of possibility that he strategically planted in the mind of his grandson during each visit.

After several moments of celebration, Papa looked at his grandson and said, *"Son, it moved for me and now it moved for you."* Then, they joined each other in one last joyful jump, twisting of the hips and shuffling of the feet, as they exhaled together, *"MOVE MOUNTAIN MOVE!!!"*

A quote from Norman Vincent Peale summarizes this chapter's parable perfectly. He stated, *"Stand up to an obstacle. Just stand up to it, that's all, and don't give way under it, and it will finally break. You will break it. Something has to break, and it won't be you, it will be the obstacle."*

Mountains in your life represent obstacles that prevent you from pursuing your purpose and releasing your full potential. Mountains are common and indiscriminate. In fact, sometimes people are mountains in your life. They seek to hold you down, stop your success, limit your potential, and treat you unfairly without just cause. Alternatively, sometimes economic conditions, cultural traditions and social influences are troubling sources of mountains in your life, as well.

No matter the origin or reason why the mountain exists in your life, the options are either stand up and believe in a successful outcome or give way and doubt. Let's revisit the introductory story. There are 10 valuable points to consider listed below:

- Sometimes mountains in your life seem to be overwhelming and impossible to overcome.

- Sometimes challenging circumstances exist because of no fault of yours.
- Issues that can rob you of your destiny in life may result from various factors such as the country you live in, economic or financial problems, cultural barriers and the list goes on.
- Sometimes you cannot remove the mountain in your life using physical means. Conquering the mountain may require mental stamina and transformation.
- Mountains seek to block your momentum and create mental instability.
- You should not blame yourself for every mountain in your life as some appear without provocation.
- Mountains do not move because you cry a lot, shout, scream, feel sorry for yourself or blame others.
- Sometimes mountains appear in your life not because of what you have done, but what you will do in your life.
- Unwavering belief and faith in God will move the tallest and toughest mountains that you encounter on your path of purpose in life.
- Only two options exist when you encounter a mountain. You can allow it to defeat you, or you can decide to overcome it.

## Mountains Create Issues

Maslow's hierarchy of needs theory provides insight into how the human mind prioritizes essential needs in life. His pyramid identifies important needs and places them into five ascending categories. This means that the needs at the bottom of the pyramid always takes precedence over the pursuit of the higher ranking desires. The categories starting at base level moving upward are Physiological, Safety, Love / Belonging, Self-Esteem and Self-Actualization.

Physiological needs consist of things such as water, food, and shelter. Safety needs consist of things such as property ownership, stability, and employment. Love or Belonging needs consist of things such friendships, connection, and networking. Self-esteem needs consists of things such as confidence, respect of others and achievements. Lastly, Self-actualization is positioned at the top of the pyramid. It consists of things such as fulfillment of purpose, maximizing your potential and being everything that you are capable of being.

The hierarchy of needs theory suggests that there are other needs that are of greater importance in life than self-actualization. Which means that, for many, self-actualization is equivalent to wishful thinking. If you consider the needs as stepping-stones or positions on a pyramid, then the needs at the base would carry greater importance. According to Maslow, humans will always seek to satisfy their most pressing wishes first, before elevating their thoughts to pursuing other less essential needs. In essence, he believed that a person that struggles to afford food doesn't want to think about property ownership, friendships, respect of others or maximizing their potential, until they are able to feed themselves without worrying.

Once the basic needs are met, then people are inclined to focus their attention on satisfying the higher set of needs such as employment, property ownership, or stability in life. His conclusion about the priority of human needs is realistic and practical thinking. Remember that reality thinking means that you acknowledge the mountain or stumbling block but at the same time you seek to find a solution to the problem.

What if you live your entire life chasing better living and economic conditions or acceptance from others but never achieve those goals? What if your country is deprived of economic wealth and you are forced into poverty? These "what if's" are real issues that millions of people face worldwide. The hierarchy of needs by Maslow does an excellent job identifying reasons why most people never maximize their potential, but it fails to offer a solution or explain the consequences.

*What's Blocking you from Maximizing your Potential*   237

Life's mountains or barriers cause individuals to divert their full attention to survival and fulfilling basic needs. Therefore, it is important to be mindful that there are 7 negative effects mountains have on your mind. Chasing after the fulfillment of certain needs may span a lifetime. If you find yourself in this predicament, then you may or will be experiencing the following negative effects:

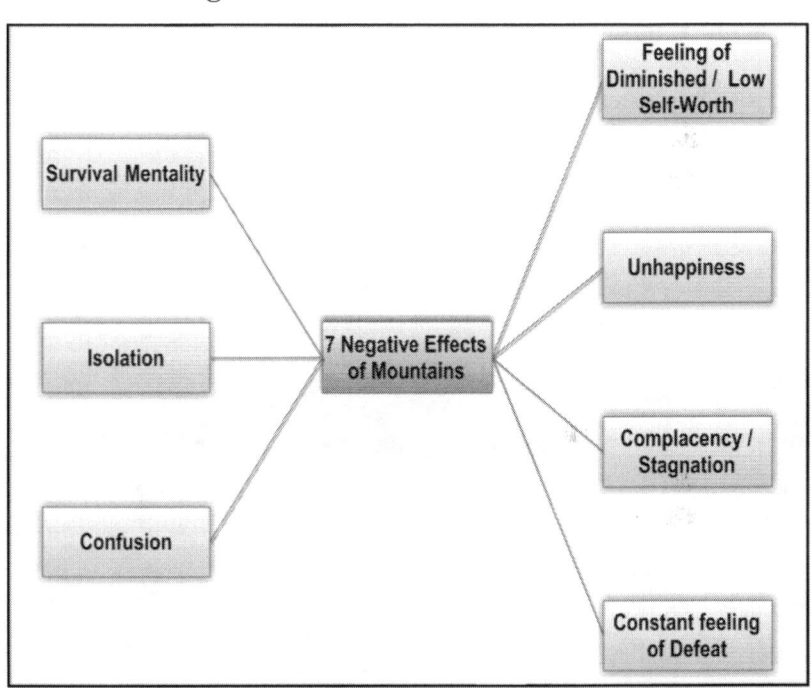

## 7 Negative Effects of Mountains Chart

- Survival Mentality
- Isolation
- Confusion
- Feeling of Diminished / Low Self-Worth
- Unhappiness
- Complacency / Stagnation
- Constant feeling of Defeat

- **Survival mentality** – Life is centered on basic survival not self-fulfillment.
- **Isolation** – Although you are surrounded by others, you feel like you are on an island all alone and nobody truly understands.
- **Confusion** – Life is confusing because it centers on survival and nothing more.

- **Feeling of diminished / low self-worth** – The pursuit of basic needs gradually leads you to believe that you have nothing of value to offer society.
- **Unhappiness** – In secret, you desire more from life than working every day just to survive.
- **Complacency / Stagnation** – Living a mundane life of pursuing basic needs is admirable because you are surviving, but you're not satisfied because you're neither maximizing your potential nor pursuing your purpose for living. Consequently, you disregard self-fulfillment because survival takes precedence.
- **Constant feeling of defeat** – Mountains or barriers tend to cause a feeling of defeat when you see the huge obstacle stopping your progression in life.

Good News!!! You do not have to accept Maslow's conclusion or anyone else's about your life. If you are living a life of pursuing basic survival needs and have given up on self-fulfillment, then please note that there is a way out. Be encouraged by the words of Dr. Myles Munroe. Based on his years of travelling the world meeting and teaching people, he concluded, *"You weren't born just to live a life and to die; you were born to accomplish something specifically. Matter of fact, success is making it to the end of your purpose; that is success... Success is not just existing. Success is making it to the end of why you were born."*

## Alternative Response to Maslow's Theory

*"Truly I tell you, if anyone says to this mountain, Go throw yourself into the sea, and does not doubt in their heart but believes that what they say will happen, it will be done for them. Therefore, I tell you, whatever you ask for in prayer, believe that you have received it, and it will be yours."* Jesus spoke those words of assurance to his disciples after an encounter with a fig tree. As discussed in a previous chapter, they were on their way to Bethany and Jesus was hungry. As you recall, he saw a fig tree in the distance and went towards it expecting to eat of its fruit. However, when he reached it, there was no fruit.

According to Mark, the writer of the scripture, there was no fruit because it was not fig season.

After not finding fruit, Jesus said to it, *"May no one ever eat fruit from you again."* Did you know that God pronounces a curse for disobeying His plan, instructions or will? Listen to the words that Moses spoke to the Hebrews, *"If you do not obey the LORD your God and do not carefully follow all his commands and decrees I am giving you today, all these curses will come on you and overtake you."* So, what is the issue with the fig tree and Jesus being hungry?

As previously concluded, it is evident that the purpose of that fig tree was to bear fruit for Jesus to eat from it at that appointed time. It was not under the law of seasons. God granted it the privilege and opportunity to bear fruit for a specific cause on a specific day and time, without hindrances. In other words, it existed to feed Jesus at that moment. However, for whatever reason, it was disobedient to its purpose and failed to produce its fruit, as expected.

Additionally, there are two other points to learn from the encounter. The first point is that mountains, obstacles, or distractions are susceptible to being removed from a purpose driven life. The second point is that God has given you the authority over the obstacle or need blocking your progression. His instructions are *"Say unto the mountain be removed and be cast into the sea."* Based on this encounter, it is obvious that the relevance of potential and purpose supersedes the things or circumstances that hinder you from accomplishing the objective.

In consideration of these points, it is time to introduce a viable response to Maslow's theory. In my view, releasing your potential and pursuing your purpose are basic essential needs for every human. As we have discussed previously, your potential and purpose give meaning to life and fulfills the internal voids. In other words, releasing your potential and pursuing your purpose adds value to acquiring food, water, shelter, friends, etc. Furthermore, self-actualization is a proven method to having your basic needs met, becoming influential, acquiring wealth, peace of mind and achieving success.

Now, considering what you know about potential, purpose, and self-actualization, would you consider these ingredients as necessities for a healthy and stable mental outlook on life? Additionally, are you now convinced that releasing your potential and fulfilling your purpose in life can alter the circumstances that seem impossible to change? As mentioned, Maslow's theory gives insight to the reality thinking, as it highlights the mountains in the path to finding true fulfillment and satisfaction in life. However, the essence of personal leadership and accountability is to find solutions to problems not making excuses to succumbing to problems.

Let's pause for a moment. I have given you a lot to think about. Perhaps, now would be a good time for you to spend a few moments meditating on these concepts before moving forward. Do you believe in the power of your potential and purpose to elevate the quality of your life?

## Climbing Out of the Pit of Despair

Are you ready for more information about the alternative response to Maslow's theory? I understand that basic needs, huge barriers, or mountains in your life will cause moments of despair or hopelessness. There have been periods in my life when the obstacles seemed too large to overcome. I will admit that sometimes there is the tendency to worry. If so, be mindful that Jesus said, *"Therefore, I tell you, do not worry about your life, what you will eat or drink; or about your body, what you will wear. Is not life more than food, and the body more than clothes? Look at the birds of the air; they do not sow or reap or store away in barns, and yet your heavenly Father feeds them. Are you not much more valuable than they?"*

I have experienced many needs, disappointments, and difficulties, but I never quit or ran away from the challenge. Yes, the thought entered my mind, but with God's strength, I kept moving forward and upward. The way out of the turbulent mental seas is to ride the wave of potential and purpose. As previously mentioned in earlier chapters, there is natural power associated with each that can pull you up and establish a brighter future in life. Take a moment to review this self-help chart:

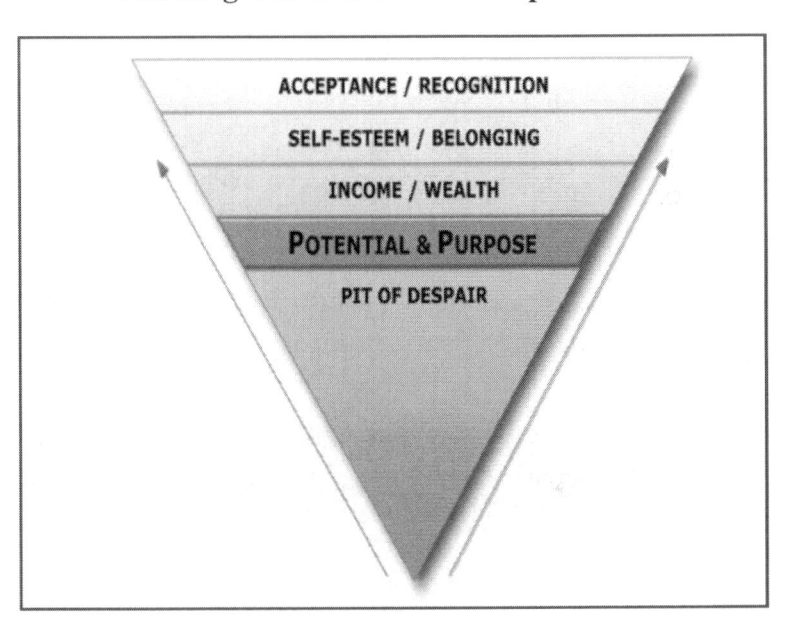

## Climbing Out of the Pit of Despair Chart

```
ACCEPTANCE / RECOGNITION
SELF-ESTEEM / BELONGING
INCOME / WEALTH
POTENTIAL & PURPOSE
PIT OF DESPAIR
```

Maslow's theory is outlined in the shape of a pyramid, but the alternative response takes the shape of an inverted pyramid. The relevance is that his theory highlights the needs of human existence but the alternative highlights the approach to breaking through the feeling of despair which is a symptom of needs. John Keats once said, *"I must choose between despair and Energy – I choose the latter."* Like Keats, I don't believe that you or anyone else enjoys living in despair or being constantly reminded about pressing needs.

The chart above identifies the benefits of focusing on your innate power to propel you up out of the pit of despair. It emphasizes the necessity of using your potential and purpose as platforms to satisfying physical, mental, and emotional needs. As you master your gift, opportunities to increase your income and personal wealth is a natural consequence. Furthermore, releasing your potential and living a purposeful life enhances your self-esteem and gives you a sense of self-worth and value. Eventually, acceptance and recognition from others will catapult you out of despair, as you use your potential on a consistent basis. The following are examples of people who used the power of their potential and purpose as energy to elevate the quality of their lives:

**Elvis Presley**

Elvis Presley was an American music icon and legend. His fame and unique style mesmerized millions of fans worldwide. It is reported that over one billion copies of his records have sold in America and around the world. During his early years, his family struggled financially depending on government assistance to meet basic needs. Nevertheless, young Presley exhibited a natural talent for music and singing. Although not having any formal music training, he excelled and rose to stardom. Equally as important, he made millions of dollars releasing his potential and pursuing this purpose in life.[36]

Commenting on his secret desires of the heart, he stated, *"When I was a child, I was a dreamer. I read comic books, and I was the hero of the comic book. I saw movies, and I was the hero in the movie. So, every dream I have ever dreamed has come true a thousand times."* Having a lack of resources does not mean there is a lack of dreams. Presley's financial and physical needs were real, but not strong enough to limit the power of his potential to elevate the quality of his life. Potential and purpose can change your quality of life in an instant. He also said, *"Ambition is a dream with a V8 engine. Ain't nowhere else in the world where you can go from driving a truck to Cadillac overnight."* Presley rose to stardom using his natural innate ability. In 1977, he died, but his international appeal still lives to this day.

## Hank Aaron

Hank Aaron was one of the most noteworthy former Major League Baseball players in the history of the game. His legendary abilities catapulted him to stardom and recognition. Exhibiting a passion and talent for the game at an early age, he practiced his batting skills using scraps found on the street. Although extremely poor and disadvantaged by racial discrimination, he never quit because of the mountains in his life. In fact, when he retired from baseball, he held the prestigious title of being the home run king.[37]

Aaron's life was also a modern-day rag to riches story. Following a lengthy career in baseball, he became a very successful businessman. His natural potential and pursuit of purpose brought fame, fortune, and a life worthy of recognition. This great baseball legend gave very good advice about barriers in your life. Aaron commented, *"You may not think you're going to make it. You may want to quit. But if you keep your eye on the ball, you can accomplish anything."*

Those words were spoken from a man that received many death threats because of the color of his skin and his unprecedented success in the game of baseball. Like Aaron, life will also grant you an opportunity to put your potential on exhibit to meet your basic needs and find your purpose for living. When it happens for you, remember these valuable words of Aaron, *"In playing ball, and in life, a person occasionally gets the opportunity to do something great. When that time comes, only two things matter: being prepared to seize the moment and having the courage to take your best swing."*

## Indra Nooyi

In pursuit of her dreams, Nooyi desired to move to America for educational and employment opportunities. Although already accomplished educationally, her parents really did not believe that she would get accepted into Yale to further her education. She proved them wrong. Reflecting on the situation she said, *"I asked my parents for permission to study in America and they were so sure that I wouldn't get in that they encouraged me to try. So, I applied to Yale and got an excellent scholarship."* Getting accepted into an Ivy League school is a tremendous accomplishment, but to also receive a scholarship as well, speaks to the necessity of pursuing purpose.[38]

For Nooyi, potential and the pursuit of purpose exalted her to one of the highest pinnacles in corporate America. Her unparalleled success as the former CEO of PepsiCo is very impressive. Under her admirable leadership, PepsiCo's gross profits rose exponentially. Through natural potential and education, she blazed a trial for other Indian born women to dream big and expect greatness. Her life is a testament that supports the alternative approach to Maslow's hierarchy of needs. Listen to her words of wisdom, *"An important attribute of success is to be yourself. Never hide what makes you, you."*

Nooyi's life is a testament that supports the alternative approach to Maslow's hierarchy of needs. Based on the information above, what did purpose and potential do for her when she left the security of home, the comfort of familiarity and having her basic needs met by family?

**Leonardo Del Vecchio**

Although born into poverty, Del Vecchio is now one of the wealthiest persons in the world. He is the founder of Luxottica, the world's largest manufacturer of eyewear. In fact, several major eyewear brands are owned exclusively by his company. With a net worth of over $20 billion dollars, a super yacht, private plane, and several luxury homes, it is fair to say that Leonardo's natural potential elevated him to an amazing level in life.[39] What do you think motivated him and the others to overcome opposition?

---

**Y**our potential and purpose can pull you over the mountain blocking your path.

---

## Sources of Behavior

Sometimes you may not be able to control the circumstances that bring obstacles or mountains in your life. Nevertheless, you can control how you respond mentally to the challenge. According to Plato, *"Human behavior flows from three main sources: desires, emotion and knowledge."* Thousands of years ago, Plato suggested that human behavior centers on desires of the heart, things you are passionate or emotional about and knowledge. Essentially, he concluded that we are products of our thoughts.

Dr. Martin Luther King Jr. once said, *"Rarely do we find men who willingly engage in hard, solid thinking. There is an almost universal quest for easy answers and half-baked solutions. Nothing pains some people more than having to think."* Dr. King's comments suggest that some people accept their present predicaments because of an inability to think of a solution capable of improving their circumstances. Therefore, if Plato and Dr. King's assessments are correct, then the solution to the problem related to human motivation would begin with thoughts and end with a solution. In other words, the right thoughts will lead to the right desires, emotions and knowledge that equips you with the mental tools to overcome the mountains in your life.

## The Power of Potential & Purpose

Using your natural potential along the path of purpose is the beginning of establishing a means to change the end. This is the reason why focusing your thoughts on releasing your potential and pursuing your purpose is better than falling or remaining in despair over the lack of basic needs. Perhaps, you have or will discover that having positive thoughts about the value of your potential and purpose will change your life in positive ways. Moreover, there are other good changes that will take place in your life, as shown on the following chart:

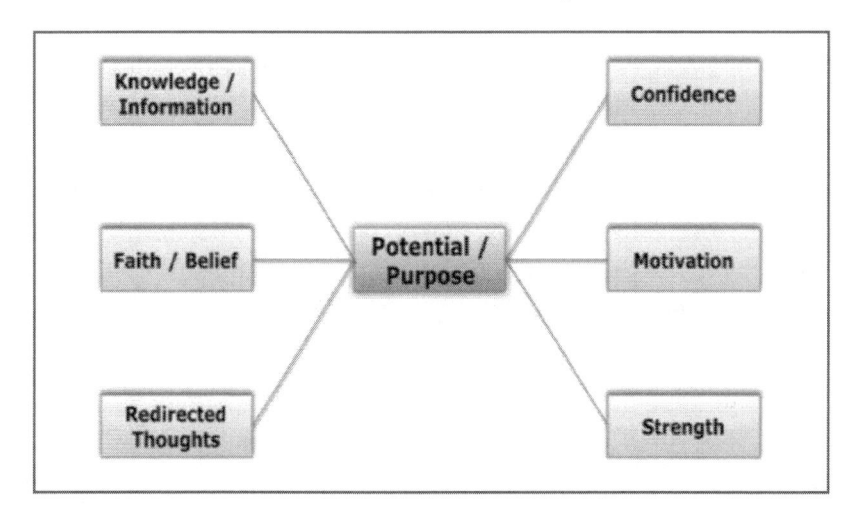

## The Power of Potential & Purpose Chart

```
Knowledge /                              Confidence
Information
                    Potential /
Faith / Belief      Purpose              Motivation

Redirected                               Strength
Thoughts
```

Identifying what would be considered a successful outcome is necessary when you are confronted with challenging circumstances. Hopefully, you will accept this advice instead of thinking of survival only. Remember that the objective when confronted with barriers or mountains is success. Success is defined as climbing over or removing the mental, physical, or emotional obstacle.

*"Life is 10% what happens to you and 90% how you react to it."* Do you agree with that assessment made by Charles Swindoll? His words suggest that your reaction to life events determines your future. Therefore, your response to barriers or mountains that you experience in life should be based on achieving a positive outcome. The above chart highlights how potential and purpose enhances your ability to be victorious. Potential and purpose enhance your life in the following ways:

- **Knowledge / Information** – You gain knowledge about yourself. This means that you begin to know who you are and what you are naturally equipped to do in life.

- **Faith / Belief** – Your belief in a positive outcome is increased when you realize that you are already equipped with the power to influence the outcome. Your faith leads to a victorious outcome.
- **Redirect thoughts** – Your thoughts are redirected towards expecting a positive outcome as your mind focuses on a long-term solution that promotes fulfillment, joy, and peace of mind.
- **Confidence** – Confidence in yourself and your life is a positive side effect of knowing your purpose and releasing your potential. This confidence dictates how you view challenges and your ability to defeat them.
- **Motivation** – Motivation is another side effect. It leads to a sense of urgency to accomplish specific objectives. This means that your thoughts, desires, objectives are motivated by the accomplishment of an expected successful end.
- **Strength** – Purpose and potential reinforces the perimeters of your mind so that you stand strong when confronted with issues that could lead you down the wrong path.

## Life on the other side of the Mountain

Once you successfully cross over to the other side of the mountain, then it is important that you move ahead in the right direction. According to Dr. Myles Munroe, *"People generally fall into one of three groups: the few who make things happen, the many who watch things happen, and the overwhelming majority who have no notion of what happens. Every person is either a creator of fact or a creature of circumstance. He either puts color into his environment, or, like a chameleon, takes color from his environment."* What category do you fall into?

Based on the assessment stated by Dr. Munroe, what category would you fall in? Are you one of the few that will make things happen through persistence, determination, and passion? Have you concluded that following popular norms, beliefs or customs is the only way to achieve success in life? Has your released potential put color in your environment? At this point, take a few minutes to think about your life and your responses to these questions.

Welcome back. As you move ahead towards self-actualization, you must set your aim on the mark of complete maximization of your potential. The key is to take your natural TAGs to the next level of manifestation. This is how you expose your identity to yourself and the world. It is also the best approach to making positive things happen for you related to your purpose for living.

*"Nothing stops the man who desires to achieve. Every obstacle is simply a course to develop his achievement muscle. It's a strengthening of his powers of accomplishment,"* according to Thomas Carlyle. His reference to the fact that obstacles develop achievement muscle is true. Sometimes, tests and trials in life come to make you stronger and wiser. Overcoming obstacles build stamina and strength. These qualities are invaluable and will fuel the perseverance and determination needed to achieve your goals. At this stage, quitting is not a realistic or viable option if peace of mind, contentment and fulfillment of purpose are your priorities.

*"Every great dream begins with a dreamer. Always remember, you have within you the strength, the patience, and the passion to reach for the stars to change the world."* That statement made by Harriet Tubman, famed American abolitionist, holds a wealth of knowledge. Released potential on the path of purpose equips you for achieving your dreams on the opposite side of the mountain. After going through a challenging period in your life, be mindful not to fall for negative thoughts associated with impatience. Tubman's advice is good news because you have the strength to reach the mark. Remember to press forward and let the tide of passion carry you towards destiny and greatness.

## THE NEXT STEP

It is my hope that at this point in your reading you realize there is significant power in releasing your potential and fulfilling your purpose for living. The mountains that you experience in life come to make you stronger not remove your bright future. Each challenge builds mental strength and creates more intensity to pursue peace of mind. Although the mountain appears to be invincible, you can conquer it and climb to the level of self-actualization.

My family and I have moved internationally three times without any financial assistance or a corporate relocation package. Each time, I had to adjust to a new environment, unfamiliar surroundings, and starting over in life. The entire process was mentally, emotionally, and physically exhausting. In addition, the tremendous financial strain and adjustment required to get reestablished was hard to accept. Yes, there were many days of difficulty, but we prevailed, and I continued pursuing my purpose and releasing my potential.

Releasing the many thoughts and personal quotes contained in this book wasn't an option, it was a requirement. My peace of mind was tied to this project because it is my destiny to share this information with you. Succumbing to the challenges presented by life's mountains was an option that I could not accept, because purpose was calling me to prevail. The same is true for you as well.

The mountains that you face are real, but they are not impossible for you to overcome. You were born to lead in your area of gifting and succeed along life's journey. The words of wisdom from Michael Jordan are very encouraging. Jordon believes, *"Obstacles don't have to stop you. If you run into a wall, don't turnaround and give up. Figure out a way to Climb It, Go Through It, or Work Around It."*

Jordan's success in life is noteworthy. How did his journey begin? His journey began by developing his natural potential and pursuing his purpose. The next time you are faced with a mountain in your life, I challenge you to look at that obstacle and say with confidence, "Move Mountain, Move!!!" "Move Mountain, Move!!!" **"MOVE MOUNTAIN, MOVE!!!"**

> **Quick reference to what's blocking you from maximizing your potential principles.**

1. Mountains in your life represent obstacles that prevent you from pursuing your purpose and releasing your full potential.
2. Sometimes, circumstances prevent you from progressing and circumstances prevent you from retreating.
3. Mountains in your life tend to seem overwhelming and impossible to overcome.
4. Issues that can rob you of your destiny in life may result from various factors such as the country you live in, economic or financial problems, cultural barriers and the list goes on.
5. You cannot remove the mountains in your life using physical means. Conquering the mountain requires mental stamina and transformation.
6. Mountains seek to block your momentum, create mental instability, and rob you of your destiny.
7. You should not blame yourself for every mountain in your life as some appear without provocation.
8. Mountains do not move because you cry a lot, shout, scream, feel sorry for yourself or blame others.
9. Sometimes, mountains appear in your life not because of what you have done, but as preparation for what you will do in your life.
10. Unwavering belief and faith in your TAGs will move the tallest and toughest mountains that you encounter on your path of purpose in life.
11. Your potential and purpose can pull you over the mountain blocking your path.
12. Sometimes, tests and trials in life come to make you stronger and wiser.
13. After going through a challenging period in your life, be mindful not to fall for negative thoughts associated with impatience.

# Chapter Eleven

## Born to Lead and Succeed

> *"You must decide if you are going to rob the world or bless it with the rich, valuable, potent, untapped resources locked away within you."*
> **Myles Munroe**

He sat at his desk with a stack of mail before him. He looked up, greeted me, and said, *"John, I have over 350 invitations requesting my presence in countries around the world."* He went on to say, *"These requests are from governments, Prime Ministers, corporations, business leaders, churches, universities and the list goes on."* For Dr. Myles Munroe, it was a year-end challenge that he approached with much appreciation, respect, and prayer. Although it was physically impossible to accept every invitation, each request was read, kept in an organized file, and given consideration.

I was shocked to know that Dr. Munroe received so many requests each year, not to mention the additional invitations that came after he traveled to an area. As he explained, the initial requests within one year would soon balloon to exceed over 800 based on impromptu invitations received after he arrived in a city or country. His response to the demand was, *"I travel between 300,000 – 400,000 miles every year but there are still so many invitations that I cannot accept."*

I replied, *"Dr. Myles can you send someone else on your behalf?"* Looking into my confused eyes, he stated calmly and confidently, *"Son, you see, they want me. They want what I have to offer. I have a lot of great leaders here, but these requests are for what I have to offer."*

Admittedly, I did not understand his comments. For years, he labored to train many talented people to become leaders in their area of gifting. To me, Dr. Myles Munroe was the greatest and most dedicated teacher that I have ever met. He possessed an extraordinary level of discipline, dedication, brilliance, knowledge, commitment, wisdom, and abilities. In addition to those qualities, he was loaded with many gifts that he refined and developed daily.

Some of his students were leaders of corporations, attorneys, doctors, politicians to name a few. Why would he not send these great leaders to those places he could not go? It is important to understand that Dr. Munroe welcomed taking his students with him on any trip. Additionally, he gave tremendous opportunities for students to showcase their abilities.

Why would he refrain from allowing someone to accept his invitations? Often, he would say during one of his inspirational, motivational, and insightful messages, *"You'll get it when I am gone."* Regarding this issue, he was correct again. A few months after his tragic death, I began the process of understanding why his response was the right approach and in the best interest of everyone involved. Now, after months of questioning and personal reflection, I understand that an original can never be replaced or duplicated.

Before each message, Dr. Munroe would say, *"The person you are standing next to is an original. You don't know who they will become."* I am convinced that the reason he refrained from passing personal invitations to others is based on his in-depth understanding of originality and leadership. **Attached to every purpose there is an original specimen created exclusively with the potential to fulfill their unique assignment**. When Dr. Munroe said, *"They only want me,"* he was referring to his originality and his assignment in life.

One of the most important points about originality is the fact that you are not a copy. As Dr. Munroe would say, *"The manufacturer made you an original based on the blueprint he has for your life."* He believed that you came to earth loaded with the innate attributes to be the solution for the issues and problems that you are uniquely designed to address. *"The people that you were born to influence, impact or help are waiting for you to arrive and to be revealed."* He spoke those words frequently.

Ralph Waldo Emerson once said, *"The mind once stretched by a new idea, never returns to its original dimensions."* The relevance of this quote is that Dr. Munroe's words of wisdom stretched the minds of those listening like no other. Oftentimes, the revelations revealed by him were spontaneous and thought provoking. For these reasons and more, his audiences sent an invitation for the original version because he was loaded with wisdom, knowledge, passion and understanding. Listen to his instructions, *"You must decide if you are going to rob the world or bless it with the rich, valuable, potent, untapped resources locked away within you."*

> **The most important person on this planet that you will meet is YOURSELF.**

Previously, has anyone told you that you possess the attributes to be a great leader? If not, I am happy to share this undeniable truth with you. According to John Buchan, *"The task of leadership is not to put greatness into people, but to elicit it, for the greatness is there already."* This statement gives you a reason why I had to write this book. From the beginning, I have attempted to get you to understand the greatness of your potential and purpose in life. Hopefully, I have succeeded in accomplishing this objective.

It is understood that there are widespread misconceptions about leaders and who qualifies for leadership. Many believe that leadership is designed for a select and privileged few. Nevertheless, the truth is that assigned to your

*Born to Lead and Succeed* 255

potential is an exclusive domain where your TAGs are needed. This means that you were born and uniquely equipped to become a leader in a specialized area. Since your area of leadership is based on what you have on the inside, you don't need the acceptance of others to become yourself or a leader.

## Leadership is the Goal of Potential

The Biblical account of Nehemiah is an excellent example of individual potential, purpose, dominion, and leadership. One day, while serving in exile as cupbearer for the King of Persia, he received word that his countrymen, the Israelites, were scattered abroad and the city of Jerusalem was left defenseless without perimeter walls or entrance gates. Upon hearing this distressing news, he immediately petitioned God for favor. Listen to his request, *"Lord let your ear be attentive to the prayer of this your servant and to the prayer of your servants who delight in revering your name. Give your servant success today by granting him favor in the presence of this man,"* referring to the king.

After praying, an opportunity was given to him to address the king. He used it to request a leave of absence to attend to the matter in his country. The king granted him leave, letters of authority and supplies to rebuild the walls and gates. It took a lot of time and effort to complete the task, but Nehemiah prevailed. What motivated him to persevere against the many obstacles? Perhaps, these words that he gave to a request from his enemies to meet and discuss his intentions gives insight. Nehemiah said, *"I am engaged in a great work, so I can't come. Why should I stop working to come and meet with you?"*

The story of Nehemiah makes no mention of any previous experience as a governor, building contractor, project manager or national leader. Yet, he served in those capacities after he decided to change the circumstances for his countrymen and hometown city. Clearly, Nehemiah possessed tremendous potential and confidence in his talents, abilities, and gifts. It is also obvious that he believed that it was his purpose in life to change the dynamics surrounding the city of Judah and the Israelites.

Nehemiah activated his dormant potential and pursued his purpose. When he did these things, it led to him having dominion over circumstances and influence to transform his status in life. One important goal of potential is to catapult you from virtual obscurity to a position of prominence. To reach this level, you must navigate through the treacherous waters created by comfort zones, mental obstacles that form mountains and the pit of despair resulting from personal struggles. It is my hope that the information, quotes, and principles contained in the previous chapters will bridge the gap between the invisible TAGs and the manifested YOU. The manifested you is the locked image of yourself that you see through your dreams and desire through your reoccurring thoughts.

Years ago, when I moved to the Bahamas, I had an entry level position at an insurance company. From that platform, I rose to the position of General Manager for an independent insurance agency and Vice President of another agency. In addition, I became the personal assistant for Dr. Myles Munroe at the height of his popularity. I also found time to write my first book. What am I trying to say? By no means do I feel as though I have arrived. I am mentioning these things because of the power of potential to change and improve your circumstances when you follow the path of purpose.

Before reading this book, you may not have known that your invisible TAGs can transform into visible realities that you manifest along the path of purpose. In other words, the things that you desire related to your TAGs and purpose are possible, but you must undergo a process to create the manifested result. This process that I am referring to is known as the transformational stage. The transformational stage is the cycle that turns your invisible TAGs into visible manifestation. In addition, it creates an environment whereby your potential is directed towards purposeful opportunities for personal growth and leadership.

*"Personal leadership is the process of keeping your vision and values before you and aligning your life to be congruent with them,"* according to

Stephen Covey, a well-known leadership guru. Guess What? Your personal leadership is more real than you may have imagined. Your vision is with you all the time. In fact, true vision cannot be removed only denied or prevented from manifesting. Your core values are formed by knowledge, information, relationships, and experiences. Your values are subject to change, but you can never remove the influence that values have on the decision-making process.

> **P**ersonal leadership is the highest recognition and acceptance of potential and purpose.

Covey's statement is a testament to something that you have access to, but may be unaware that you have it. When you align your potential and purpose to coincide with the vision for your life, then you are walking in your personal leadership. Therefore, personal leadership is not something that you acquire from an employment position or assignment, it is something that you recognize and accept as a part of your destiny. Successful completion of the transformation stage occurs when you recognize and accept the importance of living an intentional life of purpose through the maximization of your potential.

By now, I am sure that you understand the principles of potential. Nonetheless, it is imperative that I share with you, at least, four common goals associated with potential. These goals of potential attest to the fact that you were made with the tools to succeed in life. The goals are *leadership, purpose, dominion, and continuous impact*. When you recognize your potential, then you must understand that you can rise to a level of leadership, fulfilling a unique purpose, having dominion in a specialized area, and maintaining a continuous impact in your area of gifting.

> **P**ersonal leadership is the guarantee of potential and true destination of purpose.

Leadership is the guarantee of your potential because you were created as an original not a copy or clone. When your potential is released, it is a product of your TAGs, experiences, knowledge, and thoughts. These things make you uniquely different and standout from others. Since no one else can duplicate every aspect of your life, then the work produced by your potential carries your own fingerprint and signature.

During my military tenure, I experienced a situation that confirms the validity of the above statements about leadership and potential. My tour of duty in South Korea was a wonderful experience but not without several challenging situations. I worked in the Accounting & Finance Department and my job related to inputting and balancing travel pay advances. All computer entries had to be inputted and balanced prior to noon every day.

There was an aged tradition that every new airman in the section would go downtown and get intoxicated to the point of losing control over all senses and bodily functions. Everyone followed that tradition no matter the rank or gender. When I arrived, it did not take long before I was placed in a very uncomfortable position. I do not drink alcohol or go to nightclubs. Furthermore, I refused to be influenced by peer pressure. As a result, the reaction that I received from others within my section was firm and adamant, *"You will do it, everyone does it."*

I was harassed and continually subjected to many negative comments and experiences, but each day I refused to honor the tradition. My rejection was taken personally by everyone in my department. It was universally agreed that I would pay a price until I honored the tradition. I was given many uncomfortable assignments no one else had to do. For example, I was required to spend winter days walking around the base in cold weather picking up litter or working through the weekends while everyone else had time off.

Nevertheless, there was one issue that my tormentors did not take into consideration. I believed that it was my purpose to join and succeed in the Air Force. Therefore, I was determined not to allow anyone or anything to turn me away from my mission. From the very beginning, I took considerable pride in maximizing my potential and increasing my knowledge daily. As a result, I was the most skilled and knowledgeable person in my section. In fact, I received the Air Force Achievement Medal because of my knowledge, abilities, and proficiency.

Although I was mistreated daily, I held fast to the notion that one day they would have to apologize for their inappropriate actions. I believed that a situation would arise whereby my knowledge would be needed. Eventually, that day arrived, and the apology came from the highest-ranking member in our department. All morning, the entire department was tense and frightened by the consequences of not being able to fix the problem that was brought to their attention by the commanding officer. The problem had to be fixed that day before noon. Failure to fix the problem would result in extreme consequences for each of the noncommissioned officers (NCOs).

Since I was not a NCO, the problem did not rest on my shoulders. Therefore, I watched as they pondered the solution. Their fear and anxiety created a thick cloud of tension for everyone, but me. Eventually, after numerous futile attempts, the department head slowly walked towards me contemplating how to ask for my assistance. I was the last option, some tried while others conceded that they could not solve the problem, even if they tried.

I established my leadership potential, by having dominion in a specialized area, and exceeding the designated performance standards for the position. Everyone in the department realized that I was likely the only person able to solve the problem. For hours, they tried in vain without asking me for help. They wanted to avoid having to submit their egos and pride to someone that they despised and mistreated. However, it was destined to be the price they had to pay for discriminating against me.

Finally, in a quiet and humble tone, the senior NCO said to me, *"I know that we don't treat you fairly and we shouldn't require you to do something so stupid. I am much older than you and should know better. I did it and it was a stupid decision. I got so drunk I tried to climb a fence with barb wire and got all cut up."* His honesty did not illicit a response from me as I looked into his eyes and said nothing. After that, with a slight hesitation and timid voice, he asked *"Do you think that you can fix the problem?"* I knew it would only take a minute to resolve the issue, but I said, *"Maybe I can."*

Although I said, *"Maybe I can,"* my facial expression spoke the sentiments, *"Why should I help you?"* He understood my vibes. The apologetic sergeant said, *"John, I am sorry about what has happened, will you do this for me?"* After his apology, I fixed the problem. From that point onward, he ensured that everyone else in the section treated me fairly and with a degree of respect. That situation taught me a vital lesson about the power of potential.

One of the most important points is that potential changes your circumstances and improves your situations. If you develop it, then it transforms you from being a follower into a leader. I established myself as a leader not by rank but by recognizing, developing, and releasing my potential. This leads to this statement made by Dr. Myles Munroe, *"Every human has the instinct and capacity for leadership, but do not have the courage or will to cultivate it."*

Unfortunately, I believe that this statement is true for many because of issues surrounding comfort zones, pits of despair, mental obstacles, lack of wisdom, and knowledge. Nevertheless, since you have acquired the valuable information contained in this book, this statement should not apply to you. I believe that you are now the exception to the rule. I am excited about the fact that you will recognize that leadership is not an entitlement but an inalienable right. It is your right because of the importance of your purpose in life.

## Leadership is the Goal of Purpose

At this point, hopefully you have also grasped the concepts and decided to move towards developing your area of leadership by maximizing your potential. Since potential points you in the direction of your path of purpose, there is no need to live a life of uncertainty or insignificance. I have articulated that you were born with potential and because of this, you have a purpose in life. For this reason, your life, TAGs, and the things that you are destined to accomplish are inseparable. In fact, your purpose answers the questions of who you are, why you exist, where you are going and what you can do. Your potential and purpose also lead to discovering your area of dominion in life.

## Leadership is the Goal of Dominion

When Joseph Addison said, *"Nothing is more gratifying to the mind of man than power or dominion,"* I believe that he was partially correct. Everyone is seeking power or dominion over something. Some seek it over poverty, negative opinions, lack of confidence or other circumstances. Others seek power or dominion over debt, bills, and basic needs. In my opinion, maximizing potential and pursuing the purposeful path provides gratification because both give you power and dominion. Regardless of the reason, the human spirit wants to be in control over life not fall victim to it. Why is this statement true?

The statement is true because of the spirit of dominion. Are you aware that the spirit of dominion was transferred to you and now resides in you? Listen to a portion of this scripture, *"And God said, Let us make man in our image, after our likeness: and let them have dominion..."* First and foremost, God is the authority of dominion and He made us to be like Him. Our likeness to God included the transfer of the concept of dominion into our minds. Therefore, it is impossible to separate the spirit of dominion from the mind. This means that our thoughts, dreams, talents, abilities, and gifts are influenced by the impartation of dominion. It is not a mystery, God expects us to live victoriously with power, authority, and strength, because of our dominion nature.

Let's review a personal story to emphasize the dominion concept. My godparents, Rev. Walter and Lena Williams lived across the street from us and were very close friends with my parents. Rev. Williams was the neighborhood baseball coach, counselor, and mentor for all the young boys. He was aware of the many pitfalls and challenges that plagued young male teenage kids from our area. This knowledge led him to become a positive influence and role model. Unfortunately, he watched as many of them fell victim to drugs, alcohol, and illiteracy.

During one of my visits, Rev. Williams commented, *"I would like to see you write on the keys to becoming a victor and not victim."* His request was based on our family dynamics and the desire that we had to achieve a successful outcome, although we experienced many challenging circumstances and disappointments. As he stated, *"Your parents died when you guys were young, but you did not turn out like the other kids."* He proceeded to say, *"I observed you guys, and I am proud of you, but I am curious."* He continued with this question, *"What made you different?"*

There were many answers to that question but one of the most important was the desire to succeed or to be a victor. Fortunately, my siblings and I possessed the will to dominate the circumstances and not fall victim to the many difficult experiences and challenges. Furthermore, we did not succumb to the negative peer pressure. Thankfully, each one of us was able to pay our way through college and graduate. However, none of us had the pleasure of seeing the joy on our parent's faces. We succeeded against challenging odds. The same success awaits you when facing difficult circumstances in life.

> **Y**ou were born to have dominion
> over your circumstances.

The information contained in this book will help you to become a victor and understand your personal dominion. Personal dominion is a form of leadership designated for all. Specialized dominion is a normal aspect of nature. For instance, the bird has dominion over flight, the bee over production of honey, fish over the ability to swim and, seeds over fruit, the list goes on. Likewise, you were born with the natural ability to have an area of specialization. The area of specialization is your purpose in life, and it is manifested through your potential.

*"You can have no dominion greater or less than that over yourself,"* according to Leonardo da Vinci. His comments suggest that the highest form of dominion is over yourself. Invariably, dominion over self includes refining, mastering and maximizing your TAGs. Centuries later, da Vinci still receives accolades and recognition for his remarkable pieces of artwork. Guess What? You have the capacity to leave your own indelible mark as well.

Becoming skilled and masterful in the utilization of your potential should be one of your highest priorities in life. As you now know, the world is searching for those that are skilled in their specialized areas. *"Do you see a man skillful in his work? He will stand before kings..."* King Solomon's words of wisdom suggests that your developed potential will attract attention from people in high places in life. Can you imagine living a life whereby individuals seek after your dominion in your area of gifting?

## Continuous Impact

*"You cannot get through a single day without having an impact on the world around you. What you do makes a difference, and you have to decide*

*what kind of difference you want to make."* That observation was made by Jane Goodall, the internationally acclaimed anthropologist and primatologist. Each day brings an opportunity for you to make an impact on the world around you. The good thing about having potential is that you do not need to guess about where you can make the most impact. Furthermore, your potential enables you to have a fulfilling life on a consistent and continuous basis. It also establishes your continuous position of leadership and dominion.

Do you believe these words spoken by Tony Robbins, *"The only limit to your impact is your imagination and commitment?"* Can you imagine being a leader in your area of gifting for a continuous duration? If so, are you committed to overcoming the pitfalls and pressing forward until you reach the mark? It is my desire that you accept your leadership role and enjoy years of continuous fruitful results in life. Always remember that you were born to lead and not follow in your area of TAGs.

## Living as a Leader not Follower

Did you know that it is God's desire to *"make you the head and not the tail, and ...to always make you to be on top and never at the bottom?"* Dr. Munroe said, *"One key to maximizing your potential is to become dissatisfied with the circumstances that restrict, limit, and stifle your potential."* Persons that are followers tend to be led by circumstances that seem out of their control. Whereas, leaders that are led by their pursuit of purpose tend to change circumstances that are within their control. Changing the present circumstances that are restricting, limiting, or stifling your potential is an indication that you have accepted your leadership role and responsibility.

Living a life of personal leadership means that maximizing your potential is not an option but a responsibility. Therefore, if you are plagued by a lack of passion, an attitude of laziness and pessimism, then it is time to change your habits. As you look around you, I am sure that you would agree with the conclusion that the world needs more leadership options. As John Quincy Adams said, *"If your actions inspire others to dream more, learn more, do more and become more, you are a leader."* Based on what you now know about the value of your life, do you believe that you are the perfect candidate for leadership in your country, community, and place of employment?

Everything in this book points to the conclusion that the world needs to see the hidden you, as much as you need to see the manifested version hidden on the inside of you. It's time to rise to the occasion and accept your rightful leadership position. Remember these words from Leonardo DiCaprio, *"A single idea from the human mind can build cities. An idea can transform the world and rewrite all the rules."*

When you follow your purpose and release your potential, you will transform the world and rewrite all the preconceived notions about your race, color, gender, size, or social economic background. When I started this project over 5 years ago, I started with a single idea to write a book about potential and purpose. I did not have a stockpile of quotes or a library full of books written about the subjects. That idea quickly turned into a passion, then a responsibility and later into a requirement or obligation.

Along the way, this recurring thought never left me, *"You have to do this. It does not matter how you feel or whether it is difficult or not. It is your responsibility and destiny,"* I grew into understanding my personal leadership role related to bridging the gap between understanding what I was born to do and walking into it. *Have you discovered and accepted who you are?* It does not matter what others think, it matters what you think and do in life. It is my hope that I am now speaking to a person that is a focused leader ready to act upon your responsibility to change the world. The following 7 points about personal leadership will add to your wealth of knowledge:

- You are born with a personal leadership trait that designates your assignment and path in life.
- Your personal leadership comes with the natural power to have dominion over things that come to restrict, prevent, and stifle your potential.

- Disregarding the recurring cry of your heart and TAGs will lead to you rejecting your personal leadership opportunity.
- Your personal leadership position affords the opportunity to create change and bring into existence creations that never existed before. You hold the solution or answer to problems, questions, inventions, and situations that the world is waiting for.
- Your dreams, visions and desires of the heart are proof that your personal leadership position is obtainable, permissible, and already justified.
- Your personal leadership position comes with power, authority, strength, dominion, and provisions to destroy the myths about what is possible or impossible to do. You are an agent of change. It does not matter if the required change is big or small, easy, or difficult. Obstacles cannot hold up against your will and vision for a better outcome.
- Personal leadership is your greatest gift and contribution to the world and yourself. Walking in your leadership role answers the core life questions.

> **D**reams are hidden realities waiting for the leader in you to free them.

Release your dreams and let them fly. You deserve to experience the joy, success and satisfaction that comes to those that live a purpose driven life. God *"holds success in store for the upright, He is a shield to those whose walk is blameless."* Repeat after me, *"I am a possibility creator and an impossibility destroyer. I am a possibility creator and an impossibility destroyer. I am a possibility creator and an impossibility destroyer."*

# THE NEXT STEP

I realize that some of the information, concepts and principles may have been difficult to process during your initial reading. Therefore, I would encourage you to use this book as a reference guide and refer to it throughout your purposeful journey. Much of this information that I have written, I learned at various stages in life. Some aspects of this material may be more relevant at various stages of your life as well. Nevertheless, all of the information is necessary. Remember that your purpose is a journey. Never quit or give up on your dreams and the desires of your heart. You can overcome and succeed. I am convinced that you were created to be a great leader in your designated area.

When you develop your potential to its fullest and pursue your path of purpose, then you will become a natural spring that provides refreshing water to yourself and others. The demand for your potential will create a host of followers looking to taste your unique water. You may ask, "What is my water?" Your water is your released potential. Because of the uniqueness of it, others from near and far will demand to drink from it

In conclusion, *"Leadership is not an elite club for a certain few. It is the true essence of all human beings,"* as statement by Dr. Myles Munroe. As previously stated, your personal leadership authority begins and ends with your potential. This means that there is a specific leadership role designated and waiting just for you. It is a role and position that fits your natural talents, abilities, and gifts. Although the position is reserved for you solely, you must travel along the right path to discover its location along the journey of life.

It is my sincere hope that your journey in life is influenced by purpose, as leadership is the destiny of your purpose and potential. Dr. Munroe also said, *"Leadership is the capacity to influence others through inspiration motivated by passion, generated by vision, produced by a conviction, ignited by a purpose."* When you become a master at releasing your potential, then others are inspired and motivated by your passion. The key is to recognize and accept that your leadership position is waiting for you. Where you begin is not as important as where you are destined to go and what you can achieve in life. Remember these words, *"The greatest ending started with a beginning. Without a beginning, you cannot have a successful ending."*

## Quick reference to born to lead and succeed principles:

1. The most important person on the planet that you will ever meet is yourself.
2. One important goal of potential is to catapult you from virtual obscurity to national or international prominence and personal satisfaction.
3. The manifested you is the locked image of yourself that you see through your dreams and through your recurring thoughts.
4. Your values are subject to change, but you can never remove the influence that values have on the decision-making process.
5. Personal leadership is the highest recognition and acceptance of potential and purpose.
6. If you recognize your potential, then you must understand that you can rise to a level of leadership, fulfilling a unique purpose, having dominion in a specialized area while maintaining a continuous impact on earth.
7. Personal leadership is the guarantee of potential and true destination of purpose.
8. Leadership is a guarantee of your potential because you were created as an original not a copy or clone.
9. You were born to have dominion over your circumstances.
10. The concept of dominion in life stems from the belief that you were born to dominate in a specialized area.
11. Becoming skilled and masterful in the utilization of your potential should be one of your highest priorities in life.
12. When you refine and master your potential along the path of purpose, you become a master at your craft.
13. Living a life of personal leadership means that maximizing your potential is not an option but a responsibility.
14. Releasing your amazing potential along the path of purpose will inspire others to dream more, learn more from you, do more and become more than a victim of circumstances.

15. When you follow your purpose and release your potential, you can transform the world into a better place and rewrite all of the incorrect stigmas about your race, color, gender, size, or social economic background.
16. Dreams are hidden realities waiting for the leader in you to free them.

# Chapter Twelve

## God's Purpose Is In The Name

*"The beginning of wisdom is to call things by their proper name."*
**Confucius**

One of the greatest misconceptions is the belief that God's plan for your life has no impact on self-awareness. Contrary to this belief, God's plan for your life has a direct reflection on who you are and what you are to become in life. This means that God knows everything about you from the beginning of your life. In fact, He gives you a name and records it in His book of life before you are born. The name that He gives you is directly associated with your purpose and potential.

Furthermore, there are two additional important concepts about God's naming. The name that He gives you is a name of recognition and a name of identification of your purpose for living. His name of recognition is the name that you use to identify yourself such as Michael, Richard, etc. Whereas, the name of purpose that He gives you identifies your gift to the world such as teacher, counselor, etc. It is also important to realize that the world will get to know you by both names. For example, when you hear the name Michael Jordan, you associate him with his gift of playing basketball. Alternatively, when you hear the word Redeemer, the name Jesus Christ comes to mind.

God's thoughts are for you to prosper in your life. Prosperity is associated with the name he has reserved for you. Understanding your purpose in life should not be unknown. God's plan is available to you, but you must ask Him to confirm your assigned name and seek to understand its meaning related to your life. When He answers you, then you will have the information necessary to start your journey towards fulfilling your purpose and living an intentional life.

In Ancient Hebrew culture, the name held symbolic meaning, as it would reveal something about the person, character, or their life. In this regard, if the name given by the parents did not coincide with their God given purpose, then God would change the name accordingly. In other words, the name and the thing were unified. Therefore, the name or names that God gives you holds a wealth of knowledge about your character, purpose, and destiny in life.[40]

## God Assigns Your Name

The first person recorded in the Bible to have their name changed by God was Abraham. His original name was Abram, which means "exalted father." Whereas, the name Abraham means "father of a multitude."[41] Others that had their names changed by God included Sarah, Jacob, Saul, and Peter to name a few.

Jesus is also the perfect example of God's intentions reflected through the name given. During my research, I found a source that lists over 150 different names and attributes used to describe Jesus' potential and purpose. The Apostle Paul talked about the importance of the name of Jesus when he said, *"Therefore, God elevated him to the place of the highest honor and gave him the name above all names."* In addition, Isaiah mentioned these names for Jesus, *"For a child is born to us, a son is given to us. The government will rest on his shoulders. And he will be called: Wonderful Counselor, Mighty God, Everlasting Father, Prince of Peace."* Each name represents either a function, task, duty, or assignment that He performed during His life on earth.[42]

Accordingly, the name or names that God attaches to your existence gives meaning and value towards you discovering yourself. *"Everything has already been decided. It was known long ago what each person would be. So there's no use arguing with God about your destiny."* The Hebrew word used in the scripture for decided is "qara." This word also means to call, name, give name to or call by.[43] Therefore, when you insert the various meanings into the scripture, it would read as follows:

- Everything has already been called by...
- Everything has already been given a name...

The summation of the first sentence in the quote is that everything about a person is known before the person is born. It also concludes that everyone has a name which is given by and recognized by God prior to birth. The next sentence in the scripture indicates that God attaches a specific purpose with every name prior to birth. Emphasis is put on the fact that purpose is attached to the name that God gives, which may differ from the name given by the parents.

In Chapter 5, the concept of a predetermined or predestined future was discussed. This concept derives from the viewpoint that God has already chosen a path specifically for you. The last sentence of the above scripture indicates that God decides the path of destiny for each person in addition to giving them a name that coincides with their purpose. The conclusion to King Solomon's quote is that the name written in God's book of life for a person corresponds with and attaches significance to their hidden potential and purpose for living. This explains why the purpose given to each person is not debatable or questionable.

Although purpose is preassigned and foreknown by God, there is an obvious challenge with connecting His purpose to life. Unfortunately, these words of Albert Einstein are true, *"Strange is our situation here on earth. Each of us comes for a short visit, not knowing why, yet sometimes seeming to divine a purpose."* One of my primary objectives is to stop the turn of events mentioned by Einstein. His synopsis was accurate. Our visit on earth is short and sometimes filled with uncertainty about purpose and the meaning of life.

The first approach to stopping the tide of uncertainty about your purpose is to examine the issue related to the name given to you by God. The life of the Hebrew patriarch Jacob is one of many examples in scriptures that confirms God's intentions in the naming process. Jacob was the younger of twin boys born to Isaac, a man of God. During her pregnancy, the twins struggled in the womb which caused concern for their mother, Rebekah. The Lord answered Rebekah's concern by saying:

*The sons in your womb will become two nations. From the very beginning, the two nations will be rivals. One nation will be stronger than the other; and your older son will serve your younger son.*

When Jacob was preparing to give the firstborn blessing, Rebekah remembered God's words to her concerning her sons while they were in her womb. At birth, Jacob held the heel of his brother Esau as they were coming out of the womb. As a result, he was given the name Jacob which means heel holder. As the boys grew older, their father favored Esau and Rebekah favored Jacob.

During that era, before the father died, it was customary for him to speak a blessing over the oldest son. Rebekah, remembering the words of the Lord that the older son will serve the younger, intervened and arranged with Jacob to trick Isaac into giving him Esau's blessing. Their scheme worked and Isaac pronounced the first-born blessing over Jacob instead of Esau.

When Esau discovered that Jacob took his firstborn blessing, he was furious and plotted to kill him. Fearing for his life, Jacob moved away from the family for many years. Eventually, Esau discovered the location of his brother and set out to meet him. Again, fearing for his life, Jacob departed from his home with his wives, servants and all his possessions.

While on the run, he had a spiritual encounter with an angel of God. After the encounter, God advised him that his name would be called Israel. Therein, the prophecy about his life and his purpose was confirmed. The descendants of Israel are called Israelites and their nation is called Israel.

When God revealed to Jacob his preordained assigned name, Israel, He clarified that Jacob's life meant more than being a deceiver and heel catcher. The meaning of Israel is God prevails. The words God spoke to Rebekah about her son prior to birth were fulfilled, as He prevailed in the life of Jacob and his descendants, even to this day. There are other accounts in scripture supporting the fact that the name God gives you and your purpose in life are inseparable.

There is a clear message in the above story of Jacob's transition to Israel. The message is that God created you in a unique fashion, equipped you with special tools and decided that your life should follow a designated path. At the end of that path is success, an abundant life, and a fruitful existence. This also means that everything about your creation, potential and purpose was thought out by God himself. God desires that you live intentionally and deliberately to satisfy a specific need in the world that exists during your lifetime or in generations to come. Below is the flow of life chart that highlights God's process to making you special:

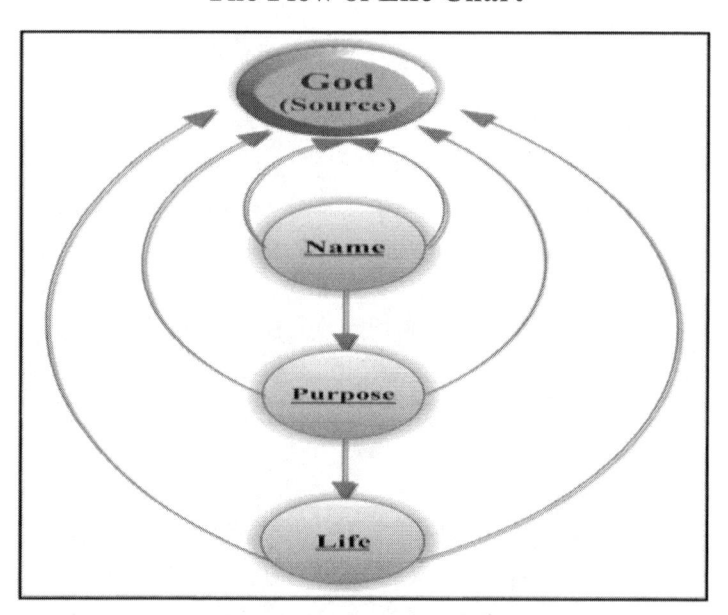

## The Flow of Life Chart

**Name**

The above chart brings visualization to the fact that key aspects regarding your life flows from God and leads back to Him. The process begins when He records your name in His book of life. This action indicates that He has a plan for your life that attaches to your purpose. It also means that the resources necessary to achieve success have been given or have already been made available to you.

Your name is recorded evidence that you deserve to receive the benefits made available when you maximize your potential along the path of purpose. Listed below are additional benefits associated with your name:

- Name reveals purpose – *1 Chronicles 22:9*
- Name provides order, focus and structure – *Gen. 3:20*
- Name determines your dominion & authority – *Is. 9:6*
- Name reveals knowledge of self – *Gen. 17:5*

- Name is confirmation and justification in the spirit realm – *Luke 10:20*

The life of Gideon is another amazing true story that exemplifies the inherent power associated with the name that God gives you. Gideon, along with all his countrymen, was in great distress due to the actions of their powerful neighbors known as the Midianites. The Midianites routinely ravaged the land and everything of value from the Israelites. Under this brutal treatment, the Israelites suffered immensely. According to the Biblical account, they cried out to God for help, and He heard their prayers.

Having foreknowledge that the Midianites would severely oppress and dominate the people, God planted a seed of deliverance in advance to confront the foreign power. He placed the deliverance that the Israelites needed inside of a man called Gideon. The gift was that of a mighty warrior. According to the writer of the historical Book of Judges, *"The angel of the Lord came and sat down under the oak in Ophrah that belonged to Joash the Abiezrite, where his son Gideon was threshing wheat in a winepress to keep it from the Midianites. When the angel of the Lord appeared to Gideon, he said, "The Lord is with you, mighty warrior."*

The name used to greet Gideon is significant, as it was not common for him to hear it or to be called it by others. In other words, it was a name that was unfamiliar to him prior to hearing it from the messenger of God. The angel of the Lord called Gideon a mighty warrior. Mighty warrior was the name assigned to him to match his potential and purpose in life. The designation of mighty warrior represented his predestined future or the fruitful stage of his purpose and gift. This means that the seed of a mighty warrior was inside of him from the beginning of his life. He was God's instrument and the gift of a mighty warrior made Gideon the solution to the problem.

Sometimes it is possible to disregard your recurring thoughts about purpose because you believe that there are other more valuable candidates to complete the assignment. It is plausible to believe that Gideon's recurring thoughts and true desires of the heart pointed him in the direction of becoming a great leader for his nation, tribe, and family. Although this may be true, the initial response given by him suggested otherwise. When the LORD said, *"Go in the strength you have and save Israel out of Midian's hand. Am I not sending you?" "Pardon me, my lord," Gideon replied, "but how can I save Israel? My clan is the weakest in Manasseh, and I am the least in my family."*

At first glance, it is possible to interpret Gideon's response as a denial of his latent potential in the form of talents, abilities, and gifts. It is important to understand that he never said, *"I don't have the natural ability to deliver the people."* His response suggested that God mistakenly chose the smallest group of people and the person with the least ability in the family. His next response in Judges 8:17 reveals an awareness of his natural gift and a sense of value, *"Gideon replied, "If now I have found favor in your eyes, give me a sign that it is really you talking to me."*

His statement suggests that he spent time refining and developing mighty warrior abilities in secret without others knowing. In other words, he was saying *"God if you are pleased with my preparation and it is time to reveal my hidden self to my family, people and the Midianites, give me a sign that it is you challenging me to move forward."* God gave Gideon the confirmation and he never wavered or hesitated. His response after receiving the confirmation clearly indicates an acceptance of his destiny and an awareness of his capacity to lead.

As indicated, the name that God gives you is very important for you to know and understand. You are relevant in the eyes of God. Everything that you were given is necessary to fulfill His plan for your life. David's words confirmed this truth when he said the following:

> *Your eyes have seen my unformed substance; and in Your book were all written the days that were ordained for me, when as yet there was not one of them. How precious also are Your thoughts to me, O God! How vast is the sum of them!*

These words confirm that God knew you and decided what you would do in life prior to your birth. The words of David also confirm that God's plan for your life is a plan of purpose. This means that you came to the earth with purpose already on the inside of you.

## Purpose in the Name

*"Purpose is when you know and understand what you were born to accomplish. Vision is when you see it in your mind and begin to imagine it,"* according to Dr. Myles Munroe. Therefore, purpose is understood when you connect to the normal flow of life that starts with an appreciation for God's role as your parent or source. Having knowledge about what you are born to accomplish comes naturally when you discover His plan. When that happens, you will also gain a sense that you are perfectly made, equipped, and entitled to fulfill your assignment in life.

In his own words, Gideon stated that he was not born into a privileged situation with great personal status, opportunities, and recognition. None of these things mattered when he accepted God's purpose for his life. In the end, he became his future in the form of a mighty warrior, great leader, and judge. His future was inside of him in the beginning. That is the reason why the messenger of God referred to Gideon as a "mighty warrior" before he led successful military campaigns. Your reason for life is just as important and necessary. When God addresses your purpose, He speaks to the end-result because it represents the designated path that He has chosen for you.

Having knowledge about what you were born to do will also open your personal vision receptacle. Your vision receptacle is the area in your mind that perceives and eventually identifies the path that you believe your life should follow. In other words, it creates the ability to envision a comprehensive plan for your life that is fueled by the desires of the heart. This means that the vision you have for your life is a mental visualization and manifestation of your purpose that leads to self-actualization. Based on this information, it is important to understand God's thoughts about your life because His thoughts lead to understanding your purpose. Your purpose leads to developing a vision and your vision helps chart a course to fulfill the right career path or assignment in life.

**Life**

Although sometimes life seems unfair, challenging, and unpredictable, your predestined future remains unaffected when you follow God's path for your life. Gideon's life and accomplishments are evidence of this truth. His life was difficult in the beginning. Daily, he experienced constant oppression and a lack of basic physical needs.

Hopefully, you accept that there are many choices that lead to a life of despair but very few that lead to God's desired life for you. The right path is found when you establish a relationship with God, recognize your purpose and manifest the hidden you. Therefore, the greatest responsibility is for you to discover the life you are born to live. Failure to make the right connection will ultimately lead to some form of mental destruction.

*"If you want to live a happy life, tie it to a goal, not to people or things."* That statement from Albert Einstein suggests that establishing and accomplishing your goals are critical to having a happy life. This is true but it is necessary that you have the right goals and objectives for your life. Focusing your goals in life on the opinions of others to gain their trust or approval is very dangerous because you risk being someone other than who God created you to be. In the same regard, tailoring your life around acquiring things or material wealth as your primary focus is equally dangerous.

What makes acquiring things or material wealth mental pitfalls in your life? This remark from Jesus Christ helps to answer that question, *"Enter through the narrow gate. For wide is the gate and broad is the road that leads to destruction, and many enter through it. But small is the gate and narrow the road that leads to life, only a few find it."* Pursuing things and issues that contradict or distract you from God's assigned plan for your life is counterproductive. Your life is supposed to follow a straight path that leads to a designated end. Unfortunately, as Jesus stated, only a few people find the narrow path that leads to their purpose for living.

The story of a rich young ruler found in Matt. 19:16-30 is an example of the tendency to make the wrong decision because of a lack of knowledge regarding God's purpose and assigned name for you. By all accounts, the young man was good hearted and well respected. The story does not give an account of how he acquired his wealth, but it does say that he was rich. Nevertheless, he seemed to possess a sincere desire to do right in life and treat others with respect. Even though, he had considerable wealth, possessions, and servants, he lacked one important thing, peace of mind.

One day, he approached Jesus for a solution to his mental unrest and desire to maximize his relationship with God. Jesus replied to the young man asking him about his faithfulness towards adhering to the commandments. He was a righteous young man and was able to confirm his compliance to each commandment very quickly. After doing so, Jesus asked him to sell his possessions, give the proceeds to the poor and to follow Him as one of his trusted students. Unfortunately, after calculating his potential financial loss, wealth, power, and riches, he chose to forgo the teacher's invitation and went away dejected. What did the young man give up by refusing to accept the invitation?

The above Biblical account of the rich young ruler and Jesus had a very unfortunate ending. Presumably, the encounter would have been different if the young man possessed the knowledge about his name assigned by God. The name assigned by God would have given him an indication of his purpose. His purpose in life was to become a disciple of Christ. It was Jesus' intention for him to have a rich and satisfying life, not to cause him to feel sad or rejected.

Listen to Jesus' comforting words, *"Yes, I am the gate. Those who come through me will be saved. They will come and go freely and will find good pastures."* Unfortunately, one decision made because of a lack of knowledge resulted in three major life issues for the young man. The decision resulted in a failure to maximize his potential, failure to discover his purpose in life and a failure to impact the world in a substantial way.

The rich young ruler's peace of mind was attached to the wrong things, at the expense of his potential and purpose. He was born with the potential and purpose to become a disciple, but he rejected his destiny. In doing so, he rejected key elements that life had to offer him. The best that life has to offer includes maximizing your potential, fulfilling your purpose, and bearing much fruit. These things lead to experiencing life more abundantly.

*"You can only become truly accomplished at something you love. Don't make money your goal. Instead pursue the things you love doing and then do them so well that people can't take their eyes off of you."* Take a moment to digest those words from Maya Angelou.

If you read the entire Biblical account about the rich young ruler, then it becomes clear that the young man loved following God's commandments, but it also reveals that he was not happy. Jesus addressed his lack of peace of mind by stating that, *"If you want to be **perfect** go and sell all your possessions and give the money to the poor, and you will have treasure in heaven. Then come follow me."* The word used for perfect is also interpreted to mean complete. Therefore, Jesus was appealing to his lack of happiness or peace of mind by offering a solution. The solution was an introduction to his purpose and assignment in life.

Many years ago, Benjamin Franklin said, *"Many be die at twenty-five and aren't buried until they are seventy-five."* When the young ruler rejected the offer, he also rejected to pursue his purpose in life. In other words, he rejected the path that leads to life for the path that leads to mental and physical destruction. If he knew God's will for his life, then it is likely that the story would have had a different ending.

## THE NEXT STEP

*"So also will be the word that I speak – it will not fail to do what I plan for it; it will do everything that I send it to do."* These are God's words to you about your future. You are not destined to be a failure. Let me rephrase that for those who still have doubt, **"You are a winner. You were not created to be a failure!!!"** God's purpose for your life will succeed. The evidence of this truth is revealed in your innate potential. As indicated, God already set into motion the circumstances regarding your success in life.

The last and most important step involves understanding God's will for your life. Everything that you have learnt thus far has prepared you for this moment. The name that He gave you and wrote in His book of life gives you an indication about His intentions. When you successfully link His will to your potential and purpose, then it makes for a formidable combination that creates possibilities and destroys impossibilities. You can do great and unimaginable things because God's name for you is associated with your life, purpose, and authority.

I am excited that you have continued the journey through each chapter and have arrived at this point. You are almost at the top of the pyramid which is where self-actualization reigns supreme. Are you ready to move forward living the life that you were born to live? If so, proceed to the last chapter and learn about discovering God's plan for your life.

### Quick reference to God's purpose is in the name principles:

1. Although purpose is preassigned and foreknown by God, there is an obvious challenge with connecting His purpose to life.
2. The first approach to stopping the tide of uncertainty about your purpose is to examine the issue related to the name given to you by God.
3. God desires that you live intentionally and deliberately to satisfy a specific need in the world that exists during your lifetime or in generations to come.
4. Everything that you were given is necessary to fulfill His plan for your life.
5. When God addresses your purpose, He speaks to the end-result because it represents the designated path that He has chosen for your life.
6. Purpose is understood when you connect to the normal flow of life that starts with an appreciation for God's role as your parent or source.
7. Your vision receptacle is the area in your mind that perceives and eventually identifies the path that you believe your life should follow.
8. Your purpose leads to developing a vision and your vision helps chart a course to fulfill the right career path or assignment in life.
9. The right path is found when you establish a relationship with God, recognize your purpose and manifest the hidden you.
10. Focusing your goals in life on the opinions of others to gain their trust or approval is very dangerous because you risk being someone other than who God created you to be.
11. Pursuing things and issues that contradict or distract you from God's assigned plan for your life is counterproductive. You are a winner. You were not created to be a failure.

# Final Chapter

## God's Plan For Your Life

> *"To walk outside of God's will is to step into nowhere."*
> **C.S. Lewis**

By all accounts, it started out as a typical Sunday morning that included Sunday school and morning worship service. I was an inquisitive eight-year-old kid that enjoyed participating in church events. During and after church meetings, I tended to quietly question the spiritual commitment and dedication of some older members. To my young mind, as I observed the actions and attitudes of some attendees, it seemed as though they were not fully committed to understanding God's plan for their lives. Many seemed more interested in their denomination and religious routines.

This opinion was formed after close observation of their attitudes and actions during and after the service. In fact, when challenged about certain scriptures related to a more dedicated walk with God, they would respond, *"We don't teach on these subjects or We don't believe that it is necessary to do these things because that related to the Bible days."* Nevertheless, I was eager to know as much as possible about God's plan for my life and I also tried my best to live up to His standards.

On this particular morning, as I watched others go through the familiar routines of standing, singing and talking, I distinctly heard the voice of God through my thoughts say, *"One day you will teach them the truth."* The voice didn't say anything else regarding the topic or timeframe when my teaching purpose would begin. Although I was sure about what I heard, it did little to quench my thirst for answers about my purpose in life. Each day, I wanted the assurance of knowing why I existed. At that time, the issue overwhelmed my thoughts every day, but I found no answers from church, family, or friends. It seemed as though; I was marooned on an isolated island trapped by my environment. I prayed, I asked questions and I wondered but no answers materialized.

Later in life, my quest for answers to the meaning of life led me to make the decision to move to the Bahamas and become a student of Dr. Myles Munroe. Although I did not fully understand that God was still ordering my steps, I realized that Dr. Munroe was an amazingly gifted teacher with special insight into purpose, potential and leadership. While serving as his personal aide, there were many valuable lessons and experiences that I cherished. In addition, there were several insightful messages that I received from God during this period.

The first event was subtle but memorable. I was working diligently on finishing my first book and one day the voice of God entered my thoughts again and said, *"You are the bridge that will take the people over from understanding their purpose and potential to living in it."* I recall mentioning to a church leader that "I am the bridge." He looked at me directly and said, *"If this is true, then time will tell."*

Although I didn't take the words lightly, it was still hard to understand how and when it would happen that I would become a bridge to help others understand the vital issues necessary to live a successful life. The next memorable personal experience came in the form of a dream. In the dream, I was travelling with Dr. Munroe to another country but there was a major issue. It was very clear that something significant had happened in the life of Dr. Munroe. He did not look the same. He was frail, weak and could not speak or walk.

When we arrived at our destination, I put him on my back and started walking in the direction of the event. I could hear the people around us say, *"Why are you carrying him on your back, he is not the same."* I responded by saying, *"I am doing this because I am supposed to. I will carry him all the way."* I will admit that the thought entered my mind, *"Why did God place you in a position to carry the legacy of a world-renowned teacher on your back."* Nevertheless, I never explored understanding the dream because Dr. Munroe was alive and doing a tremendous work for the Kingdom of God. In fact, I kept the disturbing dream a secret, but I never forgot it.

Years later, Dr. Munroe and eight others died in a plane crash that shocked thousands around the world. After that event, the messages that God spoke and revealed to me started to make sense. It became very apparent that God was ordering my steps since I was that eight-year-old kid sitting in church seeking a greater understanding about life. God revealed his purpose for my life, He gave insight into the name that is reserved for me and He confirmed what he wants me to teach.

I also received clarification regarding the dream about Dr. Munroe. The reference in the dream regarding his change of appearance and influence represented the fact that he would not be able to physically deliver the message on earth. This meant that as his student, trainee, and former aide, I would be positioned to continue what he started related to enlightening others about God's plan for their lives. Listen to Dr. Munroe's words, *"The greatest tragedy in life is not death but a life without a purpose."*

A life without knowledge of purpose has various consequences for the individuals and the world. One of the major consequences is the fact that life becomes an experiment. Often, this also means that there is no definitive strategy or intentional objective in life that satisfies the desires of the heart related to purpose. This issue leads to confusion, uncertainty, and questions regarding the meaning of life because things or achievements cannot fill the void created by unknown purpose. Unknown purpose creates internal voids in life because it is God's will that everyone lives a fruitful and productive life.

## Understanding God's Will

The first and most important point to realize about God's will is the fact that His thoughts and ways are not like yours or mine. He said, *"My thoughts are nothing like your thoughts, says the LORD. And my ways are far beyond anything you could imagine."* When you consider these words, it would be wrong to attempt to insert your opinion about God's plan for your life. For parents, this is sometimes hard to consider when you have children. Often, parents expect children to pursue the career path that they choose for them. This approach is wrong because God has certain thoughts about each person and a plan for their existence. So, when you begin to consider God's will for your life, bear in mind that it may differ from your thoughts and that of others.

David spoke this enlightening testimony about God's will:

> *You made all the delicate, inner parts of my body and knit them together in my mother's womb. Thank you for making me so wonderfully complex! It is amazing to think about. Your workmanship is marvelous—and how well I know it. You were there while I was being formed in utter seclusion! You saw me before I was born and scheduled each day of my life before I began to breathe. Every day was recorded in your book!*
>
> *How precious it is, Lord, to realize that you are thinking about me constantly! I can't even count how many times a day your thoughts turn toward me. And when I waken in the morning, you are still thinking of me!*

These scriptures validate the point that God (Source / Creator) did not make a mistake when He made you with potential and a purpose in life. In fact, He equipped you with potential to fulfill the purpose that He gave you. To ensure or guarantee your success along the path of destiny, He recorded the plan for your life in His book. Now, it is critical that you understand this next point.

*God's Plan for your Life*                                                289

Believe it or not, God has thoughts about your life and the things He has already allocated for you to have. This means that God's will and your life are inextricably woven together.

The phrase "God's will" is used to explain or acknowledge His desires, intentions or wishes for your life. This phrase is interchangeable with the concept of God's purpose for your life. As noted in the previous chapter, God has a detailed plan for your life which is accessible to you. Information contained in His book of life about your purpose is available. In this regard, God's will for your life is not intended to be a secret. On the contrary, *"But you have received the Holy Spirit, and he lives within you, so you don't need anyone to teach you what is true. For the Spirit teaches you everything you need to know and what he teaches is true-it is not a lie."*

Throughout this chapter, God's will and God's plan are used interchangeably. Although these concepts are used to mean the same thing, it is essential for you to understand that His will is a plan. His plan is also His purpose for your life. God spoke these words to Isaiah, *"I make known the end from the beginning, from ancient times, what is still to come. I say, My purpose will stand, and I will do all that I please."* God's purpose prevails over plans that are inconsistent with His will for your life. Although His plan is the best course of action, sometimes the process of receiving direct and clear information is misunderstood or unknown.

Think for a moment, do you believe that God wants to keep His plan for your life a secret, yet hold you accountable for it? It would be pointless for Him to write about you in His book of life, bless you with tremendous potential, establish a rewarding path of purpose and guarantee your future success, then fail to make His plans known or available to you. On the contrary, it is very important for you to understand that God wants you to know the truth about your existence. This assurance that He gave to Jeremiah applies to you as well, *"Ask me and I will tell you remarkable secrets you do not know about things to come."*

To assist in finding answers, there are five helpful attributes to have when seeking to understand God's plan for your life. Since the internal elements influence how you process information, it is essential that you begin your quest to understand His plan with an open mind. Having an open mind means that you remove or disregard any perceived thoughts suggesting that God must or will follow a set pattern to answer your questions. In other words, He can choose any means necessary to make His plan known to you. Albeit, it is extremely helpful for you to possess the attributes shown on the following chart, when seeking to understand His will for your life:

## Understanding God's Will Chart

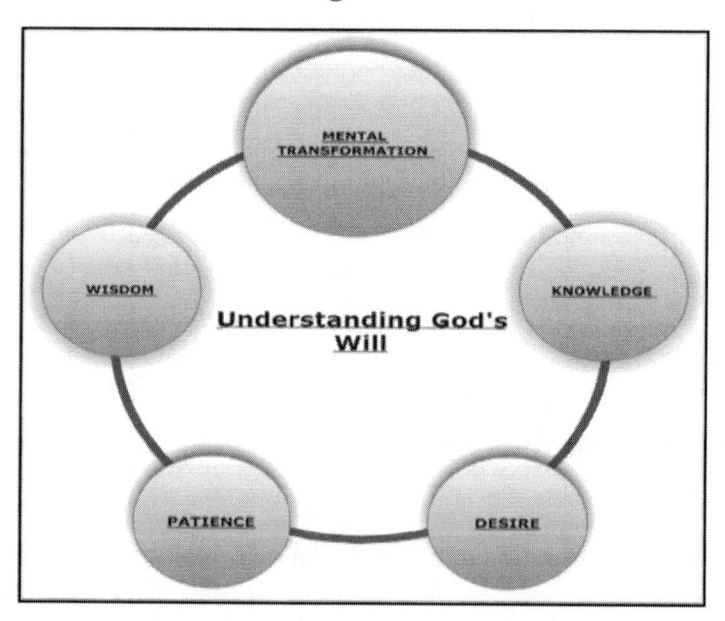

*"There are two kinds of people. Those who say to God, thy will be done and those to whom God says all right, then have it your way!"* That C.S. Lewis statement is based on the premise that God's will is readily made known to all and some follow it while others decide to do as they please. Nevertheless, based on my experience, there are countless individuals that are uncertain about His plan for their lives. If you fall into this category, then rest

assured that the above characteristics are helpful. The process of understanding begins with a transformation of your thoughts.

**Mental Transformation**

*"Don't copy the behavior and customs of this world, but let God transform you into a new person by changing the way you think. Then you will learn to know God's will for you, which is good and pleasing and perfect."* With that being said, it is essential that you undergo a drastic change in how you perceive God's desire to reveal your purpose. A transformation of your thoughts means that you trust, seek, and obey the leading of the Holy Spirit. When describing the role of the Holy Spirit in your life, Jesus said, *"When the Spirit of truth comes, he will guide you into all truth. He will not speak on his own but will tell you what he has heard. He will tell you about the future."*

Based on the words of Jesus, information about your predetermined future is accessible to you. To ensure that you are in step with God's plan, it is imperative that you read and study His word. You are guaranteed to be blessed if you *"take delight in God's word and meditate on it day and night."* In fact, *"you will be a tree planted by streams of water, which yields its fruit in season and whose leaf does not wither-whatever they do prospers."* Having a mental transformation also means that you meditate frequently on His promise to direct your path while praying for clarification about the correct path to take. I encourage you to remain committed. His will becomes easier the more you acquire knowledge and seek to live by His principles and standards.

**Knowledge**

President Theodore Roosevelt once made this profound statement about knowledge and God's word, *"A thorough knowledge of the Bible is worth more than a college degree."* For clarification, I don't believe that Roosevelt was suggesting that you not pursue a college education. I interpret his comment to mean that the knowledge that you receive from having a thorough understanding of God's word is unmatched by any other knowledge that you will acquire in life. In other words, a college degree is valuable to your career path, but knowledge of the Bible is valuable for all aspects of your life, to include discovering His plan.

Unfortunately, one of the most tragic ways to fall into a pit of despair is a lack of knowledge about God's plan, your self-worth, and your future. In fact, God says, *"My people are destroyed because they lack knowledge of me."* When you lack sufficient knowledge about God's principles, standards, and values, then you are susceptible to being led astray from His plan. Thomas Aquinas said, *"We can't have full knowledge all at once. We must start by believing; then afterwards we may be led on to master the evidence for ourselves."* His words are true, as you must acquire knowledge about God's will for your life and start to believe it.

*"For if you call out for insight and cry aloud for understanding, and if you look for it as for silver and search for it as for hidden treasure, then you will understand the fear of the LORD and find the knowledge of God."* This scripture is another guarantee that God will give you insight and knowledge about His plans. For these reasons, it is imperative that you desire with all your heart to know God's planned future for your life.

**Desire**

Previously, it was discussed in a past chapter that there are things that you need to do in order to experience peace of mind. These needs manifest in the form of recurring desires of the heart. Having a sincere desire to know God's plan will lead to a mental transformation of your thoughts and desires. This will occur in your life because of the knowledge you receive from reading God's word and having a desire to live according to His will. His *"word is a lamp to guide your feet and a light to guide your path."*

*"Take delight in the Lord, and He will give you the desires of your heart. Commit your way to the Lord; trust in him and He will do this."* Sincerely desiring to know God's plan for your life is confirmation that a mental

transformation has begun to take place. However, be mindful of the necessity to commit your way or path and to also trust in Him. When you do these things, He will do it. What will He do? God will make known His plan for your life by showing you which path to take and guiding you in the decision-making process. Therefore, it is important that you wait patiently with an expectant heart for Him to make His plan known to you.

**Patience**

One of the fruits of the Spirit referred to in Galatians 5:22 is longsuffering, which also means patience. The fruits of the Spirit are personal characteristics that God gives you to assist with life. Patience is necessary when you are seeking to understand God's plan for your life. He can reveal to you His full plan at any given point but if He chooses to reveal it in phases, then patience is key. Listen to these words of Paul, *"...if we look forward to something we don't yet have, we must wait patiently and confidently."*

You don't want to make the wrong decision about your career or life's path because you are too impatient. Again, let's go back to the wisdom of Harriet Tubman. Do you recall that she said, *"Every great dream begins with a dreamer. Always remember, you have within you the strength, the patience, and the passion to reach for the stars to change the world?"* Tubman's suggestion that you have the capability to be patient is true because God gives patience once you receive the Holy Spirit.

On the other hand, strength and passion are essential characteristics that you must ask Him to give you to help in your quest to release your potential and pursue your purpose. David said, *"I remain confident of this: I will see the goodness of the Lord in the land of the living. Wait for the LORD; be strong and take heart and wait for the LORD."* The conclusion is that being patient when it comes to waiting for God to direct your path is a wise thing. It is better to go the right way than experience heartache because you rushed and made the wrong decision.

**Wisdom**

*"Knowledge comes, but wisdom lingers. It may not be difficult to store up in the mind a vast quantity of facts within a comparatively short time, but the ability to form judgments requires the severe discipline of hard work and the tempering heat of experience and maturity."* Those comments by President Calvin Coolidge hold a wealth of information. As you read God's word you will receive knowledge, but the best use of that knowledge will require wisdom. This is necessary because wisdom helps you form the judgments needed to understand and to follow God's path for your life. *"For wisdom is better than rubies, and all the things that may be desired are not to be compared to it."*

## Features and Benefits of God's Will

Finding or receiving wisdom positions you to discover the life God intends for you to live. When this happens, you also receive favor from Him because He is pleased with your actions, decisions, and thoughts. Pursuing God's plan is a wise choice because it is the only plan that guarantees you will experience peace of mind and success in life. From the very beginning of your life, He desired that you should prosper. His will is the only comprehensive plan that covers all the key elements of your life. It is also designed to remove any misconception surrounding your existence and path in life. Listed below are the key features and benefits of His plan for your life:

- **Name**: Function, Reservation, Domain, Authority
- **Purpose**: Assignment(s), Course, Career, Desires, Recurring Thoughts
- **Potential**: Talents, Abilities, Gifts
- **Path**: Destination, Destiny

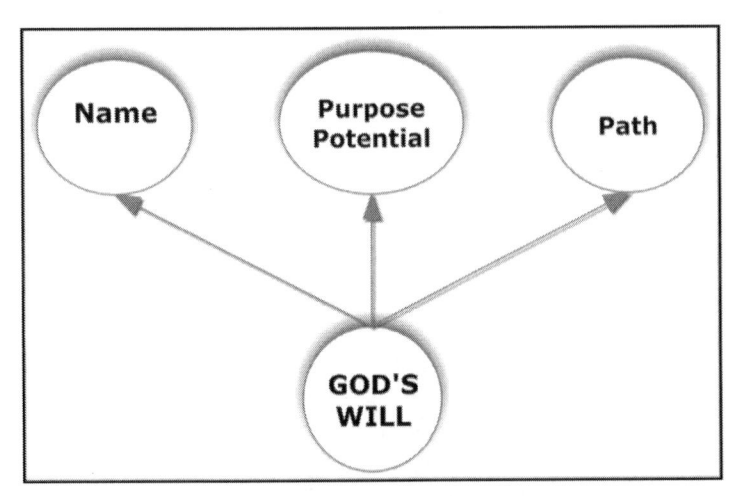

## Features & Benefits of God's Will Chart

```
   Name      Purpose        Path
             Potential
              ↑
           GOD'S
           WILL
```

As shown above, God's plan comes with an assigned name, purpose, potential and a designated path. When you accept His plan for your life, then you have access to receiving helpful and useful information. This information will remove the mystery surrounding His will and the plan for your life. In fact, you will be held accountable for either using the information to accomplish the right objectives or for failing to ask for it. God's first directive to us is the reason why you must know His will and apply it to your life.

## God's Promise to Give Answers

To understand God's will for your life, you must pray to Him and solicit this information. He says, *"Call to me and I will answer you and tell you great and unsearchable things you do not know."* Jesus also gives an assurance that you can expect to receive answers to questions, receive information pertinent to your life and given access to things needed to live successfully. Listen to his promise, *"Keep on asking, and you will receive what you are asking for. Keep on seeking, and you will find. Keep on knocking and the door will be open to you. For everyone who asks, receives. Everyone who seeks, finds, and to everyone who knocks, the door will be opened."*

This promise is all inclusive and guarantees a solution to uncertainty and answers to questions relative to your purpose. In other words, if you need God to clarify why He gave you life and what you should do with it, then He will give you the answers at the right time. The great news is that you qualify to receive information about your designated name, potential, purpose, and His plan for your life. The chart below is a visual aide showing His promise:

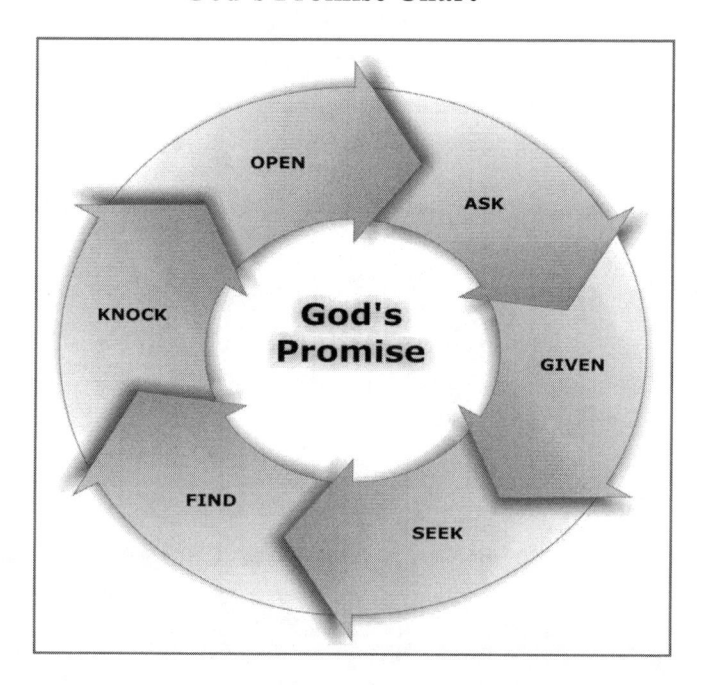

## God's Promise Chart

The scripture promises that when you ask for things relevant to His will you receive them. When you seek to find information about His plan for your life, you will find it. When you knock at the door waiting for it to open, then eventually it will open. These promises confirm His intentions to make known the answers to your core life questions.

The introductory quote from C.S. Lewis, says that walking outside of God's will is a journey to nowhere. A journey to nowhere is not necessary and it is counterproductive. I shared with you a brief glimpse into my life concerning my purposeful journey. I am thankful that I have received answers to questions necessary for me to understand who I am, what I need to do, when I need to do it, how to do it and why it is important to do it. By no means am I the exception. You have access to the same information, provisions and possibilities related to your purpose.

> God's will is an optional requirement.

Although God's will is required to satisfy your reason for living, it is optional because you have a right to choose which path you will pursue in life. You can choose what is popular, convenient and provides the most income or you can choose what is right according to God's plan. Knowing and pursuing God's will is a requirement that you can choose to follow or reject.

The Apostle Paul said, *"I have the right to do anything, you say – but not everything is beneficial. 'I have the right to do anything' – but not everything is constructive."* Everyone is born with the inherent power of choice. Unfortunately, there are situations whereby the power of choice is either taken away or limited. Nevertheless, my advice to you is to fear not, because God sees and knows about every situation. Either way, when God made the directive to be fruitful it came with His personal guarantee. Those circumstances that are beyond your control and created by national or economic challenges are never too great for Him to solve. Have you heard that Jesus said, *"For nothing is impossible with God?"*

After reading this book, it is my hope that you will be one of those individuals that will say *"Thy will be done."* For this to happen, you must first know what His will is for your life. No one can answer the questions regarding your purpose with complete certainty other than God himself. This means that you must position yourself to receive information from Him. Praying daily for information is a good start but you must also have faith, patience, perseverance, wisdom, and clarity of thought. Additionally, if you are experiencing one or all the following situations, then you must reconsider your position in life.

- Recurring thoughts and desires to pursue a path that coincides with your natural potential and passion.
- Your life seems directionless and void of personal goals that will allow you to maximize your potential.
- You are not sure if your job or career is the right path for you to follow.
- You are not content with the work that you are doing in life.
- You believe that your TAGs are not being fully used.

Reconsidering your position in life will require that you rethink your approach to discovering God's will. *"Don't copy the behavior and customs of the world, but let God transform you into a new person by changing the way you think. Then you will learn to know God's will for you, which is good and pleasing and perfect."* According to Paul, discovering God's will for your life requires that you become a new person and think differently from the norm. Following the norm means that you...:

- Disregard your hidden potential and pursue a path that will allow you to earn a living.
- Allow others to influence your thoughts about purpose based on their personal views about life and how to become successful.
- Believe that God's will is either a secret or not a prerequisite to discovering your purpose.
- Acquiring wealth, fame, and the admiration of others as the hallmarks for a successful life.

- Don't believe that releasing your TAGs is necessary to find peace of mind or live a fruitful life.

When you become a new person then discovering and pursuing God's will for your life becomes a priority every second, minute and hour of the day. I realize that this statement sounds too conservative or strange in a world that is filled with many opinions, distractions, opportunities, challenges, and paths to take. Nevertheless, if you are willing to let God transform your thought process and priorities then discovering His will for your life will happen. It happened for me and it can happen for you.

Remember that God gave you potential with the expectation that you would become a leader in your area of gifting and live a fruitful life. *"If you listen to these commands of the LORD your God that I am giving you today, and if you carefully obey them, the LORD will make you the head and not the tail, and you will always be on top and never at the bottom."* This scripture promises that if you listen and follow God's instructions, then you will succeed. Are you aware of the first command that God gave to creation related to potential?

## Be Fruitful Mandate

The parable of the talents is discussed in Matthew 25:14-30. It is an interesting message of the responsibility related to predetermined talents, abilities and gifts given by God. It emphasizes the fact that everyone receives something from God. However, it also outlines God's expectation related to what you receive and what you do with it. This message delivered by Jesus to his disciples makes it clear that it is God's will that everyone is productive and a good steward with what they have. Unfortunately, he leaves no room for individuals to make excuses, be complacent, doubtful, or unproductive.

Did you know that God desires that you have a fruitful life? Listen to the words Jesus spoke to His disciples that also applies to you, and me as well. Jesus said *"You didn't choose me, I chose you. I appointed you to go and produce lasting fruit, so the Father will give you whatever you ask for, using my name."* It is exciting to know that God appointed us to produce lasting fruit and that He will give us whatever is necessary to be successful.

It is my prayer that *"you may be filled with the knowledge of His will in all wisdom and spiritual understanding."* So that *"you may walk worthy of the Lord, fully pleasing Him, being fruitful in every good work and increasing in the knowledge of God."* As previously mentioned, being fruitful in life is an essential requirement of having potential. Therefore, another important point about understanding God's will for your life is to have wisdom and spiritual understanding about His mandate to be fruitful.

In Chapter 1 of Genesis, the mandate to be fruitful is the first directive issued by God to every living thing. This directive leaves no room for doubt or debate. The command also establishes His expectation for your life based on His gift to you. Moreover, it signifies that you possess the capacity to produce something of value on a consistent basis. God's command was not to be a fruit. If He said be a fruit, then that would mean to manifest your TAG, on one occurrence or for one event.

His first command related to potential was *"Be Fruitful..."* which implies that your life should produce continuous consistent successful returns. This directive also highlights the ability to be self-manifesting. Self-manifesting means that you are constantly exhibiting the qualities and characteristics that makes you unique. Also, it confirms the fact that you possess a valuable seed that can achieve unimaginable and unlimited end-results.

Think for a moment about the principal that governs seeds. By nature, the purpose of seeds is continuous production of plants, trees, and fruits. Therefore, the beginning of recurring success starts with one seed. The seed undergoes the process of becoming a healthy fruit tree capable of producing much fruit. Each fruit on the tree possesses at least one seed with the inherent capacity to produce a tree with fruit and seeds. Following this thought, it is possible to see how one seed can produce a forest and how a forest can produce an unimaginable number of fruits.

As you know, the true confirmation of your purpose in life comes from the originator of the purpose. God gave you your purpose. Therefore, He is able and willing to confirm the plan He has for your life. Listen to His words, *"For I know the plans I have for you," declares the Lord, "plans to prosper you and not to harm you, plans to give you hope and a future."* God's plan is a plan to prosper you.

God's plan for your life is also a plan of success. To ensure your success in fulfilling your purpose, He issued a guarantee to direct your path. Therefore, *"Trust in the LORD with all of your heart; do not depend on your own understanding. Seek his will in all you do, and He will show you which path to take."* His promise is a written guarantee that your path is prearranged exclusively for you.

I cannot recall a single day in my life wherein either discovering, understanding, or pursuing God's will wasn't a priority. You were created to know God's will and pursue it with passion as well. His will is calling you to introduce you to yourself and your future. It is also calling you to expose you to the vision and destiny that He has for your life.

**Personal Vision**

What is vision? Vision is being able to perceive and articulate the path to follow prior to beginning the journey. Additionally, according to Dr. Myles Munroe, *"Vision is a conception that is inspired by God in the hearts of humans."* A positive step to prove your commitment to releasing your potential and fulfilling your purpose in life is the creation of a personal vision. Much of the information that you need to create your vision is already on the inside of you. Any additional information that you need will come directly from the Source (God).

> **A** personal vision for your life formalizes your awareness of self, confirms your belief in the power of potential and acknowledges your purpose for living.

Think for a moment about how exciting it would be to have a clear picture regarding the direction you should take in life. I am sure that your outlook on life would be completely different because having a road map in the form of your personal vision adds value to knowing how to maximize your potential and live a purposeful life. Vision also creates an attitude of optimism.

*"When you have vision it affects your attitude. Your attitude is optimistic rather than pessimistic,"* according to Charles Swindoll. An optimistic outlook regarding your potential is necessary to sustain your motivation to continue until your purpose is fulfilled. Ask yourself, "Am I truly motivated to discover my potential and purpose in life?" Motivation is the key, as it will dictate whether you take the next step towards developing your own personal vision for your life.

Bob Marley, legendary and internationally renowned Jamaican reggae artist, had good advice regarding a personal vision. Marley believed, *"Life is one big road with lots of signs. So when you riding through the ruts, don't complicate your mind. Flee from hate, mischief and jealousy. Don't bury your thoughts, put your vision to reality. Wake up and Live!"* He was correct in stating that there are many things that occur in life that could cause you to bury your dreams under a pile of mental blocks.

> **V**ision of the heart is a snapshot of the domain where seeds of potential bear purposeful fruit.

One day a farmer decided to explore the cliffs that surrounded his farm in the valley. Upon climbing a high ledge, he noticed a large nest full of eggs just below the top. Realizing that the clutch of eggs belonged to an eagle, he decided to take one and place it in his pack. Understanding the necessity of placing the egg with a surrogate mother, he put it in a chicken coup under the care of an affectionate hen. When the egg hatched, the eagle grew up with the other chicks learning to do things that chickens do.

The eagle's actions completely resembled that of the chickens. He ate, walked, and balked like a chicken. The actions of the eagle confirmed its belief that it was a chicken just like the other birds. In its latter years, the eagle looked up and noticed a bird flying high in the sky while eating with the other chickens in the yard. Curious about the eagle soaring effortlessly and gracefully, the "eagle," who thought he was a chicken, asked one of the chickens about this magnificent creature.

The other chicken replied, it is an eagle and it's a majestic bird that soars high in the sky, but we are chickens that stay low to the ground. Upon hearing this, the eagle and the chickens continued the daily routine of digging and pecking the ground. The eagle lived and died experiencing the life of a chicken. Unfortunately, the environment and chicken culture influenced it to accept a life beneath the power of its true potential and purpose destined for it at birth.[44]

The message of this fable speaks to the issues of potential, purpose, and vision. Circumstances and its environment prevented the eagle from living a life that coincided with its natural potential. As a result, its habits, goals, and desires of the heart produced an inferior quality of life. It saw a brief glimpse of its destiny through its eyes, but did not recognize it through the vision of the heart. The heart validates your vision and desires the contentment that comes from living a purposeful life.

An important lesson from the story is that your potential, purpose, and personal vision should reflect the same image. In other words, the life that you choose to live should reflect your potential and purpose. Vision supports a direction in life that focuses on pursuing the desires of the heart by releasing talents, abilities, and gifts. The key is that you must believe in yourself by believing in your vision. At this point, let's "circle back" and listen again to the wisdom of Dr. Myles Munroe, *"When you believe in your dream and your vision, then it begins to attract its own resources. No one was born to fail."* I agree with his sentiments. What about you, do you agree? I believe that you can and will succeed in releasing your potential and fulfilling your purpose in life.

## Features and Benefits of Vision

There are many tools and resources available to you that will help you construct a personal vision for your life. Like Gideon, you may not understand why God chose you to pursue the path that you see through the window of your heart, but if you accept the opportunity then success awaits you. In my experience, a personal vision according to the will of God is merely putting pen to paper the information that God gives you about your name, potential, purpose, and life's path. In addition, Dr. Myles Munroe mentioned, *"Purpose is when you know and understand what you were born to accomplish. Vision is when you see it in your mind and begin to imagine it."* Furthermore, the following 14 statements will also provide you with insight about the subject of vision:

- Vision must come from God and point you in the direction of His will for your life.
- Although vision is planted in your mind, it is revealed through your recurring dreams and desires of the heart.
- Vision is a glimpse of your intended future prior to the manifestation of it.
- Vision is an intentional and purposeful plan outlining your directed path or future destiny.
- Vision from God comes to give you insight into the things that are possible, necessary, and required to fulfill His purpose for your life.

- Vision is not a wish list but a process of identifying the plans, objectives, and accomplishments that you desire to achieve through your natural talents, abilities, and gifts (TAGs).
- Vision is a focused perspective on the things you intend to achieve at a future time in your life.
- True vision clarifies your assignment without contradicting or violating God's will.
- Vision is not haphazard, it has a definitive start, and finish associated with your released potential along the path of purpose.
- True vision from God is enhanced through the purposeful experiences, actions, achievements and completed assignments.
- A personal vision is the written or unwritten path that God has established for you to pursue that you visualize through your dreams and desires.
- Vision expires when life ends and begins when you can imagine pursuing your purpose for living during the pre-conceptualization season.
- A personal vision for your life formalizes your awareness of self, confirms your belief in the power of potential and acknowledges your purpose for living.
- Vision of the heart is a snapshot of the domain where your seeds of potential bear purposeful fruit.

According to Steve Jobs, *"If you are working on something exciting that you really care about, you don't have to be pushed. The vision pulls you."* Your answers to the following 5 questions will determine what happens next:

1. Do you care about maximizing your potential?
2. Do you care about using your TAGs to the fullest?
3. Do you care about pursuing your purpose for living?
4. Do you care about overcoming comfort zones and stumbling blocks?
5. Do you care about fulfilling God's will for your life?

"Vision is the Source and hope of life. The greatest gift ever given to mankind is not the gift of sight, but the gift of vision. Sight is a function of the eyes; vision is a function of the heart. 'Eyes that look are common, but eyes that see are rare.' Nothing noble or noteworthy on earth was ever done without vision." Those words were spoken by Dr. Myles Munroe. It is God's desire to give you the gift of vision so that you can answer the core question of life and live a fruitful existence. Hopefully, at this stage, you answered YES to each of the questions. If so, then you don't have to be pushed, just allow your vision to pull you. The concept of pulling you towards your future is the same as the calling of your heart.

God predetermined that you should have dominion and authority. He carved out a specific assignment just for you. He gave you the special TAGs to make a profound impact in the world and a path that leads to destiny. He also gave you a future and something to hope for. When you consider His promises and desires for your life, then you should have the confidence to say and believe, *"I am a possibility creator and an impossibility destroyer."*

## THE FINAL STEP

I discovered over the years that God's will is not a secret but a plan that is revealed to those capable of understanding His messages. His will for you is synonymous with His purpose for your life. Unfortunately, our society does not promote the concept of positioning the will of God in the priority seat related to success and peace of mind. The lack of knowledge about the process of discovering God's purpose leads many to believe that His will for their life is a mystery that is very difficult to solve. Nevertheless, *"For the LORD God is our sun and our shield. He gives us grace and glory. The LORD will withhold no good thing from those who do what is right."*

The knowledge necessary for a fruitful life centers on the discovery of self, potential and purpose. The starting point to initializing the Potential Effect in your life begins when you can answer 5 core questions that influence your life's journey. In order to have a successful life a person must be able to ask, answer and pursue the most important questions surrounding self-awareness. Consider those things that you enjoy doing, your natural talents, abilities, gifts, and desires of the heart as you review the following core life questions:

- Who am I? (Potential)
- What should I do? (Purpose)
- When should I do it? (Period of Time / Timeframe)
- How should I do it? (Path / Plan)
- Why should I do it? (Destiny)

God already knows the path that your life should take to ensure that your work on earth is successful. He wants your work to shine brightly so that men will glorify Him for blessing you. Therefore, I encourage you to *"Let your light shine before men in such a way that they may see your good works, and glorify your Father who is in heaven."*

Benjamin Franklin once said, *"If you fail to plan, you are planning to fail."* Accepting the fact that potential is given for an expressed purpose is the first step in recognizing the need to develop a plan on how to use it. At this stage, spend time thinking about your plan of action to release your potential. If you have thoughts, dreams, and desires without a plan to release them from captivity, then you become a prime candidate for internal voids and a lack of fulfillment. Again, these words of wisdom from Henry David Thoreau will help, *"What you get from achieving your goals is not as important as what you become."* The objective is for you to become the person that you were born to be.

The final step on Maslow's Hierarchy of Needs is the position of self-actualization. He was quoted as saying, *"What a man can be, he must be. This need we call self-actualization."* Self-actualization is the final step of this book as well because what you can be, you must be. You can be what and who you dream about becoming, and you must be it.

Therefore, *"...whatever is true, whatever is noble, whatever is right...if anything is excellent or praiseworthy think about such things."* Your purpose in life is true, noble, excellent, and praiseworthy. Think about it and let it open the doors to confirming God's will for your life. Jesus said, *"The thief's purpose is to steal and kill and destroy. My purpose is to give them a rich and satisfying life."* Don't let the thief steal your potential, kill your dreams, or destroy your future. God has ordained that you should have a productive and satisfying life.

---

**D**estiny calls to the person holding the potential prompting them to make a positive impact on earth by leaving an indelible mark that is impossible to erase from either history or the hearts of mankind.

# God's Plan for your Life

Your journey through this book has taken you through many challenging concepts and principles. Everything that you have read is relevant, and necessary for you understand to live effectively. Furthermore, it is important for you to understand what Benjamin Franklin said about knowledge. He said, *"An investment in knowledge pays the best interest."* Your life will be more enriched, and your decisions should be more intentional because you understand how important your life is to God.

Although you have knowledge you must decide to apply the principles in the right way and for the right reasons. I believe in you. You can do great things in life. Stay on the right path. The right path is the way that leads to maximizing your potential and fulfilling your purpose for living. As you now know, God is with you and will make His plan known to you. For the last time say with me, *"I am a possibility creator and an impossibility destroyer."* MAY GOD BLESS YOU AND CONTINUE TO KEEP YOU.

## Quick reference to God's plan for your life principles:

1. A life without knowledge of purpose has various consequences on the individual and the world.
2. God has a detailed plan for your life which is accessible to you.
3. God's purpose prevails over plans that are inconsistent with His will for your life.
4. Transformation of your thoughts is a critical aspect in understanding God's plan for your life.
5. Unfortunately, one of the most tragic ways to fall into a pit of despair is lack of knowledge about God's plan, your self-worth, and your future.
6. Having a sincere desire to know God's plan will lead to a mental transformation of your thoughts and desires.
7. Patience is necessary when you are seeking to understand God's plan for your life.
8. Pursuing God's plan is a wise choice because it is the only plan that guarantees you will experience peace of mind and success in life.
9. Every seed possesses the natural capacity to produce recurring successes.
10. God's plan for your life is a plan of success.
11. Whenever you begin the process of understanding His will, you must first believe that His plan is the reason for your potential, purpose, and destined path in life.
12. Failure to properly link your potential with the right career, job or assignment will result in temporary gratification.
13. Pursuing God's will for your life is an optional requirement that promises to give your life positive and supernatural returns.

## Scripture References

### CHAPTER ONE

p. 18: "Have mercy on us…" – Mark 9:22.
p. 19: "What do you mean…" – Mark 9:23.
p. 24: "You saw me…" – Psalm 139:16.
p. 25: "I can do all things…" – Philippians 4:13 (KJV).
p. 28: "I knew you before…" – Jeremiah 1:5.
p. 32: "What will a man…" – 1 Samuel 17:26.
p.37. "Don't be afraid…" – Isaiah 41:10.

### CHAPTER TWO

p. 43: "For in him all…" – Colossians 1:16 (NIV).
p. 43: "All things were made…" – John 1:3 (ESV).
p. 44: "Who should I say…" and "I AM…" – Exodus 3:13-14 (KJV).
p. 44: "Every good and …" – James 1:17 (NIV).
p. 52: "As each has received…" – 1 Peter 4:10 (ESV).
p. 54: "A gift opens the way…" – Proverbs 8:18 (NIV).
p. 66: "Ask and it will…" – Matthew 7:7-8 (NIV).
p. 68: "There is a time…" – Ecclesiastes 3:1 (NIV).
p. 68: "They are trees planted…" – Psalm 1:3.

### CHAPTER THREE

p. 76: "For we are each…" – Galatians 6:5.
p. 76: "Are you the king…' – See John 18:33-37.
p. 77: "I am the way…" – John 14:6.
p. 77: "Remain in me, and I will" – John 15:4-5
p. 79: "…call into being things" – See Romans 4:17 (NIV).
p. 81: "For as he thinks within…" – Proverbs 23:7 (NKJV).
p. 84: "This is the confidence that we have…" – 1 John 5:14 (NIV).
p. 84: "Faith is the confidence that…" Hebrews 11:1
p. 90: "…not by might.." Zechariah 4:6 (NIV)

p. 90: "The eyes of the LORD watch…" – Psalm 34:15.

p. 90: "… eyes of the LORD range throughout…" – 2 Chronicles 16:9 (NIV).

p. 91: "Suddenly, a fierce storm struck…" – See Matthew 8:24-26.

p. 92: "…press to reach the end…" – Philippians 3:14.

p. 93: "The Lord hears His people when they call…" – Psalm 34:17.

p. 93: "…For it gives your Father great happiness…" – Luke 12:32.

p. 94: "…God will meet all your needs…" – Philippians 4:19 (NIV).

p. 94: "Seek the Kingdom of God above all else…" – Matthew 6:33.

p. 94: "Until John the Baptist…" – Luke 16:16.

p. 94: "The time promised by God has come…" – Mark 1:15.

p. 94: "Jesus replied…" – John 3:3 (NIV).

p. 94: "Jesus answered… – John 3:5 (NIV).

## CHAPTER FOUR

p. 104: "Would anyone light a lamp…" – Mark 4:21.

p. 111: "…Who do you say I am..." – Mark 8:29 (NIV).

p. 111: "I am the good shepherd…" – John 10:11.

p. 111: "I am the bread of life" – John 6:48 (NIV).

p. 115: "Every tree is known by its own fruit" – Luke 6:44 (NKJV).

p. 122: "Those who know your name…" – Psalm 9:10.

p. 123: "Faith shows the reality of what we hope for…" – Hebrews 11:1.

p. 123: "… those who hope in the LORD…" – Isaiah 40:31.

## CHAPTER FIVE

p. 129: "As each one has received a gift…" – 1 Peter 4:10 (NKJV).

## CHAPTER SIX

p. 151: "To everything there is a season…" – Ecclesiastes 3:1 (NKJV).

p. 151: "Teach me to realize the brevity…" – Psalm 90:12.

p. 154: "God has made everything beautiful…" – Ecclesiastes 3:11.

## CHAPTER EIGHT

p. 185: "For God has not given us a spirit of fear..." – 2 Timothy 1:7.

p. 186: "Don't be afraid, for I am with you..." – Isaiah 41:10.

p. 186: "But when you ask him, be sure that your faith is in God..." – James 1:6.

p. 187: "Then you will know the truth, and the truth will..." – John 8:32 (NIV).

p. 188: "...I have not achieved it, but I focus on this one thing..." – Philippians 3:13-14.

p. 189: "For at the proper time you will reap..." – See Galatians 6:9 (NIV).

p. 189: "For God is not the author of confusion, but of peace..." – 1 Corinthians 14:33 (NKJV).

p. 190: "Work hard so you can present yourself to God..." – 2 Timothy 2:15.

p: 192: "...God causes everything to work together for the good..." – Romans 8:28.

p. 192: "Every word of God proves true. He is a shield..." – Proverbs 30:5.

p. 192: "...prepare your mind for action; and exercise self-control." – 1 Peter 1:13.

p. 194: "My soul is overwhelmed with sorrow to the point of death." – Mark 14:34 (NIV).

p. 194: "My father, if it is possible, may this cup be taken away..." – See Matthew 26:39 (NIV).

p. 194: "My father, if it is not possible for this cup..." – See Matthew 26:42 (NIV).

## CHAPTER NINE

p. 213: "Wisdom is the principal thing..." – Proverbs 4:7 (NJKV).

p. 214: "If any of you lacks wisdom, you should ask God..." – James 1:5 (NIV).

p. 214: "For the LORD grants wisdom..." – Proverbs 2:6 (NIV).

p. 214: "you position yourself for long life, riches and honor. – See Proverbs 3:16.

p. 215: "For whoever finds me finds life and receives favor from the LORD. – Proverbs 8:35.

p. 215: "I had a dream, and no one can interpret it…" – Genesis 41:15 (NIV).

p. 218: "I will guide you…" – Psalm 32:8.

p. 221: "whatever is true, whatever is noble, whatever is right…" – Philippians 4:8 (NIV).

p. 221: "Do not conform to the pattern of this world…" – Romans 12:2 (NIV).

p. 222: "Getting wisdom is the wisest thing you can do…" – Proverbs 4:7.

p. 222: "I turned my heart to know and to search out…" Ecclesiastes 7:25 (ESV).

p. 222: "Wisdom is a tree of life to those who embrace her…" – Proverbs 3:18.

p. 222: "prepare you mind for action; be self-controlled." – See 1 Peter 1:13.

p. 223: "So be careful to do what the LORD your God…" – Deuteronomy 5:32-33.

p. 223: "Do not be anxious about anything, but in every situation…" – Philippians 4:6-7.

p. 225: "Then the man and his wife heard the sound…" – Genesis 3:8 (NIV).

p. 225: "The woman you put…"– Genesis 3:12 (NIV).

p. 226: "And the LORD God said, The man has become…" – Genesis 3:22 (NIV).

## CHAPTER TEN

p. 238: "Truly, I tell you, if anyone says to this mountain…" – Mark 11:22-23 (NIV).

p. 239: "May no one ever eat fruit from you again." – See Mark 11:14 (NIV).

p 239: "If you do not obey the LORD you God…" – Deuteronomy 28:15 (NIV).

p. 239: "Say unto the mountain be removed…" – See Mark 11:22-23.

p 240: "Therefore, I tell you, do not worry about…" – Matthew 6:25-26 (NIV).

## CHAPTER ELEVEN

p. 255: "Lord let your ear be attentive to the prayer..." – Nehemiah 1:11 (NIV).

p. 255: "I am engaged in a great work, so I can't come..." – Nehemiah 6:3.

p. 261: "And God said, Let us make man in our image..." – Genesis 1:26 (KJV).

p. 263: "Do you see a man skillful in his work..." – Proverbs 22:29 (ESV).

p. 264: "make you the head and not the tail..." – See Deuteronomy 28:13.

p. 266: "holds success in store for the upright..." – Proverbs 2:7 (NIV).

## CHAPTER TWELVE

p. 272: "Therefore, God elevated him to the place of the highest..." – Philippians 2:9.

p. 272: "For a child is born to us, a son is given to us..." – Isaiah 9:6.

p. 272: "Everything has already been decided. It was known..." – Ecclesiastes 6:10.

p. 274: "The sons in your womb will become..." – Genesis 25:23.

p. 277: "The angel of the LORD came and sat down..." – Judges 6:11-12 (NIV).

p. 278: "Go in the strength you have and save Israel..." – Judges 6:14-15 (NIV).

p. 278: "Your eyes have seen my unformed substance..." – Psalm 139:16-17 (NASB).

p. 280: "Enter through the narrow gate. For wide is..." – Matthew 7:13-14 (NIV).

p. 281: "Yes, I am the gate. Those who come..." – John 10:9.

p. 283: "So also will be the word that I speak..." – Isaiah 55:11 (GNT).

## FINAL CHAPTER

p. 288: "My thoughts are nothing like your thoughts..." – Isaiah 55:8.

p. 288: "You made all the delicate, inner parts of my body..." – Psalm 139:13-18.

p. 289: "But you have received the Holy Spirit..." – 1 John 2:27.

p. 289: "I make known the end from the beginning, from..." – Isaiah 46:10.

p. 290: "Ask me and I will tell you remarkable..." – Jeremiah 33:3.

p. 291: "Don't copy the behavior and customs of this world..." – Romans 12:2.

p. 291: "When the Spirit of truth comes, he will..." – John 16:13.

p. 291 "take delight in God's word and meditate..." – See Psalm 1:2.

p. 291: "you will be a tree planted by streams..." – See Psalm 1:3.

p. 292: "My people are destroyed because..." – See Hosea 4:6.

p. 292: "For if you call out for insight..." – See Proverbs 2:3-5.

p. 292: "word is a lamp to guide your feet..." – Psalm 119:105.

p. 292: "Take delight in the Lord, and He will..." – Psalm 37:5 (NIV).

p. 293: "...if we look forward to something..." – Romans 8:25.

p. 293: "I remain confident of this..." – Psalm 27:13-14 (NIV).

p. 294: "For wisdom is better than rubies..." – Proverbs 8:11 (KJV).

p. 295: "Call to me and I will answer you..." – Jeremiah 33:3.

p. 296: "Keep on asking, and you will..." – Matthew 7:7-8.

p. 297: "I have the right to do anything..." – 1 Corinthians 10:23.

p. 297: "For nothing is impossible with God." – See Matthew 19:26.

p. 298: "Don't copy the behavior and customs of the world..." – Romans 12:2.

p. 299: "If you listen to these commands..." – Deuteronomy 28:13.

p. 299: "You didn't choose me. I chose you. I appointed..." – John 15:16.

p. 300: "...you may be filled with the knowledge..." – See Colossians 1:9 (NKJV).

p. 300: "...you may walk worthy of the Lord..." – See Colossians 1:10 (NKJV).

p. 300: "…Be fruitful…" – See Genesis 1:28.
p. 301: "For I know the plans I have for you…" – Jeremiah 29:11 (NIV).
p. 301: "Trust in the Lord with all of your heart…" – Proverbs 3:5-6.
p. 307: "For the LORD God is our sun and our shield…" – Psalm 84:11.
p. 307: "Let your light shine before men in such a way…" – Matthew 5:16 (NASB).
p. 308: "…whatever is true, whatever is noble…" – Phil. 4:8.
p. 308: "The thief's purpose is to steal…" – John 10:10.

# Endnotes

## PREFACE

[1] Gipson, J. Arthur, 12 Steps to a Highly Rewarding Career: *Discovering the Secrets to Defeating Comfort Zones* (New York: iUniverse, 2004), xi.

## CHAPTER ONE

[2] <http://law2.umkc.edu/faculty/projects/ftrials/mandela/mandelaspeech.html> (September 9, 2019).
[3] <https://www.merriam-webster.com/dictionary/potential> (September 9, 2019)
[4] <https://atlantablackstar.com/2014/10/31/50-facts-about-the-wizard-of-tuskegee-inventor-george- washington-carver/5/> (September 9, 2019) and <https://www.britannica.com/biography/George-Washington-Carver> (September 9, 2019)
[5] <https://www.wnd.com/2018/01/the-secret-to-george-washington-carvers-success> (September 9, 2019)
[6] <https://www.britannica.com/biography/Michelangelo> (February 10, 2020)

## CHAPTER TWO

[7] <http://www.historyplace.com/speeches/reagan-parliament.htm> (February 10, 2020)
[8] <https://www.globalsecurity.org/military/world/russia/soviet-collapse.htm> (February 10, 2020)
[9] <http://www.en.antiquitatem.com/know-thyself-socrates-plato-philosophy> (February 10, 2020)
[10] <https://www.etymonline.com/search?q=potential> (September 9, 2019)
[11] <https://www.biography.com/artist/leonardo-da-vinci> (February 10, 2020)

## CHAPTER THREE

[12] <https://people.utm.my/wanfahminfaiz/meaning-of-life> (February 10, 2020)
[13] <https://www.unfpa.org/resources/quotes-culture-and-culturally-sensitive-approaches> (February 10, 2020)
[14] <https://www.imdb.com/name/nm0001856/bio> (March 11, 2020)

## CHAPTER FOUR

[15] <https://en.wikipedia.org/wiki/Steve_Jobs> (March 11, 2020)
[16] <https://www.marketwatch.com/investing/stock/aapl/financials> (March 11, 2020)
[17] <https://www.thoroughbredracing.com/articles/remembering-unbridled-classic-influence-gone-too-soon/ > (March 11, 2020)
[18] <https://www.thoughtco.com/mary-anderson-inventor-of-the-windshield-wiper-1992654> (March 11, 2020)
[19] <https://www.dictionary.com/browse/self-actualization?s=t> (March 11, 2020|)
[20] <https://www.imdb.com/name/nm0309540/bio> (March 11, 2020)
[21] <https://www.abc.net.au/news/rural/2015-09-03/mango-manipulation-trial-bearing-fruit-near-darwin/6743794> (March 11, 2020)
[22] <https://www.merriam-webster.com/dictionary/hope> (March 11, 2020)

## CHAPTER FIVE

[23] <https://www.merriam-webster.com/dictionary/purpose> (March 11, 2020)
[24] <https://www.conference--board.org/press/press-board.org/press/pressdetail.cfm?pressid=7528 > (March 11, 2020)
[25] <https://www.cnbc.com/2013/09/17/nearly-half-of-the-worlds-employees-unhappy-in-their- jobs-survey.html> (March 11, 2020)
[26] <https://www.biography.com/business-figure/mary-kay-ash> (March 11, 2020)

## CHAPTER SIX

[27] <http://www.whyville.net/smmk/whytimes/article?id=75> (March 11, 2020)
[28] <https://www.merriam-webster.com/dictionary/image> (March 11, 2020)

## CHAPTER SEVEN

[29] < https://www.merriam-webster.com/dictionary/calling> (March 11, 2020)
[30] <https://www.merriam-webster.com/dictionary/development> (March 11, 2020)

## CHAPTER EIGHT

[31] <https://www.forbes.com/sites/travisbradberry/2015/07/21/7-challenges-successful-people- overcome/#333c0b5e13a3> (March 11, 2020)

## CHAPTER NINE

[32] <https://www.merriam-webster.com/dictionary/wisdom> (March 11, 2020)
[33] <http://blackinventor.com/jan-matzeliger/ >(March 11, 2020)
[34] <https://www.merriam-webster.com/dictionary/mind> (March 11, 2020)
[35] <https://www.merriam-webster.com/dictionary/conscience> (March 11, 2020)

## CHAPTER TEN

[36] <https://www.biography.com/musician/elvis-presley> (March 11, 2020)
[37] <https://www.biography.com/athlete/hank-aaron> (March 11, 2020)
[38] <https://www.notablebiographies.com/news/Li-Ou/Nooyi-Indra-K.html> (March 11, 2020)
[39] <https://www.famous-entrepreneurs.com/leonardo-del-vecchio> (March 11, 2020)

## CHAPTER TWELVE

[40] <https://hebrew4christians.com/Names_of_G-d/Introduction/introduction.html> (March 11, 2020)
[41] <https://www.allaboutbible.com/names-were-changed/> (March 11, 2020)
[42] <http://blog.adw.org/2012/05/150-titles-of-christ-from-the-scriptures/> (March 11, 2020)

[43] <https://www.blueletterbible.org/lang/lexicon/lexicon.cfm?Strongs=H7121&t=NLT> (March 11, 2020)

## FINAL CHAPTER

[44] <https://lifelessons4u.wordpress.com/tag/the-eagle-who-thought-he-was-a-chicken/> (March 11, 2020)

## NOTES

**NOTES**

## NOTES

**NOTES**

## NOTES

## Additional Material For This Book

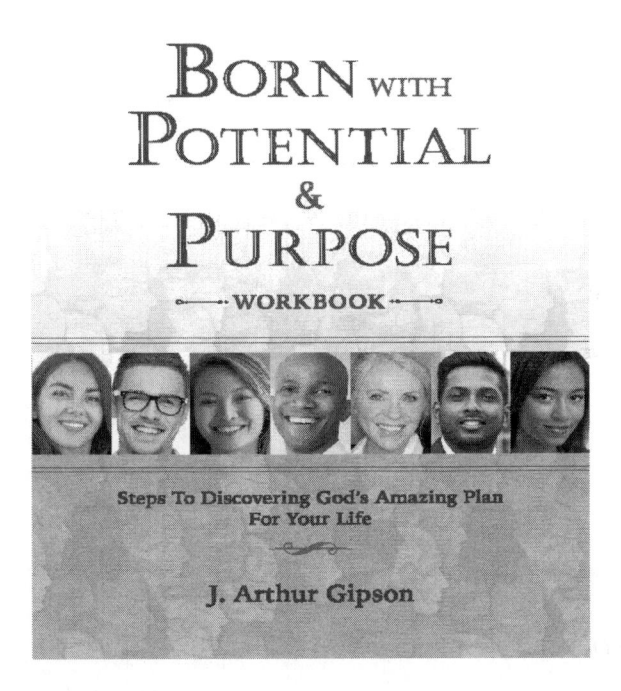

### BORN WITH POTENTIAL & PURPOSE
— WORKBOOK —

Steps To Discovering God's Amazing Plan For Your Life

J. Arthur Gipson

This study guide is dedicated to assisting you in discovering God's amazing plan for your life. It will reinforce the fact that God knows you and has given you the natural resources to become successful in life. It will also help you customize your path to success using the potential and purpose information.

ISBN: 979-8-9850385-2-1

# Additional Reading Material From J. Arthur Gipson

**12 Steps to a Highly Rewarding Career** – *Discovering the Secrets to Defeating Comfort Zones*

In 12 Steps to a Highly Rewarding Career, author J. Arthur Gipson, takes a unique approach to finding peace of mind through fulfillment in your job, career or assignment. Follow the 12 Steps to the top of the pyramid. Along the way, you will learn the true benefits of applying Faith, Perseverance, Positive Thinking, Positive Speaking and Vigilance and discover:

*Your true assignment in life
*How to identify true needs of the heart
*The untold secrets and dangers associated with comfort zones
*How to climb out of pits of despair

The benefits of tests and trials and how they can be beneficial. This amazing book will equip you with the tools to launch out into a more rewarding job or career. The principles of the Fortune 5 System will guide you into success and satisfaction in the workplace. Get ready-It's time to experience your greatest joy in life and with life.

ISBN: 0-595-26937-0 * Paperback * 146 pages

# JOIN THE GROUP OF BELIEVERS FROM AROUND THE WORLD

*"Potential never quits, it always says, 'one more time, just one more time,' until purpose is finally fulfilled."* **J. Arthur Gipson**

*"Purpose recognizes your potential and opens the door of success."* **J. Arthur Gipson**

Made in the USA
Columbia, SC
01 August 2024